HEROES' TWILIGHT
a Study of the Literature
of the Great War

Bernard Bergonzi

HEROES' TWILIGHT

a Study of the Literature
of the Great War

Second Edition

For Gabriel

© Bernard Bergonzi 1965, 1980

First published in 1965 by Constable
Second edition 1980

Published by
THE MACMILLAN PRESS LTD
London and Basingstoke
Companies and representatives
throughout the World

Printed in Hong Kong

British Library Cataloguing in Publication Data

Bergonzi, Bernard
  Heroes' twilight – 2nd ed.
  1. English literature – 20th century – History
  and criticism
  2. European War, 1914–1918, in literature
  I. Title
  820'.9'3   PR478.E8

  ISBN 0–333–28126–8
  ISBN 0–333–28157–8 Pbk

CONTENTS

Preface to the Second Edition

Since this book was first published in 1965 several poets and novelists who endured and survived the Great War and were then still living have died: Edmund Blunden, David Jones, Sir Herbert Read, Siegfried Sassoon, Sir Osbert Sitwell, Henry Williamson. Before long the events of more than sixty years ago will have faded from living memory. But as the war recedes into history the literature it produced receives increasing scholarly and critical attention. In 1964, as I was completing this book, John H. Johnston published *English Poetry of the First World War*, a substantial and well-documented but selective study, which provides a discriminating discussion of the poetry of victims and survivors. Mr Johnston's book is, I think, somewhat distorted by the application of a particular thesis. He argues that most of the war poets were limited by their restriction to the lyric mode, which is necessarily brief and subjective, expressing a single moment of experience, and that they were unable to rise to the full demands of war as a subject, which should be given extended treatment in a narrative or epic manner. Mr Johnston argues that only David Jones's *In Parenthesis* and, to a lesser degree, Herbert Read's *The End of a War* are properly adequate to their subject. His thesis seems unconvincing to me, particularly in its strictures on the inadequacy of the lyric mode. It was hard to write anything other than short poems in the trenches or when recovering from service at the Front. In a larger context, the whole movement of poetry since Romanticism has been towards moments of lyric concentration, even if they are sometimes articulated into larger structures. Like Mr Johnston, I greatly admire *In Parenthesis*; but I try to show why it is hardly appropriate to call it an epic. Nevertheless, his book has many valuable things to say about particular poems and poets. This is true, too, of a later work, Jon Silkin's *Out of Battle: The Poetry of the Great War*, which covers more ground than Mr Johnston's. Mr Silkin is convinced of the centrality of the two victims of 1918, Wilfred Owen and Isaac Rosenberg, whom he discusses at length, making large claims for Rosenberg's actual achievement as opposed to his potentiality. Mr Silkin's book is also marked by a limiting thesis, of an ethical and ideological kind. Writing from a position of absolute pacifism, he believes that the point of war poetry is to be anti-war poetry, a stark protest against mass destruction and waste of life. There is a certain failure of historical imagination in Mr Silkin, which means that ancient codes of human response to war are inaccessible to him, so that he is unable to understand, let alone sympathise with, the patriotic emotions and high aspirations which inspired so many Englishmen in 1914, before the bitterness and disillusionment of 1916 and after set in. Writing about *In Parenthesis*, Mr Silkin is baffled when David Jones evokes and praises the positive aspects of soldierly life, in the Great War and in earlier wars. But despite my reservations about the books by Mr Johnston and Mr Silkin, I have to say that their discussion of the poetry of the Great War is far more extensive and detailed than my own.

In 1975 Paul Fussell published *The Great War and Modern Memory*, a subtle, sophisticated and highly illuminating combination of literary criticism and cultural history. It seems to me by far the best book yet on the subject, and I discuss it at some length in the appendix to this edition. In the preface to the first edition I expressed the hope that one day there would be some account of the international literary reactions to the war. An interesting attempt at such a study has been made in *The First World War in Fiction*, edited by Holger Klein, a collection of essays by various hands, discussing fiction by English, American, French, German, Austrian, Italian and Czech writers; 'fiction' is interpreted widely enough to include *Goodbye to All That* and *In Parenthesis*. The critical level of the essays is uneven, but the best of them—such as those on Cummings, Barbusse, Jünger, Martinetti, Ford and Dos Passos—are very good, and on the level of plot summary and content analysis the book offers a useful comparative guide to the fiction produced in several different literatures during or, more often, after the war. Mr Klein's volume can be supplemented by Frank Field's *Three French Writers and the Great War*, which discusses the life and work of three novelists who were profoundly affected by their wartime service and later turned to the extremism of left or right: Barbusse, Drieu la Rochelle, and Bernanos.

Individual English writers, particularly the poets, have been widely written about during the past fifteen years. In 1965, at about the time this book was published, there appeared the third and final volume of Harold Owen's life of his brother Wilfred in the setting of their family. This was followed by Owen's collected letters, Jon Stallworthy's biography and a new edition of Dennis Welland's critical study. Rupert Brooke's collected letters came out in 1968. Since the first edition of *Heroes' Twilight* there have been books about Julian Grenfell, Siegfried Sassoon, Edward Thomas, David Jones and Ivor Gurney; R. George Thomas's fine edition of Thomas's *Collected Poems* came out in 1978. No less than three studies of Isaac Rosenberg appeared during 1975, followed in 1979 by the handsome, definitive *Collected Works*. The same year saw Jon Silkin's *Penguin Book of First World War Poetry* and Andrew Rutherford's *The Literature of War* which contains an excellent essay on the literature of the Western Front. The interest continues.

In the last chapter of this book I discussed the way in which, as the Great War receded from memory into history, it became an engaging source of myth and imagery for living writers and their readers. The process has been very evident since 1965, and has been well described by Paul Fussell. Television series about the Great War, whether documentary or fictional, have proved very popular, particularly those exploiting the nostalgic appeal of early air warfare, with daredevil pilots in ramshackle but romantic bi-planes. The war on land and in the air has been re-enacted in popular fiction, while in 1971 Susan Hill, a writer of high literary aspirations and seriousness, published *Strange Meeting*, a sensitively and sharply written novel about the friendship of two young officers in the trenches.

I excluded historiography from this book, finding the field full enough with the more immediately literary forms of poetry, fiction and autobiography. But I should like to mention a recent work of history that deals in part with the Great War. This is John Keegan's *The Face of Battle*, which describes three battles fought by the British Army in Northern France or Flanders over several centuries: Agincourt, Waterloo and the Somme. Mr Keegan's book is very absorbing; it brings together detailed and vivid military history and wide-ranging reflections on the philosophical and moral implications of battle, past and present. The book is so well-written, in a lucid and vigorous prose, and so satisfyingly constructed, that it certainly qualifies as literature in its own right.

When I was writing this book I missed a couple of important

books by survivors, which later appeared in new editions. The first of them was Henry Williamson's *The Patriot's Progress*, originally published in 1930 as a text accompanying a series of wood-engravings by the Australian artist, William Kermode. Although it can be loosely regarded as a novel, *The Patriot's Progress* does not attempt to convey character in depth; its hero, John Bullock, is a flat Everyman figure, whom we follow from his enlistment as a patriotic young volunteer in 1914, through four years in the trenches, to his discharge, minus a leg, after the Armistice. *The Patriot's Progress* is a rapidly-moving narrative and a work of some literary distinction, though in a quite different style from the wartime volumes of Williamson's *A Chronicle of Ancient Sunlight*. Compared with Williamson's later expansive and leisurely recreation of Phillip Maddison's war, *The Patriot's Progress* is narrower in focus and sharper in manner, with a satirical edge to the prose. The earlier book was part of the anti-war reaction of c.1930, and in a note at the end of the 1968 edition of *The Patriot's Progress* Williamson said he thought the anti-Staff bias was overdone. Referring to the treatment of the war in *A Chronicle of Ancient Sunlight*, Williamson added, 'I wanted to write balanced novels; the Staff also had their problems.' It is possible, though, that *The Patriot's Progress* may turn out to be Williamson's more enduring literary response to the war.

The other book, Guy Chapman's *A Passionate Prodigality*, is an autobiography first published in 1933. Against all the odds, Chapman survived three years in France as a young officer. His recollections are extraordinarily detailed, set down in plain but careful prose, and in places are very harrowing, particularly when he describes the horrors of the waterlogged battlefields around Ypres in 1917. His tone is undoubtedly disillusioned, as in most English war-writing of the late twenties and early thirties, but it is never shrill or sensational. *A Passionate Prodigality* is clearly a work of pondered maturity. Chapman abundantly illustrates Paul Fussell's account of the intensely literary way in which many educated young Englishmen reacted to the Great War. The title of the book comes from Sir Thomas Browne, and the sections and chapters are prefaced with quotations from many different authors, from Skelton and Shakespeare and Dryden to Verlaine and Arnold Bennett and Ezra Pound. *A Passionate Prodigality* came out rather too late for the great wave of war-writing of which the memoirs or autobiographies of Blunden and Graves and Sassoon formed part and it has never achieved an equal celebrity, though I think it deserves it.

After fifteen years, *Heroes' Twilight* seems a little remote to its author. Parts of it, where literary history touches on history proper, appear vulnerable in their assumptions. I was perhaps too ready to accept without question the passionate conviction of some of the soldier-writers that the war not only should have been stopped in 1916 or 1917, but that it *could* have been stopped if it were not for the stupidity and bad faith of Allied politicians and generals. The historical evidence suggests that the truth was more complex; some historians have argued that a negotiated peace was never a real possibility and that the long war of attrition on the Western Front was the only way of bringing the war to a conclusion, however high the cost. This is an argument for historians, which I am not expert enough to engage in, except to repeat my conviction that entering the war at all was a disaster for Britain. Methodologically this book now strikes me as remarkably simple, even naïve, in the way in which it combines bits of proper history, literary history and biography with the close analysis of poems and prose passages. The problems of relating the texts of literature and the texts of history now loom larger and more dauntingly. So it is as well that I wrote it when I did. Readers of the first edition were good enough to find it interesting and useful, and I hope that will still be true of this second edition. I have not changed the substance of the text, apart from correcting typographical errors, but the chronology of publications at the end has been brought up to date.

I incurred a number of debts in writing this book: in particular, I am grateful, for intellectual or material assistance, to Marcus Cunliffe, Tony England, Christian Hardie, Sylvia Mulvey, Fr Brocard Sewell, and Dennis Welland. My thanks are also due to the editors of the *Critical Quarterly*, in whose pages Chapter 2 first appeared.

1

Between Hotspur
and Falstaff:

Reflections on the Literature of War

WE can begin with Shakespeare, who may or may not have
been a soldier, but who wrote about war with uncommon completeness: showing us the glory and the trumpets in *Henry V*
and the sickness and the taste of death in *Troilus and Cressida*.
In *Henry IV*, Part I, he invents two characters who stand for
two opposing attitudes to war, and who illustrate these attitudes with great lucidity and an almost clinical exaggeration.
Hotspur exemplifies the moral virtues of heroism and the
single-minded pursuit of honour, but carries them to a ludicrous
pitch:

> By heaven methinks it were an easy leap,
> To pluck bright honour from the pale-fac'd moon,
> Or dive into the bottom of the deep,
> Where fadomline could never touch the ground,
> And pluck up drowned honour by the locks,
> So he that doth redeem her thence might wear
> Without corrival all her dignities.
> But out upon this half-fac'd fellowship.

To which Worcester sourly replies that Hotspur does not
know what he is talking about:

> He apprehends a world of figures here,
> But not the form of what he should attend.

At the end of the play Hotspur has died in battle and his
body is discovered by Sir John Falstaff, who habitually puts life
before honour. Falstaff embodies the biological virtue of cowardice: he combines the blind impulse to survive of a low writh-

ing organism with the human burden of consciousness and a far more vivid imagination than Hotspur's:

> Well, 'tis no matter, honour pricks me on; yea, but how if honour prick me off when I come on? how then? can honour set to a leg? no, or an arm? no, or take away the grief of a wound? no, honour hath no skill in surgery then? no, what is honour? a word, what is in that word honour? what is that honour? air, a trim reckoning. Who hath it? he that died a'Wednesday, doth he feel it? no, doth he hear it? no 'tis insensible then? yea, to the dead, but will it not live with the living? no, why? detraction will not suffer it, therefore I'll none of it, honour is a mere scutcheon, and so ends my Catechism.

By constant reiteration Falstaff evacuates the word 'honour' of all the densities of meaning that it held for Hotspur, and reduces it to 'a word . . . air'. Shakespeare does not endorse either of these attitudes: each of them is an unacceptable extreme, though stemming from a genuine value: Falstaff's will arouse a more immediate response, since it flatly embodies, in its most basic form, the desire for self-preservation.

One or other of these attitudes, though usually expressed in a more moderate form, will certainly be present when war is talked about. Thus, a year or so ago, a film was released which depicted an attempted escape by a number of British officers in a prisoner-of-war camp during the last war; the attempt failed and many of them were shot. A lady critic, reviewing this film, complained of the futile heroics that led these men to make the attempt. They were well out of the war, she implied; wouldn't they have been better off taking correspondence courses in some useful pursuit, and so preparing themselves for peacetime, instead of throwing their lives away in a futile gesture? A male correspondent replied, in somewhat Hotspurian tones, that they were by no means out of the war; they were still serving soldiers, obliged to harass the enemy wherever possible, and this their attempted escape succeeded in doing.

In Renaissance images of war, Hotspur was likely to be in the dominance, whether seen as the helmeted, gesturing superman of Verrochio's statue of Bartolommeo Colleoni, or the loud-mouthed colossi who strode across the dramatic stages of the time: Tamburlaine, Coriolanus, Bussy D'Ambois. (Shakespeare, however, would sometimes permit his heroes to be undercut by the scoffing, sceptical intellect of a Falstaff or a Thersites.) In the Romantic era, Scott exploited a nostalgia for the clear-cut heroics of a past age of chivalry. Byron, on the other hand, savagely castigated the inglorious pursuit of glory in those cantos of *Don Juan* that deal with the siege of Ismail:

> "Let there be light! said God, and there was light!"
> "Let there be blood!" says man, and there's a sea!
> The fiat of this spoiled child of the Night
> (For Day ne'er saw his merits) could decree
> More evil in an hour, than thirty bright
> Summers could renovate, though they should be
> Lovely as those which ripened Eden's fruit,
> For war cuts up not only branch, but root.

General Suvorov, who might have been seen as a figure of traditional heroic splendour, is calmly stripped of his pretensions:

> Suwarrow, who was standing in his shirt
> Before a company of Calmucks, drilling,
> Exclaiming, fooling, swearing at the inert,
> And lecturing on the noble art of killing,—
> For, deeming human clay but common dirt,
> This great philosopher was thus instilling
> His maxims, which, to martial comprehension,
> Proved death in battle equal to a pension.

In his stress on the physical horror of death in battle Byron is close to what one might think of as a characteristic note of twentieth-century war poetry:

> The groan, the roll in dust, the all-white eye
> Turned back within its socket—these reward
> Your rank and file by thousands, while the rest
> May win perhaps a riband at the breast!

Mocking Wordsworth, for unguardedly referring in his 'Thanksgiving Ode' to Carnage as the daughter of God, Byron seems to anticipate the angry gibes that Siegfried Sassoon and other poets of 1914-18 directed at the crass utterances of civilian propagandists. (Wordsworth wisely removed the reference when he came to revise the poem.) Byron eloquently condemns war, but not without reservations: he runs up against the hard paradox that to be a complete pacifist is to acquiesce in tyranny. *Some* wars—wars in defence of freedom, as opposed to wars fought for mere empty glory—are just. And here the paradox closes its jaws, for *all* wars are claimed as being in defence of freedom by those who initiate them.

> History can only take things in the gross;
>   But could we know them in detail, perchance
> In balancing the profit and the loss,
>   War's merit it by no means might enhance,
> To waste so much gold for a little dross,
>   As hath been done, mere conquest to advance.
> The drying up a single tear has more
> Of honest fame, than shedding seas of gore.
>
> And why? because it brings self-approbation;
>   Whereas the other, after all its glare,
> Shouts, bridges, arches, pensions from a nation,
>   Which (it may be) has not much left to spare,
> A higher title, or a loftier station,
>   Though they may make Corruption gape or stare,
> Yet, in the end, except in Freedom's battles,
> Are nothing but a child of Murder's rattles.
>
> And such they are—and such they will be found.
>   Not so Leonidas and Washington,
> Whose every battle-field is holy ground,
>   Which breathes of nations saved, not worlds undone.
> How sweetly on the ear such echoes sound!
>   While the mere victor's may appal or stun
> The servile and the vain, such names will be
> A watchword till the future shall be free.

It is in the novel, the dominant literary form of the nineteenth century, which in its very nature is realistic, bourgeois-centered, anti-heroic, and frequently ironic, that the Hotspurian or heroic attitude to war is most radically undermined. Stendhal, Byron's contemporary, provides in *La Chartreuse de Parme* a superbly written account of Fabrice del Dongo's misadventures on the field of Waterloo. Overflowing with martial aspirations and eager for a place in the fight, Fabrice plunges into the battle and meets a scene of inextricable confusion.

Neither he nor anyone else can grasp the pattern of what is going on, and there is little opportunity to play the part of a hero: Fabrice day-dreams of glory and is thrilled to catch sight of the red-faced Marshal Ney, one of his idols; but Stendhal ironically contrasts his state of mind with the reality that surrounds him, the carnage and the spreading disorder of an army in retreat. He provides the sharply observed and bloody detail that one more readily associates with Barbusse or Remarque:

> Fabrizio sat on, horror-struck. What most impressed him was the mud on the feet of the corpse, which had been stripped of its shoes and of everything else, indeed, except a wretched pair of blood-stained trousers . . . The corpse was hideously disfigured. A bullet had entered near the nose and passed out at the opposite temple. One eye was open and staring.

A little later Fabrice comes upon a wounded horse, its hooves entangled in its own entrails, and reflects, 'Well, I am under fire at last. I have seen the firing. Now I am a real soldier.'

Thackeray, too, dealt with Waterloo, though not with the actual fighting; his irony, though a good deal less subtle than Stendhal's, is sharply anti-heroic. He expresses that typically British attitude which, whilst prepared to be actively patriotic at times of crisis, is generally contemptuous of the military virtues as such, an attitude of which Kipling complained in 'Tommy':

> Yes, makin' mock o' uniforms that guard you while you sleep
> Is cheaper than them uniforms, an' they're starvation cheap.

But the fullest treatment of the war in nineteenth-century fiction occurs in the great battle scenes of *War and Peace*, in which Tolsoy combines Stendhal's cruel detail and awareness of confusion with a huge panoramic sweep that dwarfs all the participants, whether generals or ordinary soldiers, reducing them to agents of the historical process. Also in the Tolstoyan manner, though on a far smaller scale, is Stephen Crane's astonishing re-creation of a war that he had never experienced, *The Red Badge of Courage*: Crane said of this masterpiece: 'of course, I have never been in a battle, but I believe that I got my sense of the rage of conflict on the football field, or else fighting is a hereditary instinct, and I wrote intuitively.'

English writers were less adventurous, but at intervals, when the occasional far-away wars of the period demanded it, feelings rose to an unusual pitch of patriotic fervour and were given appropriate literary expression. One of the most notorious and wretchedly unforgettable specimens, in a thoroughly atavistic mode, is Tennyson's 'Charge of the Light Brigade'. In this celebrated and self-parodying party-piece Tennyson writes with a large and confident innocence about the state of mind of the unhappy cavalrymen forced to charge the Russian guns:

> 'Forward, the Light Brigade!'
> Was there a man dismay'd?
> Not tho' the soldier knew
> Some one had blunder'd. . . .

He displays a curious and presumably inadvertent tact in *not* giving the phrase 'someone had blundered' any kind of sardonic weight: the blunder merely makes the glory of the fallen heroes all the more spectacular. One can imagine what Sassoon would have made of the incident.

In the final years of the nineteenth century, the period of self-assertive Imperialism, British writers were increasingly aware of the martial and heroic virtues; and there was at the same time an increasing preoccupation with violence: I shall say more about this in the next chapter. But the anti-heroic mode also had its energetic protagonists, of whom Bernard Shaw was one of the most illustrious and skilful. *Arms and the Man* provided a thoroughly Falstaffian view of war, and was recognized by some patriots as being a subversive work. Writing in 1916, T. E. Hulme, an intellectual militarist, complained of the humanistic (or Falstaffian) ethic: 'As *life* is its fundamental value, it leads naturally to pacifism, and tends to regard conceptions like Honour, etc., as empty words, which cannot deceive the *emancipated*.' Defending the case for heroic values, Hulme continued:

> The rationalists (though they could not have said why) seem to have known *instinctively* that this conception of heroism was the central *nerve* of the ethic they opposed; and have consequently always tried to disintegrate it by ridicule. The author of 'Arms and the Man' thus reminds one of the wasps described by Fabre, who sting their prey in the central ganglia

in order to paralyse it, in this way acting as if they were expert entomologists, though in reality they can have no conscious knowledge of what they are doing.[1]

Hulme remains a singular and exotic figure (at least in an English context), who was prepared to argue about and advance intellectually positions which most people only upheld in a blind and purely instinctive way. In the essays he published during the Great War, containing a dispute about the War with Bertrand Russell, he provided fresh manifestations of the perennial debate between Hotspur and Falstaff (though Hulme, as a serving soldier, disliked the trenches as much as anyone else). Amongst those who fought, the Hotspurian mode in time gave place to the Falstaffian, or something rather like it. Hulme may have vigorously defended the traditional heroic virtues, which had been so nobly upheld at Thermopylae and even, in Tennyson's vision, in the Crimea; but after the mechanized, large-scale slaughter on the Somme in July 1916, a certain necessary balance and proportion had been lost, and these virtues were increasingly devalued. One may contrast Julian Grenfell's hymn to battle:

> And Life is Colour and Warmth and Light,
> And a striving evermore for these;
> And he is dead who will not fight;
> And who dies fighting has increase . . .

with the depressed utterance of Arthur Graeme West (in a diary entry of 19th August 1916): 'What right has anyone to demand of me that I should give up my chance of obtaining happiness—the only chance I have, and the only thing worth obtaining here.' West was a keen admirer of Bertrand Russell, Hulme's opponent in controversy.

The war of 1914-18 can still very properly be referred to by its original name of the Great War; for despite the greater magnitude of its more truly global successor, it represented a far more radical crisis in British civilization. In particular, it meant that the traditional mythology of heroism and the hero, the Hotspurian mode of self-assertion, had ceased to be viable; even though heroic *deeds* could be, and were, performed in abundance. For recent evidence of the way in which anti-heroic attitudes to war have become dominant we can consider, finally,

B

one of the most brilliant novels of the Second World War, *Catch-22*, by the American, Joseph Heller. The hero, or anti-hero, of *Catch-22* is Captain Yossarian, a bomber-pilot who has flown gallantly on a large number of missions but has now frankly had enough of the war: his principal opponent is not the Germans, but his commanding officer, Colonel Cathcart, who for reasons of personal glory is constantly increasing the number of missions his men must undertake before being sent home. In this situation Yossarian proclaims a belief in the absolute value of survival; in the face of Julian Grenfell's passionate assurance that 'who dies fighting has increase' he would probably have replied with equal passion that 'who dies fighting is *dead*!' In the face of Yossarian's energy and conviction, the old absolute distinction between 'heroism' and 'cowardice' ceases to have much meaning: Yossarian asserts the primacy of the biological, for which 'cowardice' is a virtue. In this discussion with a fellow-officer, Yossarian gives the Falstaffian arguments a fresh emphasis:

"You are talking about winning the war, and I am talking about winning the war and keeping alive."

"Exactly," Clevinger snapped smugly. "And which do you think is more important?"

"To whom?" Yossarian shot back. "Open your eyes, Clevinger. It doesn't make a damned bit of difference *who* wins the war to someone who's dead."

Clevinger sat for a moment as though he'd been slapped. "Congratulations!" he exclaimed bitterly, the thinnest milk-white line enclosing his lips tightly in a bloodless, squeezing ring. "I can't think of another attitude that could be depended upon to give greater comfort to the enemy."

"The enemy," retorted Yossarian with weighted precision, "is anybody who's going to get you killed, no matter *which* side he's on, and that includes Colonel Cathcart. And don't you forget that, because the longer you remember it, the longer you might live."

But Clevinger did forget it, and now he was dead.

Joseph Heller takes the Falstaffian approach further by making one of his characters argue that, on the whole, it is better to lose wars than to win them. In a Roman brothel an airman called Nately, who is a normally patriotic young American, meets an old man who claims to be a hundred and seven years old and who talks like this:

"You put so much stock in *winning* wars," the grubby iniquitous old man scoffed. "The real trick lies in *losing* wars, in knowing which wars can be *lost*. Italy has been losing wars for centuries, and just see how splendidly we've done nonetheless. France wins wars and is in a continual state of crisis. Germany loses and prospers. Look at our own recent history. Italy won a war in Ethiopia and promptly stumbled into serious trouble. Victory gave us such insane delusions of grandeur that we helped start a world war we hadn't a chance of winning. But now that we are losing again, everything has taken a turn for the better, and we will certainly come out on top again if we succeed in being defeated."

There is an uncomfortable degree of truth in his remarks: under the stress of Hotspurian emotions, much blood has been spilt in the past in the pursuit of wars whose outcome made no difference at all to most of the inhabitants of the countries involved. But not all wars might as well be lost as won: in our own age, where totalitarianism and the technology of genocide go hand in hand, the price of losing a war might be the surrendering of one's fellow-countrymen to torture, deportation or mass extermination.[2]

2

Preludes

IT is always tempting to mythologize the past, and no period of recent history lends itself so readily to such a habit of mind as the years immediately before 1914. We imagine long, brilliant afternoons, with the costumes and décor out of *My Fair Lady,* the champagne and strawberries inexhaustible, premières of the Russian Ballet, yachting at Cowes, veteran motor-cars with their brass and paint-work gleaming. And for the poor, beer was cheap and the pubs were open all day. The sun always shone and the sky was triumphantly, everlastingly blue. This whole, magnificent, fragile order was shattered in pieces by a pistol shot at Sarajevo, and then trodden deep in the mud and darkness of Flanders and the Somme. It is a compelling myth, and, of course, some of it is true. When we read that David Lloyd George observed in a speech on 17th July 1914—three weeks before Britain declared war on Germany—'In the matter of external affairs the sky has never been more perfectly blue', we are struck by the poignancy of such child-like unawareness, enhanced by that familiar and characteristic image of a sky of perfect blue.

One cannot say that myths are untrue: it is not in their nature to be contradicted, but one can point out their insufficiencies. And the picture of the England of the years before the outbreak of the Great War as a peaceable Eden, happily unconscious of the fate about to sweep it away, contains very much less than the whole truth. Many people were aware of the clouds already forming in that apparently flawless sky. George Dangerfield's admirable book, *The Strange Death of Liberal England 1910-1914* provides abundant evidence of the way in which the civilized and placid surface of life in those years barely covered alarming areas of violence and disorder: huge cracks were already appearing in the structure that toppled with such apparent suddenness in 1914. Indeed, Dangerfield argues that the Great War did no more than accentuate a process that was already under way. He shows that the stability of English life was threatened by a triple outbreak of violence: from industrial troubles, from the suffragette movement, and from the Tory revolt over Ulster. If the country had not gone to war in August 1914, England would have been faced with a possible civil war in Ireland, and something like a general strike in industry,' provoked by union leaders of extremely militant temper.

As one might expect, some of the imaginative writers of the time were conscious of the spreading cracks in the social façade and the hints of impending disaster. In 1910, the year of George V's accession, two books, both quite famous, were published. One of them, Norman Angell's *The Great Illusion,* an impressive work of liberal optimism, argued that a general European war was impossible for economic reasons. The other book was *Howards End,* the fourth novel by E. M. Forster, then aged thirty-one: it advanced no propositions, save perhaps the mild argument in favour of togetherness contained in its epigraph, 'only connect'; but it contained a far more penetrating insight into the attitudes and preoccupations of its time than many overtly discursive works. Though in purely literary terms an imperfect and desperately contrived novel, *Howards End* remains highly relevant for anyone concerned with the intellectual, moral and social quality of life in the England of 1910-14. As a recent critic, Mr. C. K. Stead, has remarked,[1] its decent, worried liberalism, deeply in love with the English countryside and past, and conscious of impending dissolution, was to form the staple attitude of the Georgian poets of two or three years later, an attitude which was to find both fulfilment and catastrophe during the Great War. In many passages of *Howards End* Forster shows himself strangely prophetic, already concerned with problems that were to be dominant fifty years later: the volume of traffic in London streets, the demolition of well-loved buildings, the sprawl of suburbia into open countryside. Here, for instance, is a key passage from the final pages of the novel: Margaret, Helen and Helen's baby are arranged in a precarious tableau in the garden of Howards End, the house that has symbolized the continuity of English tradition.

"I hope it will be permanent," said Helen, drifting away to other thoughts.

"I think so. There are moments when I feel Howards End peculiarly our own."

"All the same, London's creeping."

She pointed over the meadow—over eight or nine meadows, but at the end of them was a red rust.

"You see that in Surrey and even Hampshire now," she continued. "I can see it from the Purbeck Downs. And London is only part of something else, I'm afraid. Life's going to be melted down, all over the world."

Margaret knew that her sister spoke truly. Howards End, Oniton, the Purbeck Downs, the Oderberge, were all survivals, and the melting pot was being prepared for them. Logically, they had no right to be alive.

Forster could not have viewed open violence, and still less the prospect of war, with anything other than utter repugnance. Nevertheless, there is a surprising amount of violence in his earlier novels, usually of a flatly melodramatic kind, and the topic is clearly one which the author found interesting if distasteful. As an example, one can refer to the scene in Chapter XLI of *Howards End* in which Leonard Bast, the wretched, upstart young autodidact from the lower orders, is beaten by Charles Wilcox with the flat of a sword, and falls dead; as he falls, he brings down a bookcase on top of him and so is buried, with heavy symbolism, under a pile of books.

A similar interest in violence is noticeable in many other works of the early years of this century, and in much late-Victorian literature. In authors who do not share Forster's liberal convictions it is a good deal more pronounced: Kipling is a figure who comes immediately to mind, but there were other exemplars on the Right. In 1892 the crippled Imperialist, W. E. Henley, published a strange poem called 'The Song of the Sword', which he dedicated to Kipling. This is a passionate paean to violence, perhaps inspired by early heroic poetry, in which Henley almost seems to hint at something as radically un-English as the Spanish cult of death:

> Clear singing, clean slicing;
> Sweet spoken, soft finishing;

Making death beautiful,
Life but a coin
To be staked in the pastime
Whose playing is more
Than the transfer of being;
Arch-anarch, chief builder,
Prince and evangelist,
I am the Will of God:
I am the Sword.

Or consider a very different writer, G. K. Chesterton, who was a Liberal of sorts, a Little Englander, and a Christian apologist. His fantastic novel, *The Napoleon of Notting Hill* (1904), contains some jolly accounts of street fighting in the West London suburbs in which a good deal of blood in spilt but no one is really hurt: 'down the steep streets which lead from the Waterworks Tower to the Notting Hill High Road, blood has been running, and is running, in great red serpents, that curl out into the main thoroughfare and shine in the moon.' There is something deeply innocent about such a vision, the product of a period when England had been at peace for a very long time (save for the Boer War and various colonial adventures) and peace had come to seem insupportably dull. How much more modern, by contrast, are Byron and Stendhal.

Another example of purely literary violence can be seen in an early poem by Ezra Pound, 'Altaforte', which commemorates with considerable gusto the bellicose inclinations of a Provençal nobleman:

And let the music of the swords make them crimson!
Hell grant soon we hear again the swords clash!
Hell blot black for always the thought 'Peace'![2]

One does not need to look far to find literary evidence of a concern with violence that was to erupt in the large-scale political and social turbulence of the years immediately before 1914.

A particular preoccupaton of many writers in the early years of this century was the fear of a future war and a possible invasion of England. This was not, in itself, a new theme. From the Franco-Prussian war of 1870 onwards many books and pamphlets had been published which dealt with such an invasion; some of them were written by professional soldiers and aimed at arousing the nation and strengthening its defences, while others, of a more sensational kind, merely wanted to make their readers' flesh creep. One of the earliest and most famous was *The Battle of Dorking* (1871) by General Sir George Chesney, about a successful Prussian invasion of southern England, which inspired many imitations. Representative later examples included *The Invasion of England* (1882) by General Sir William Butler, and *The Great War in England in 1897* (1894) by William Le Quex. In the same genre, but of incomparably greater literary and imaginative power, was H. G. Wells's *The War of the Worlds* (1898), which described an invasion of England, not by human enemies, but by Martians. Many of these works were of a frankly ephemeral nature, but there seems to have been a fairly steady demand for them, and no doubt their output varied according to the international situation: the hypothetical enemies involved were usually France, Germany or Russia, or a combination of two or three of these powers; but in one or two instances America was seen as a possible opponent.

After the turn of the century, however, Germany came to be regarded more and more as Britain's most likely enemy, reflecting the increasing German attempt to rival Britain as a world power; and the warning note became more urgent. As, for instance, in Kipling's impassioned rebuke in 'The Islanders' (1902) to his fellow-countrymen—'the flannelled fools at the wicket or the muddied oafs at the goals'—for their slackness in the matter of national defence:

Do ye wait for the spattered shrapnel ere ye learn how a gun is laid?
For the low, red glare to southward when the raided coast-towns
    burn?
(Light ye shall have on that lesson, but little time to learn.)

A celebrated popular novel of about the same time was Erskine Childers's *The Riddle of the Sands* (1903), a splendid adventure story, in which an English yachtsman sailing in the East Frisian islands stumbles upon plans for a German invasion of England. Childers wrote the book with an overtly didactic aim, though in later years, after fighting throughout the Great War, he abandoned his English patriotism and became an Irish nationalist; he was finally shot by the Free State Government as an adherent of the Republican side in the Civil War. H. G. Wells was another writer somewhat preoccupied with the threat of war and the menace of Imperial Germany. In 1908 he published *The War in the Air*, in which a German attempt to obtain world domination begins with an airship attack on the United States. Global war ensues and leads to the virtual collapse of civilization throughout large parts of the world. This novel embodies an apocalyptic vision of a kind which had obsessed many writers of the *fin de siècle* era and to which Wells had previously given a more profoundly imaginative embodiment in *The War of the Worlds*. But *The War in the Air*, though a shapeless book, has some powerful passages, and contains a fairly good anticipation of the horrors of aerial bombardment. Wells returned to the topic of war in *The World Set Free*, a very inferior fantasy, which appeared in 1914, not long before the outbreak of the Great War. It describes a war fought in the nineteen-fifties (it is mankind's last war, and the prelude to Utopia), but the line-up is appropriate to 1914: Britain and France, allied with the 'Slav Confederation', against Germany and the other Central European powers. Wells displays his characteristic flair for prophecy in imagining the use of atomic bombs, but gets the detail wrong by making them two feet in diameter and dropped from aeroplanes by hand. He displays a more accurate anticipation of the conflict that was to follow hard on the publication of his book when one of his characters reflects:

" 'From Holland to the Alps this day,' I thought, 'there must be crouching and lying between half and a million of men, trying to inflict irreparable damage upon one another. The thing is idiotic to the pitch of impossibility. It is a dream. Presently I shall wake up.' . . ."

More directly concerned with the German menace as it was understood by many people in the immediate pre-war period, is a novel by Saki (H. H. Munro), *When William Came*. Published in 1913, ten years after *The Riddle of the Sands*, it reflects the same basic preoccupation. Britain has already been occupied by Germany, after a brief war, not described in detail, in which the British forces were decisively defeated: the King has fled to India, and the British Isles have been annexed as a province of the German Empire, with bilingual notices and newspapers and German troops much in evidence. The story is told through the eyes of Murrey Yeovil, a Tory patriot, who had been travelling in Siberia whilst the war was being fought and returns to discover, in horror, a defeated nation. Most of the novel is set in fashionable London, among Saki's familiar circle of epigrammatic, world-weary socialites, Murrey's wife, Cicely, prominent amongst them; they are prepared to accept the new situation and collaborate, with varying degrees of enthusiasm, with the occupying power. Murrey's disgust with the prevailing decadence is heightened when an Imperial Rescript is published stating that subjects of British birth will not, as had been anticipated, he conscripted for military service, since they are not of sufficient martial calibre; instead they will be prohibited from handling arms at all, even in rifle clubs, though they will be very heavily taxed to help support the occupying German troops. Thus the will and capacity to resist of the British will be finally eradicated: it was part of Saki's didactic message in this novel, as it had previously been Kipling's, to denounce the British for their unwillingness to accept conscription in peace-time. The point is rather heavily underlined when Murrey sees a company of Bavarian infantry marching down a London street:

> A group of lads from the tea-shop clustered on the pavement and watched the troops go by, staring at a phase of life in which they had no share. The martial trappings, the swaggering joy of life, the comradeship of camp and barracks, the hard discipline of drill yard and fatigue duty, the long sentry watches, the trench digging, forced marches, wounds, cold, hunger, makeshift hospitals, and the blood-wet laurels —these were not for them. Such things they might only guess at, or see on a cinema film, darkly; they belonged to the civilian nation.

This is, perhaps, a somewhat civilian concept of the martial virtues, though a very traditional one: within a year or so the 'blood-wet laurels' were to seem a distinctly inadequate symbol for the realities of twentieth-century warfare. (Though Saki himself died in action in 1916.) At the end of his book, Saki permits a faint note of hope: the youth of Britain, it seems, have not been won over by the conquerors, and a parade of boy-scouts in front of the Kaiser in Hyde Park is boycotted and a complete failure.

German rule in the England of 1913, as Saki describes it, though irksome, is remarkably mild when compared with what we now know of Nazi or Communist occupation; but it would have been a shocking enough picture for contemporary readers. One may doubt if such works were very successful in their directly homiletic aims: but they are pointers to a deep-seated fear of German domination. They may suggest, too, that the outbreak of war in August 1914, though in one way such an unexpected event, had been imaginatively anticipated for some time. And a subconscious fear of invasion and occupation is perhaps why so many Englishmen reacted as if it were England herself that was being invaded, rather than Belgium. To this extent, a war propaganda poster showing German soldiers mounting guard in a British factory and maltreating the workers fulfilled expectations and fears aroused by books like *When William Came*.

There is another sphere, much more remote from politics and everyday affairs, in which one also finds a certain pre-occupation with violence, and an impatience with the pacific virtues. In the world of *avant-garde* art and literature there was a cult of the virile and dynamic virtues: Futurism as an inter-national artistic movement, under the leadership of the ebul-lient Italian, Marinetti, briefly flourished from about 1911; and the Futurists idolized the machine—notably the aeroplane and the motor-car—and were very excited by the dynamism manifested in modern war. Before long Futurist aspirations were to be surpassed in the artillery bombardments of the Western front: shortly before his death in 1915 the young French sculptor of genius, Henri Gaudier-Brzeska, remarked in a letter:

we have the finest futuristic music Marinetti can dream of, big guns, small guns, bomb-throwers' reports, with a great difference between the German and the French, the different kinds of whistling from the shells, their explosion, the echo in the woods of the rifle fires, some short, discreet, others long, rolling, etc.; but it is all stupid vulgarity, and I prefer the fresh wind in the leaves with a few songs from the birds.[3]

Futurism never made any great impact in England, though the painter C. R. W. Nevinson considered himself an adherent of the moment. But there were comparable currents of thought in advanced London intellectual and artistic circles during the years before 1914. One can again consider the enigmatic figure of T. E. Hulme, for instance, who was killed in 1917: had he survived he might have become the principal theoretician of English fascism—if such a movement had developed on a large scale—just as Kipling might have been its d'Annunzio. Hulme, as the begetter of Imagist poetry and the keen defender of Epstein's sculpture, was actively engaged in the various artistic manifestations of the modern movement; and whilst not a systematic thinker, he professed a number of highly influential attitudes. Hulme's aesthetic was, above all, anti-vital; just as he admired heroic values, as against an ethic based on *life*, so he desired an art—particularly in sculpture—a kind of creation that was geometrical, non-organic and more or less abstract. In his excursions into political thought Hulme strongly admired the writings of the French syndicalist, Georges Sorel, whose mystical cult of 'proletarian violence' appealed to the extreme Right as much as to the Left (Sorel himself was an admirer of Lenin, but was also a dominant influence on Mussolini). Hulme helped to translate Sorel's *Reflections on Violence* (1916), in Chapter 2 of which we find the following sentiments, a straightforward example of Fascist rhetoric:

> Proletarian violence, carried on as a pure and simple manifestation of the class war, appears thus as a very fine and very heroic thing; it is at the service of the immemorial interests of civilisation; it is not perhaps the most appropriate method of obtaining immediate material advantages, but it may save the world from barbarism.

Hulme was associated for a time with Ezra Pound and Wyndham Lewis, who founded early in 1914 the Vorticist movement, as something of an English counterblast to Futurism. There are many similarities between the two movements, though the Vorticists condemned the Futurists: the principal

28

difference, however, is that the Vorticists were less concerned with dynamism and movement; their aesthetic principle was the 'Vortex', defined variously as a point of stasis amidst the flow of 'vital' activity, or as a unit of creative energy (it also had affinities, never very clearly defined, with the Image in poetry). Hulme was suspicious of the Vorticists, and not on good personal terms with them, but they seemed to reflect his ideas: above all a stress on the abstract, geometrical, anti-human element in art. Like the Futurists, they admired machinery. This, at least, was true of the painters and sculptors in their midst: Lewis, Edward Wadsworth, and Henri Gaudier-Brzeska. Pound was in the group principally as an enthusiastic publicist, and Lewis has said that the artists secretly despised his literary interests as hopelessly old-fashioned and backward-looking, compared with their own revolutionary zeal. (Though once the war had started, Gaudier-Brzeska, a belligerent patriot who joined the French army at the outbreak, could find inspiration in Pound's purely literary bellicosity; in a letter to Edward Wadsworth in November 1914 he remarked: 'you may imagine how difficult it is to concentrate your mind upon any subject when you are obsessed by fighting. Now would be the time to read over and over again Ezra's "Altaforte".'⁴)

The first number of *Blast*, the Vorticist magazine, was dated 20th June 1914: its huge magenta cover and stark, angry typography were in themselves aggressive acts. Still more so were the manifestoes that it contained, those lists of 'blasts', more trenchant than coherent, directed at the survivals of the Victorian era and the various idols and comfortable assumptions of the philistine British middle-class. Much of the contents of *Blast* have their permanent place in the literary and artistic history of the twentieth century: the reproductions of paintings by Lewis and Wadsworth, of sculpture by Gaudier-Brzeska, the early chapters of Ford Madox Ford's *The Good Soldier*, and, in the second number, some of Eliot's first poems. But in the present context, the most poignant thing about *Blast* is the contrast between its small-scale belligerency, so emphatic at the time and so frail in retrospect, and the wave of mechanized violence, thoroughly geometrical and anti-vital, that was to sweep over Europe a few weeks later. Knowing what we do, is it sinister or pathetic to find reproduced in *Blast* an angular abstract design by Lewis with the caption 'Plan of War'?

The War provided a far greater Vortex; and this was recognized by Gaudier-Brzeska, in the manifesto that he wrote from the trenches and which appeared posthumously in 1915 in the second number of *Blast*.

I HAVE BEEN FIGHTING FOR TWO MONTHS and I can now gauge the intensity of life.

HUMAN MASSES teem and move, are destroyed and crop up again.

HORSES are worn out in three weeks, die by the roadside.

DOGS wander, are destroyed, and others come along.

WITH ALL THE DESTRUCTION that works around us NOTHING IS CHANGED, EVEN SUPERFICIALLY. LIFE IS THE SAME STRENGTH, THE MOVING AGENT THAT PERMITS THE SMALL INDIVIDUAL TO ASSERT HIMSELF.

THE BURSTING SHELLS, the volleys, wire entanglements, projectors, motors, the chaos of battle DO NOT ALTER IN THE LEAST the outlines of the hill we are besieging. A company of PARTRIDGES scuttle along before our very trench.

IT WOULD BE FOLLY TO SEEK ARTISTIC EMOTIONS AMID THESE LITTLE WORKS OF OURS.

THIS PALTRY MECHANISM, WHICH SERVES AS A PURGE TO OVER-NUMEROUS HUMANITY.

THIS WAR IS A GREAT REMEDY.

IN THE INDIVIDUAL IT KILLS ARROGANCE, SELF-ESTEEM, PRIDE.

IT TAKES AWAY FROM THE MASSES NUMBERS UPON NUMBERS OF UNIMPORTANT UNITS, WHOSE ECONOMIC ACTIVITIES BECOME NOXIOUS AS THE RECENT TRADE CRISES HAVE SHOWN US.

MY VIEWS ON SCULPTURE REMAIN ABSOLUTELY THE SAME.

IT IS THE VORTEX OF WILL, OF DECISION, THAT BEGINS.[5]

And so on.

Traditional England, prosperous, pacific, humane, optimistic, the England seen in an exalted light in *Howards End*, in Margaret Schlegel's vision of a countryside that 'would vote Liberal if it could', was sadly undermined in the years that led

Preludes

up to the Great War: attacked by strikers and suffragettes, threatened by military revolt over Ireland, and on the intellectual plane riddled with self-doubt and preoccupied with violence; berated by Tories like Kipling and Saki for being pacific, and by the artistic *avant-garde* for being philistine and bourgeois. It is not hard to see why the country should have found in the outbreak of war, that apparent thunderbolt from a cloudless sky, something very like an act both of fulfilment and deliverance.

3

POETS I
Brooke, Grenfell, Sorley

THE impact of war, on 4th August 1914, has often been described, and the details are familiar: cheering crowds outside Buckingham Palace, a surge of patriotic fervour throughout the country, the rush to the recruiting offices. One young man who volunteered has left a vivid account of his motives: J. B. Priestley has written:

> There came, out of the unclouded blue of that summer, a challenge that was almost like a conscription of the spirit, little to do really with King and Country and flag-waving and hip-hip-hurrah, a challenge to what we felt was our untested manhood. Other men, who had not lived as easily as we had, had drilled and marched and borne arms—couldn't we? Yes, we too could leave home and soft beds and the girls to soldier for a spell, if there was some excuse for it, something at least to be defended. And here it was.[1]

In the opening weeks of the war many poems appeared in the press which were impeccably patriotic in sentiment and thoroughly wretched as literary art. Thomas Hardy's 'Men Who March Away', dated 5th September 1914, is a good deal better than the average run of these. It reflects the dominant mood unpretentiously, with obvious sincerity and the kind of baffled clumsiness that characterizes so much of Hardy's writing:

> Nay. We well see what we are doing,
> Though some may not see—
> Dalliers as they be—
> England's need are we;
> Her distress would leave us rueing:
> Nay. We well see what we are doing,
> Though some may not see!

Another poem written at about the same time is Kipling's
'For All We Have and Are', which, in J. I. M. Stewart's
words, 'is adequate to its grave occasion':

> For all we have and are,
> For all our children's fate,
> Stand up and take the war.
> The Hun is at the gate!
> Our world has passed away,
> In wantonness o'erthrown.
> There is nothing left today
> But steel and fire and stone!

Kipling combines his grim acceptance of war with a certain
degree of relish about the overthrow of that 'wantonness' which
he had so often condemned in his slack fellow-countrymen.
In the second stanza Kipling seems to be echoing the poem
that Henley had dedicated to him over twenty years before:

> Once more we hear the word
> That sickened earth of old: —
> 'No law except the Sword
> Unsheathed and uncontrolled.'
> Once more it knits mankind,
> Once more the nations go
> To meet and break and bind
> A crazed and driven foe.

It was to be expected that Tory patriots like Kipling would
share the popular enthusiasm for the war and would urge
universal support for it. What was less inherently probable was
that progressive and radical writers, the idols of the Left, would
be equally wholehearted in supporting the war; but H. G.
Wells offers a curious and instructive example. He had not long
published *The World Set Free*, which exposed the futility and
horror of war, and showed the nations resolving never to undertake it again. Wells's convictions, as revealed in that novel,
were pacifist; but when the war against Germany broke out he
rapidly wrote a series of newspaper articles, soon afterwards
published in book form as *The War That Will End War*, which
urged full support for the struggle against Prussian militarism,
so that, once Germany was defeated, war itself might be abolished. Wells justified British participation—in defence of Bel-

C

gium—by seeing the war as a real-life enactment of the 'The Last War' that he had described in *The World Set Free*. He did not expect the war to last long, and was confident that France would defeat Germany within three months: he could even permit himself such confident observations as: 'a Russian raid is far more likely to threaten Berlin than a German to reach Paris' (This, of course, was written before the battle of Tannenburg).

Wells's support for the war earned him derisive comments from both Left and Right. T. E. Hulme ironically retailed an anecdote about a man suddenly taken ill who was examined by a vet, and was told, 'I don't know what's the matter with you, but I can give you something that will bring on blind staggers, and I can cure that all right.' Hulme continued:

> Now Mr. Wells had never taken the possibility of an Anglo-German war seriously—he was pacifist by profession. It was not exactly his subject then, and last August may have found him somewhat baffled as to what to say. So he gave it blind staggers, he turned it into a "war to end war", and there you are. Such writers, in dealing with a matter like war, alien to their ordinary habits of thought, are liable to pass from a fatuous optimism to a fatuous pessimism, equally distant from the real facts of the situation.[2]

On the other hand, Douglas Goldring sharply attacked Wells soon after the war (Goldring had volunteered at the outbreak of war, then fallen seriously ill and been discharged; two years later he was called up, and by that time had become a conscientious objector):

> When war broke out, while many of Mr. Wells' disciples were keeping alight the flame of those principles which by his eloquence he had instilled into their minds, Mr. Wells himself, like the majority of us, completely lost his head.[3]

Outright pacifists were few in number at the beginning of the war, though they included a number of intellectuals: Bertrand Russell, the Bloomsbury group, and various other members of Lady Ottoline Morrell's circle. But for the most part the nation had no doubts that the war against Germany was both necessary and just; fanned by atrocity stories from Belgium, hatred of the Germans grew to an intensity greater than anything that arose in the Second World War. Disenchanted innocence turned savagely sour. The feelings of diffused patriotic fervour, heightened by the painful news during August of the long retreat of the British Expeditionary Force from Mons, needed a focus, a dominating myth that could give coherence to these strong but scattered emotions. One was to arise in extraordinary fashion. On 29th September 1914 Arthur Machen published a short story called 'The Bowmen' in the *Evening News*: Machen was a professional journalist who had made his début in the 'nineties with a number of short stories of the occultist, consciously bizarre kind that were popular at that time. 'The Bowmen' was, as he admitted, a very slight piece; it described the stand made by a company of British troops during the retreat from Mons. They were hard pressed by numerically stronger German forces, and though they fought back energetically were on the point of being overrun. At that moment one of them, more educated than the rest, murmured an invocation to St. George, *'Adsit Anglis Sanctus Georgius'*:

His heart grew hot as a burning coal, it grew cold as ice within him, as it seemed to him that a tumult of voices answered to his summons. He heard, or seemed to hear, thousands shouting: "St. George! St. George!"

"Ha! messire; ha! sweet Saint, grant us good deliverance!"

"St. George for merry England!"

"Harrow! Harrow! Monseigneur St. George, succour us."

"Ha! St. George! Ha! St. George! a long bow and a strong bow."

"Heaven's Knight, aid us!"

And as the soldier heard these voices he saw before him, beyond the trench, a long line of shapes, with a shining about them. They were like men who drew the bow, and with another shout their cloud of arrows flew singing and tingling through the air towards the German hosts.

The fight turns in favour of the British, aided by these heavenly forces, and the Germans leave ten thousand dead on the field: a disastrous break-through has been averted.

The reception given to this frankly pot-boiling piece seems

to have amazed Machen, and with good reason. Within a short time of its publication he was being asked if the story were founded on fact, and was pressed for details of its source. Despite his energetic assertion that the story was pure invention, the mythopoeic imagination of the public insisted otherwise. Rumours spread declaiming that the story *was* based on a genuine incident during the British retreat and Machen's denials were ignored. Before long the legend was elaborated so that the bowmen were described as 'angels'—no doubt because of the reference to 'a long line of shapes, with a shining about them'—and thus was born the extraordinary myth of the 'angels of Mons', which was firmly believed in by a great many people during the early years of the war. And if no one had actually seen them, there were innumerable second- or third-hand accounts, allegedly stemming from soldiers involved in the retreat. The legend died hard and passed into the popular mythology of the war: there can be no doubt that it served as a genuine mythic focus for the anguish aroused by the British retreat during the early weeks of the war.

Yet of all the myths which dominated the English consciousness during the Great War the greatest, and the most enduring, is that which enshrines the name and memory of Rupert Brooke: in which three separate elements—Brooke's personality, his death, and his poetry (or some of it)—are fused into a single image. Brooke was the first of the 'war poets'; a quintessential young Englishman; one of the fairest of the nation's sons; a ritual sacrifice offered as evidence of the justice of the cause for which England fought. His sonnet, 'The Soldier', is among the most famous short poems in the language. If the Tolstoyan theory of art had any validity it would be one of the greatest—as, indeed, it is considered to be by the numerous readers for whom the excellence of poetry lies in the acceptability of its sentiments rather than in the quality of its language.

Brooke's personal legend was first embodied in Frances Cornford's epigram, written whilst he was still an undergraduate:

> A young Apollo, golden-haired,
> Stands dreaming on the verge of strife,
> Magnificently unprepared
> For the long littleness of life.

This already contains the essentials of the myth which was to develop during Brooke's life and then to burgeon luxuriantly after his death in April 1915. Already, during the poet's life, it seems to have been self-perpetuating: the image of the 'young Apollo, golden-haired' was given physical reality in the rather deplorable photograph taken by Sherril Schell in 1913, showing Brooke with bare shoulders and flowing locks, which formed the frontispiece of *1914 and other poems* (1915). Christopher Hassall records that this photograph was not well received by Brooke's friends, who referred to it as 'Your Favourite Actress'; one of them suggested that he might as well be photographed completely in the nude. The extravagances in the legend were played down in Edward Marsh's posthumous memoir, which fixed the public image of the dead poet: handsome, talented, theatrical, with a rather frenetic gaiety; a product of the Cambridge milieu which when transported to London produced the Bloomsbury ethos: Brooke disliked its upholders but shared many of its ideals—the cult of personal relations, in particular. There was also Brooke's social idealism which made him an enthusiastic Fabian, and the hints, scattered through many of his poems, of an energetic but rather soulful amorist. In Christopher Hassall's massive biography we are now told as much as we can conveniently assimilate about Brooke's short and favoured life. Hassall fills in the picture about aspects of Brooke's personality which Marsh left in tactful silence. It's interesting to know, for instance, that Brooke was psychologically unstable, with a paranoid streak, and for quite long periods was on the edge of a nervous breakdown: for several years he was involved in a singularly gruelling love affair that brought him little happiness. As his life becomes part of history, Brooke's legend, one may assume, will lose some of its former glamour; Hassall's book, by its sheer density of detail, may well hasten the process of demythologization. But Brooke's life will continue to be interesting, and will never lack some kind of archetypal quality, if only because he was such a perfect symbol of the doomed aspirations of Liberal England: a figure from an unwritten, or suppressed, novel by his friend, E. M. Forster.

To extricate Brooke's poetry from the personal legend in which it played a merely contributory role is not at all easy, but the critic and literary historian must make the attempt. In the first place, the poetry can best be undersood by placing it in its proper context in the Georgian movement: Brooke was one of the most admired contributors to Edward Marsh's first volume of *Georgian Poetry* when it appeared in 1912. Poetically, the Georgians were an ambiguous group. For more than forty years it has been customary to regard them as no more than the fag-end of late-Victorian romanticism, a poetic nadir before the advent of the triumphant modernists, Eliot and Pound. And there is some truth in this; there are good reasons for seeing the Georgians as the end of an era, as George Dangerfield does:

> Until the very outbreak of war, the poets stayed unresponsive to the changing times; stubborn, sweet, unreal, they were the last victims and the last heroes of Liberal England. And in the midst of them, a little in front of them, as one who takes his place before an effective background, there stands the engaging figure of Rupert Brooke.[4]

This is a persuasive notion: but it is too simple. A more discriminating view has been advanced in Mr. C. K. Stead's recent admirable book, *The New Poetic*. As he shows, no matter how remote and old-fashioned the Georgians may seem now, at the time they regarded themselves, and were regarded, as somewhat revolutionary. Their comparative bluntness of language, and liking for 'ordinary', unpretentious subjects, was not to everyone's taste; and Brooke found himself in a good deal of trouble over one of his early poems, 'A Channel Passage', which deals with love and sea-sickness in a self-consciously brutal fashion:

> Do I forget you? Retchings twist and tie me,
>   Old meat, good meals, brown gobbets, up I throw.
> Do I remember? Acrid return and slimy,
>   The sobs and slobber of a last year's woe.
> And still the sick ship rolls. 'Tis hard, I tell ye,
>   To choose 'twixt love and nausea, heart and belly.

It is not difficult to sympathize with the original critics of the poem. Such excursions are not, to be sure, typical of Georgian poetry, but they can serve to modify both the received picture of the Georgian movement and (in those not very familiar with his work) of Brooke's poetic personality.

Technically, the Georgians were less innovating than they thought: nothing they wrote had anything approaching the originality of, say, 'The Love Song of J. Alfred Prufrock'. But ideologically they can be seen as participating in the post-Victorian mood of revolt, which was manifested in such literary monuments as Galsworthy's *The Man of Property* (1906) as well as, later, in the avant-gardism of Wyndham Lewis and the other 'men of 1914'. As Mr. Stead has shown, the Georgians, in turning to a simple patriotism centred on images of rural England—the country cottage, the cricket match, the genial pub —were in reaction against the loud-mouthed but vague poetic imperialism associated with Kipling, and with less talented late-Victorian and Edwardian versifiers such as William Watson, Henry Newbolt, and Alfred Noyes, who dwelt heavily on the splendours of Empire and heroes like Drake and Nelson. In comparison, the Georgians were Little Englanders. Mr. Stead has summed the matter up succinctly:

The dominant images of three decades of poetry, even when they spring initially from a literary concern, carry accurately the mood, and in a sense the history, of England during that time: Drake and Nelson; rural England; fear in a handful of dust.[5]

In one of Brooke's most famous poems, 'The Old Vicarage, Grantchester', we have a lucid instance of the Georgian concentration on rural England; this poem was written in Berlin, and Christopher Hassall observes that Brooke originally intended to call it 'The Sentimental Exile', and suggests that the public might in that case have read it less solemnly. This is possibly true, and such a reading may have been closer to Brooke's intention; the fact remains that the whole poem displays a kind of switchback irregularity of tone, alternatively satirizing the Cambridge landscape (and by implication the poet) and idealizing it. Such uncertainty is a perhaps inevitable concomitant of Georgian Little Englandism: it is difficult for the retreat to a rural fastness, no matter how delectable, to be entirely whole-hearted. At the same time as he wrote 'The Old Vicarage' Brooke was concerned about the possible advent of a European war.

What we think of as the characteristic 'war poetry' of 1914-18 was, in fact, a continuation of the Georgian movement by poets who, volunteering in defence of the England they had written about so lovingly, found themselves thrust into the melting pot which Forster had envisaged at the conclusion of *Howards End*. Arthur Waugh, a critic of conservative tastes but considerable clarity of mind, remarked during the Great War:

> The Victorian poets wrote of war as though it were something splendid and ennobling; but as a matter of fact they knew nothing whatever about it. The Georgian poets know everything there is to know about war, and they come back and report it to us as an unspeakable horror, maiming and paralysing the very soul of man.[6]

Brooke was denied such knowledge, for he saw practically no fighting, save for a brief skirmish outside Antwerp in the autumn of 1914. In a prose piece he indicates the state of mind of innumerable young men like himself at the start of the war: 'An Unusual Young Man', published in the *New Statesman* on 29th August 1914,[7] supposedly describes the state of mind of a friend on the outbreak of war, though this figure is clearly a vehicle for Brooke's own opinions. He thinks about Germany, a country he knows and likes, and is incredulous at the idea of an armed conflict between England and Germany:

> But as he thought 'England and Germany' the word 'England' seemed to flash like a line of foam. With a sudden tightening of his heart, he realized that there might be a raid on the English coast. He didn't imagine any possibility of it *succeeding*, but only of enemies and warfare on English soil. The idea sickened him.

The notion of a foreign invasion of England, already played on by Tory publicists like Kipling and Saki, evoked a ready response in the consciousness of the young Fabian. Brooke continues the essay with a rhapsodic description of the Southern English landscape in a passage recalling the similar descriptions in *Howards End*. This passage has been subjected to a withering analysis by Cyril Connolly in *Enemies of Promise*; Connolly describes it in this way: ' "England has declared war," he says to himself, "what had Rupert Brooke better feel about it?" His

equipment is not equal to the strain and his language betrays
the fact . . .' As a critical judgment this is undoubtedly penetrating. And yet it is not the most interesting thing that one
can say about this piece of writing: Brooke was having to
fake up an emotional attitude precisely because the experience
of England being involved in a major war was so alien and un-
graspable. There was, too, a curious interplay between the literary cult of rural England fostered by the Georgians, and the
degree of patriotism that it is traditionally proper to feel when
one's country goes to war: Brooke's feelings are very literary
indeed in their mode of expression, but are not thereby pre-
vented from being genuine. As Connolly says, Brooke's equipment was unequal to the strain: but so was that of every other
writer in those days. The literary records of the Great War can
be seen as a series of attempts to evolve a response that would
have some degree of adequacy to the unparalleled situation in
which the writers were involved.

Brooke's '1914' sonnets were written during November and
December of that year, and were published in a miscellany
called *New Numbers*; they were not widely read at first, but
on Easter Sunday 1915, Dean Inge, preaching in St. Paul's,
quoted 'The Soldier' from the pulpit; the poem was reprinted
in *The Times* and aroused immense interest. And in a week or
so there came the news of Brooke's death in the Aegean (un-
glamorously, from blood poisoning, but on active service): the
juxtaposition of the poem in which Brooke had reflected on the
possibility of his death—'If I should die . . .'—and the news of
his actual death was sufficient to promote him to the status of
a hero and martyr. The sonnets themselves are not very amenable to critical discussion. They are works of very great mythic
power, since they formed a unique focus for what the English
felt, or wanted to feel, in 1914-15: they crystallize the powerful
archetype of Brooke, the young Apollo, in his sacrificial role of
the hero-as-victim. Considered, too, as historical documents,
they are of interest as an index to the popular state of mind
in the early months of the war. But considered more narrowly
and exactly as poems, their inadequacy is very patent. Such a
judgment needs qualification. It is, for instance, a commonplace to compare Brooke's sonnets with the work of later war
poets, notably Wilfred Owen. This seems to me to prove very

little, except, in a purely descriptive way, that poets' attitudes changed profoundly as they learned more about the war. Beyond this one might as well attempt to compare the year 1914 and the year 1918. A more useful comparison is with Brooke's own earlier poetry, and with contemporary works that express a broadly similar state of mind. Brooke's poetic gifts were never robust, and he was very far from being the most talented of the Georgian group, but at his best he had a certain saving irony and detachment of mind, which, very naturally, were absent from the 1914 sonnets. At the same time, the negative aspects of his poetry, a dangerous facility of language and feeling, are embarrassingly in evidence. To compare like with like, the sonnets seem to me inferior to Kipling's 'For All We Have and Are' and to Julian Grenfell's 'Into Battle', both products of the opening phase of the war.

One very pressing difficulty in reading these sonnets is that elements that can be called representative, expressing currents of popular feeling, are closely interwoven with others which are purely personal to Brooke himself. Thus, to take the octet of the first sonnet, 'Peace':

> Now, God be thanked Who has matched us with His hour,
>   And caught our youth, and wakened us from sleeping,
> With hand made sure, clear eye, and sharpened power,
>   To turn, as swimmers into cleanness leaping,
> Glad from a world grown old and cold and weary,
>   Leave the sick hearts that honour could not move,
> And half-men, and their dirty songs and dreary,
>   And all the little emptiness of love!

I do not think I am alone in finding these lines disagreeably lax in movement, and excessively facile in much of their detail; in a phrase like 'old and cold and weary' the words seem to be thrusting ahead of the sense. Yet there can be no doubt that they expressed quite closely a dominant state of mind, the attitude which, for instance, J. B. Priestley describes in the passage I have previously quoted: a turning aside from the stalely familiar, and an eager acceptance of new and unknown experience. Nor indeed was this attitude confined to English poets; as Sir Maurice Bowra shows in his lecture, 'Poetry and the First World War',[8] there were comparable manifestations at the outbreak of war by various Continental poets; even such an unbellicose figure as Rilke could write in these terms:

> We are others, changed into resemblance; for each
> there has leapt into the breast
> suddenly no more his own, like a meteor, a heart.
> Hot, an iron-clad heart from an iron-clad universe.

Nevertheless, Brooke was also expressing certain wholly personal preoccupations, whose nature is apparent from Hassall's biography. Professor D. J. Enright, in a sharp comment on these poems, has asked, referring to the line 'the little emptiness of love', 'whose love?'[9] On the level of intention, at least, the love in question seems to be Brooke's long and gruelling affair with 'Ka'.

This self-regarding element is very much in evidence in the poems, cutting across their apparent glad transcendence of the merely personal; the result can be called theatrical, and it is this, rather than Brooke's blank ignorance of things that no one else at that time knew much about either, that makes the sonnets hard to accept as poems. In the most famous of them, 'The Soldier', Brooke uses the Georgian concentration on rural England as a focus for a meditation on his own possible death. He identifies his own body and the soil of England in an almost mystical fashion:

> If I should die, think only this of me:
> That there's some corner of a foreign field
> That is for ever England. There shall be
> In that rich earth a richer dust concealed;
> A dust whom England bore, shaped, made aware,
> Gave, once, her flowers to love, her ways to roam,
> A body of England's, breathing English air,
> Washed by the rivers, blest by suns of home.

The oratorical tone of this seems to be part of the poem's essential intention: not for nothing has it become a set-piece for recitation at school prize-giving days and similar public occasions. Yet though the poem aims at oratorical impersonality, it is also an insistently self-regarding performance. There is an unresolved conflict between a subjective lyric impulse, not at all sure of its language, and the assumed decorum of patriotic utterance. As Mr. Enright has observed: 'The reiteration of

"England" and "English" is all very well; but an odd uncertainty as to whether the poet is praising England or himself—"a richer dust"—remains despite that reiteration.'

A similar criticism was made soon after the poems were
published by a younger and better poet than Brooke, Charles
Hamilton Sorley, who was killed in October 1915 at the age of
twenty. In a letter of April 1915 Sorley observed:

> I saw Rupert Brooke's death in *The Morning Post*. *The
> Morning Post*, which has always hitherto disapproved of him,
> is now loud in his praises because he had conformed to their
> stupid axiom of literary criticism that the only stuff of poetry
> is violent physical experience, by dying on active service.
> I think Brooke's earlier poems—especially notably *The Fish*
> and *Grantchester*, which you can find in *Georgian Poetry*
> —are his best. That last sonnet-sequence of his which you
> sent me the review of in the *Times Lit. Sup.*, and which has
> been so praised, I find (with the exception of that beginning
> "These hearts were woven of human joys and cares, Washed
> marvellously with sorrow" which is not about himself) over-
> praised. He is far too obsessed with his own sacrifice, regarding
> the going to war of himself (and others) as a highly intense,
> remarkable and sacrificial exploit, whereas it is merely the
> conduct demanded of him (and others) by the turn of circum-
> stances, where non-compliance with this demand would have
> made life intolerable. It was not that "they" gave up anything
> of that list he gives in one sonnet: but that the essence of
> these things had been endangered by circumstances over
> which he had no control, and he must fight to recapture
> them. He has clothed his attitude in fine words: but he has
> taken the sentimental attitude.[10]

By any standard, this seems to me a remarkably penetrating
criticism of Brooke; all the more so, as it was made by one who
had every right to make it and who could not be accused of
being wise after the event.

Had Brooke survived and undergone the experiences of later
war poets on the Western Front—Sorley himself, Graves and
Sassoon, Owen and Rosenberg—it is very probable that he
would have tried to respond as they did to those experiences and
achieved a correspondingly more profound mode of expression.

Brooke, Grenfell, Sorley

In Edmund Blunden's words, 'That Brooke, if he had lived to march into the horrifying battlefield of the River Ancre with his surviving companions of the Hood Battalion in the deep winter of 1916, would have continued to write sonnets or other poems in the spirit of the 1914 Sonnets, is something that I cannot credit.' As Blunden suggests, the piece called 'Fragment', written by Brooke on a troopship not long before his death in April 1915, is a sign that he was beginning to have a firmer imaginative grasp of the reality of war:

> I strayed about the deck, an hour, to-night
> Under a cloudy moonless sky; and peeped
> In at the windows, watched my friends at table,
> Or playing cards, or standing in the doorway,
> Or coming out into the darkness. Still
> No one could see me.
>
> I would have thought of them
> —Heedless, within a week of battle—in pity,
> Pride in their strength and in the weight and firmness
> And link'd beauty of bodies, and pity that
> This gay machine of splendour'ld soon be broken,
> Thought little of, pashed, scattered. . . .
> Only, always,
> I could but see them—against the lamplight—pass
> Like coloured shadows, thinner than filmy glass,
> Slight bubbles, fainter than the wave's faint light,
> That broke to phosphorus out into the night,
> Perishing things and strange ghosts—soon to die
> To other ghosts—this one, or that, or I.

The only other poem to have been written by a combatant in the opening phase of the war, expressing a similar idealizing attitude to it, which has achieved anything like the reputation of Brooke's sonnets, is Julian Grenfell's 'Into Battle', a celebrated anthology piece for almost fifty years. Grenfell died of wounds in France on 27th May 1915, a month after Brooke's death. He was an equally glamorous figure and in some respects of more conventionally heroic stature: he was born in 1888, the eldest son of Lord Desborough, and educated at Eton and Balliol, where he was part of the legendary pre-war generation who mostly perished in France. Like so many of those brilliant, semi-mythical young men, Grenfell seems to have excelled at everything. He was an accomplished classicist, a dedicated sportsman and, by all accounts, a superb athlete. He displayed, too, considerable talents at drawing and writing verse; despite his passion for physical activity—notably for riding and boxing—his letters made it clear that Grenfell also had an alert and lively intelligence. After Oxford, he went into the Regular Army, which he enjoyed immensely—he wrote in one letter, 'I'm so happy here. I love the Profession of Arms, and I love my fellow officers and all my dogs and horses'—and for several years served in India and South Africa.

For all his many talents, and the clear devotion to his family expressed in his letters, Grenfell seems to have been an enigmatic figure, even to his friends. A Balliol contemporary, Raymond Asquith, who was himself to be killed in France, has left an account of Grenfell which curiously depersonalizes him, turning Grenfell (despite Asquith's intentions) into a Renaissance statue, an emblematic embodiment of abstract heroic virtue :

> It was easy to idealize Julian, because superficially he seemed to be built on very simple lines. One might have set him up in a public place as a heroic or symbolic figure of Youth and Force. In reality he was far too intelligent and interesting to be a symbolic figure of anything. His appetite for action was immense, but it was a craving of his whole nature, mind no less than body. His sheer physical vigour, as everyone knows, was prodigious. Perfectly made and perpetually fit he flung himself upon life in a surge of restless and unconquerable energy. Riding, or rowing, or boxing, or running with his greyhounds, or hunting the Boches in Flanders, he 'tired the sun with action' as others have with talk. His will was persistent and pugnacious and constantly in motion. His mind, no less, was full of fire and fibre; lively, independent, never for a moment stagnating, nor ever mantled with the scum of second-hand ideas, violent in its movements but always moving, intemperate perhaps in its habit but with 'the brisk intemperance of youth'.[11]

Grenfell was unique among the poets of the Great War in being a professional soldier rather than a volunteer from civilian life, and his response to war was different from his contemporaries' in a number of ways. For instance, Grenfell, having served in different parts of the Empire, manifested a genuine enthusiasm for the imperialist ideal, as opposed to the more narrowly England-centred patriotism of the Georgians. On 6th August 1914 he wrote from South Africa:

And don't you think it has been a wonderful and almost incredible, rally to the Empire; with Redmond and the Hindus and Will Crooks and the Boers and the South Fiji Islanders all aching to come and throw stones at the Germans. It reinforces one's failing belief in the Old Flag and the Mother Country and the Heavy Brigade and the Thin Red Line, and all the Imperial Idea, which gets rather shadowy in peace time, don't you think? But this has proved a real enough thing.[12]

Grenfell was quickly in action and proved an extremely intrepid fighter, delighting in single-handed raiding exploits in No Man's Land: during his short wartime life, he was awarded the D.S.O. and twice mentioned in despatches. Grenfell represents the purest embodiment of the romantic, Hotspurian ideal that the Great War produced, at least among British writers; unlike the belligerent armchair patriots at home, and unlike an innocent such as Brooke, he was well acquainted with the nature of battle. He saw war, however, in the terms that came most immediately to him, as a game, and it was this that prompted him to write from Flanders in October 1914:

I *adore* War. It is like a big picnic without the objectlessness of a picnic. I have never been so well or so happy. Nobody grumbles at one for being dirty. I have only had my boots off once in the last 10 days, and only washed twice. We are up and standing to our rifles by 5 a.m. when doing this infantry work, and saddled up by 4.30 a.m. when with our horses. Our poor horses do not get their saddles off when we are in trenches.

This letter has been taken, reasonably enough, as evidence of a certain cheery callousness on Grenfell's part; but he adds, in the following paragraph,

The wretched inhabitants here have got practically no food left. It is miserable to see them leaving their houses, and tracking away, with great bundles and children in their hands. And the dogs and cats left in the deserted villages are piteous.

Although mostly fighting in infantry conditions Grenfell was a cavalryman, and had an appropriately traditional, and ana-chronistic, attitude to the war; his letters are full of a desire to see the cavalry go dashing into action. Yet Grenfell was soon experiencing something of the nature of technological war and was reluctantly sensing a certain insufficiency in traditional heroic attitudes:

About the shells, after a day of them, one's nerves are really absolutely beaten down. I can understand now why our in-fantry have to retreat sometimes; a sight which came as a shock to me at first, after being brought up in the belief that the English infantry cannot retreat.

Yet such an awareness, which was to prove central to the ex-perience of Sassoon and Owen, was here no more than a dent in Grenfell's conventional though genuine assurance. Although a romantic, he was not lacking in a sense of humour, as his 'Prayer for Those on the Staff' might suggest:

> Fighting in mud, we turn to Thee,
>   In these dread times of battle, Lord,
> To keep us safe, if so may be,
>   From shrapnel, snipers, shell, and sword.
>
> But not on us, for we are men
>   Of meaner clay, who fight in clay,
> But on the Staff, the Upper Ten,
>   Depends the issue of the Day.
>
> The staff is working with its brains,
>   While we are sitting in the trench;
> The Staff the universe ordains
>   (Subject to Thee and General French)
>
> God help the Staff—especially
>   The young ones, many of them sprung

From our high aristocracy;
  Their task is hard, and they are young.

O Lord, who mad'st all things to be,
  And madest some things very good,
Please keep the extra A.D.C.
  From horrid scenes, and sight of blood.

See that his eggs are newly laid,
  Not tinged as some of them—with green;
And let no nasty draughts invade
  The windows of his Limousine.

When he forgets to buy the bread,
  When there are no more minerals,
Preserve his smooth well-oiled head
  From wrath of caustic Generals.

O Lord, who mad'st all things to be,
  And hatest nothing thou has made,
Please keep the extra A.D.C.
  Out of the sun and in the shade.

This neat composition is good-humoured in its satire, but it points forward to Siegfried Sassoon's savage verses which expressed the front-line soldier's resentment of the imbecilities of the Staff.

'Into Battle', written in April 1915, is the one poem that demands a place for Grenfell in any discussion of the poets of 1914-18. It is made up of a variety of constituent elements: the soldier's sense of dedication to a cause, his excitement in battle, and a strain of nature mysticism, all combined in a vein of Shelleyan exalation. The opening lines of the poem offer a traditional lyric in praise of spring, and then make a large but seemingly inevitable transition to the soldier's own spirit rising like the sap around him and to a sense of sacrifice as rebirth:

The naked earth is warm with spring,
  And with green grass and bursting trees
Leans to the sun's gaze glorying,
  And quivers in the sunny breeze;
And life is Colour and Warmth and Light,
  And a striving evermore for these;

D

And he is dead who will not fight;
And who dies fighting has increase.

The fighting man shall from the sun
    Take warmth, and life from the glowing earth;
Speed with the light-foot winds to run,
    And with the trees to newer birth;
And find, when fighting shall be done,
    Great rest, and fullness after dearth.

The sentiments are those traditional in the idealistic literature of war, and the diction of these lines is not particularly
original. Nevertheless, their quality, which seems to me real,
comes largely from their rhythm and syntax, in which a major
element is the very high concentration of verbs, conveying a
sense of dynamic movement, derived no doubt from Grenfell's
own celebrated energy of mind and body. One feels that he
is at one with what he is saying: there isn't the sense of
theatricality and of the poet uncertainly striking an attitude
that is so evident in Brooke's sonnets.

Later sections of the poem are quieter and less rhetorical
than the opening, as in the stanzas which suggest a degree of
identification with nature rather closer than that habitually
achieved by the Georgians:

The woodland trees that stand together,
    They stand to him each one a friend;
They gently speak in the windy weather;
    They guide to valley and ridge's end.

The kestrel hovering by day,
    And the little owls that call by night,
Bid him be swift and keen as they,
    As keen of ear, as swift of sight.

The concluding stanza is undoubtedly vulnerable, with its personified abstractions portentously intruding, but even here I
think the poem is saved from mere neo-classical inertness by
the placing of verbs and the resultant sense of energy:

The thundering line of battle stands,
    And in the air Death moans and sings;
But Day shall clasp him with strong hands,
    And Night shall fold him in soft wings.

('Thundering' and 'clasp', in particular carry much of the force of these lines.)

The attitudes expressed in 'Into Battle' seem almost unimaginably remote now; but they came naturally enough to an aristocratic young cavalry officer of great courage, with a passion for sport and a talent for writing verse, who had not wholly discovered the way the war was shaping by the time he died. But he had already sensed that heavy artillery and the machine-gun were driving out the traditional, romantic and chivalric view of war; after the Somme it could seem only an obscene mockery. 'Into Battle' is the last memorable verbal enactment of that attitude in English literature: the poetic equivalent of some final, anachronistic battle in which cavalry (etymologically close to chivalry) played a dominant part. When Maurice Baring came to commemorate Grenfell in a memorial sonnet which began,

> Because of you we will be glad and gay;
> Remembering you, we will be brave and strong . . .

such assurance was already sounding more than a little hollow.

A third poet who died in 1915 was Charles Hamilton Sorley, killed in October, at the Battle of Loos. Sorley's upbringing was fairly conventional: the son of an academic family at Cambridge, he attended Marlborough College, where he was happy, high-spirited and popular, with the attributes of a good allrounder of unusually acute intelligence. But perhaps the most formative period of Sorley's life was the time from January to July 1914, which he spent in Germany, acquiring some knowledge of the language and the country, before, as he intended, going up to Oxford that autumn. A full account of his stay there is contained in Sorley's letters, which are singularly fascinating: he had the rare gift of conveying, simply and unselfconsciously, the essential quality of his mind and personality in letters, in a way that makes one think of the great letter-writers amongst English authors: Keats and D. H. Lawrence, in particular. It is scarcely an exaggeration to say that Sorley fell in love with Germany. Soon after his arrival he wrote about hearing German soldiers singing on the march, 'Then I understood what a glorious country it was: and who would win, if war came.' In another letter he remarked of the same experience:

And when I got home, I felt I was a German, and proud to be a German: when the tempest of the singing was at its loudest, I felt that perhaps I could die for Deutschland—and I have never had an inkling of that feeling about England, and never shall. And if the feeling died with the cessation of the singing—well I had it, and it's the first time I have had the vaguest idea what patriotism meant—and that in a strange land. Nice, isn't it?

Yet despite his admiration for the German spirit, Sorley remained critical of some of its manifestations—the aggressiveness and anti-semitism of the corps students at the University of Jena, where he spent a term, for instance: 'the students with whom I mostly go about are Jews, and so perhaps I see, from their accounts of the insults they've had to stand, the worst side of these many coloured reeling creatures.' But with unhappily misplaced optimism—he was writing in July 1914—Sorley claimed that the militaristic spirit was declining.

When war broke out Sorley was still in Germany, but he was able to return to Britain, where he joined up in a spirit of dutiful but unenthusiastic patriotism.

The letters written by the nineteen-year-old Sorley during his weeks in training in the autumn of 1914 are remarkable for their detachment and maturity of mind; all the more so, when one realizes the mood of hysteria and anti-German racialist nonsense that had descended on the country and infected many of the most admired figures in public life. Their spirit is apparent in such a passage as this:

For the joke of seeing an obviously just cause defeated, I hope Germany will win. It would do the world good and show that real faith is not that which says "we *must* win for our cause is just," but that which says "our cause is just: therefore we can disregard defeat." All outlooks are at present material, and the unseen value of justice as justice, independent entirely of results, is forgotten. It is looked upon merely as an agent for winning battles.

Very few people, in the weeks after Britain entered the war, were capable of such lucid insights. Above all, Sorley refused to accept the current abuse and hatred of Germany, the country he had grown to love (he was even able to write sympathetically about the Kaiser, whom he saw as 'not unlike Macbeth, with the military clique in Prussia as his Lady Macbeth, and the court flatterers as the three weird sisters'):

> I regard the war as one between sisters, between Martha and Mary, the efficient and intolerant against the casual and sympathetic. Each side has a virtue for which it is fighting, and each that virtue's supplementary vice. And I hope that whatever the material result of the conflict, it will purge these two virtues of their vices, and efficiency and tolerance will no longer be incompatible.

At times, Sorley's impatience with the platitudes of conventional patriotism, and his capacity for painful self-knowledge, rose to an angry intensity:

> England—I am sick of the sound of the word. In training to fight for England, I am training to fight for that deliberate hypocrisy, that terrible middle-class sloth of outlook and appalling "imaginative indolence" that has marked us out from generation to generation. Goliath and Caiaphas—the Philistine and Pharisee—pound these together and there you have Suburbia and Westminster and Fleet Street. And yet we have the impudence to write down Germany (who with all their bigotry are at least seekers) as "Huns", because they are doing what every brave man ought to do and making experiments in morality. Not that I approve of the experiment in this particular case. Indeed I think that after the war all brave men will renounce their country and confess that they are strangers and pilgrims on the earth. "For they that say such things declare plainly that they seek a country." But all these convictions are useless for me to state since I have not had the courage of them. What a worm one is under the cart-wheels—big clumsy careless lumbering cart-wheels—of public opinion. I might have been giving my mind to fight against Sloth and Stupidity: instead, I am giving my body (by a refinement of cowardice) to fight against the most enterprising nation in the world.

Sorley spent four months as an officer at the Front, and his letters written on active service preserve the same note of detached, often ironic, and always unillusioned commentary:

All patrols—English and German—are much averse to the death and glory principle; so, on running up against one another in the long rustling clover, both pretend that they are Levites and that the other is a Good Samaritan—and pass by on the other side, no word spoken. For either side to bomb the other would be a useless violation of the unwritten laws that govern the relations of combatants permanently within a hundred yards of distance of each other, who have found out that to provide discomfort for the other is but a roundabout way of providing it for themselves: until they have their heads banged forcibly together by the red-capped powers behind them, whom neither attempts to understand.

With this humorously anti-Hotspurian description we seem very remote from Julian Grenfell's passionate heroics, and not too far away from the attitudes of Captain Yossarian. In another letter written at about the same time Sorley wryly remarked: 'why the term "slackers" should be applied to those who have not enlisted, God knows. Plenty of slackers here, thank you. I never was so idle in my life.'

But Sorley was well aware that any calm was likely to be short-lived. In one of his last letters, written in August 1915, there is a grimmer note, and an anticipation of that concern with the brutalizing effect of constant exposure to violence which was to be central for Sassoon and Owen:

Looking into the future one sees a holocaust somewhere: and at present there is—thank God—enough of "experience" to keep the wits edged (a callous way of putting it, perhaps). But out in front at night in that no-man's land and long graveyard there is a freedom and a spur. Rustling of the grasses and grave-tapping of distant workers: the tension and silence of encounter, when one struggles in the dark for moral victory over the enemy patrol: the wail of the exploded bomb and the animal cries of wounded men. Then death and the horrible thankfulness when one sees that the next man is dead: "We won't have to *carry* him in under fire, thank God; dragging will do": hauling in of the great resistless body in the dark, the smashed head rattling: the relief, the relief that the thing has ceased to groan: that the

54

bullet or bomb that made the man an animal has now made the animal a corpse. One is hardened by now: purged of all false pity: perhaps more selfish than before. The spiritual and the animal get so much more sharply divided in hours of encounter, taking possession of the body by swift turns.

Sorley's surviving poetry was published in a small posthumous volume in 1916, *Marlborough and Other Poems*. A good deal of it is pleasant juvenilia, written whilst Sorley was still at school, but in some of the poems written before the outbreak of war the signs of an individual talent are already plain. In 'Rooks', for instance, which is dated 21st June 1913, we have what is on the face of it a fairly straightforward piece of Georgian nature observation; nevertheless, it is technically adroit, being based on two rhymes only, and has some imaginative touches, such as the curious and vivid phrase, 'the evening makes the sky like clay', and the transformation, in the final stanza, of the aimlessly flapping rooks to the soul flying hopelessly 'from day to night, from night to day':

> There, where the rusty iron lies,
> The rooks are cawing all the day.
> Perhaps no man, until he dies,
> Will understand them, what they say.

> The evening makes the sky like clay.
> The slow wind waits for night to rise.
> The world is half-content. But they

> Still trouble all the trees with cries,
> That know, and cannot put away,
> The yearning to the soul that flies
> From day to night, from night to day.

But it was the war, undoubtedly, that caused Sorley's rapid development towards the full artistic maturity that he had still not altogether reached at the time of his death. There is a sense in which Sorley, though not apparently influenced by the experiments of Pound and the Imagists, seems a more fundamentally 'modern' poet than his contemporaries who wrote about the war in its opening phase. One of the fundamental attributes of modern literature has been that it attempts to combine and fuse together disparate or even contradictory elements of experience, rather than concentrate on only one element to the exclusion of others. Rightly or wrongly, 'complex' has become a major term of approbation in present-day criticism (though the origins of the attitude that lies behind its use can be found in Coleridge). In this respect, Sorley's poems about the war are complex, lacking the single-mindedness of Brooke or Grenfell.

His steadfast refusal to adopt conventionally patriotic attitudes is evident in the sonnet 'To Germany', of which the octet runs:

> You are blind like us. Your hurt no man designed,
> And no man claimed the conquest of your land.
> But gropers both through fields of thought confined
> We stumble and we do not understand.
> You only saw your future bigly planned,
> And we, the tapering paths of our own mind,
> And in each other's dearest ways we stand,
> And hiss and hate. And the blind fight the blind.

Sorley saw the war as a tragic paradox, rather than as a simple cause. In a number of other sonnets he explores an even larger and more intimate paradox, death, which is at once the greatest possible experience and the cessation of all experience:

> Saints have adored the lofty soul of you.
> Poets have whitened at your high renown.
> We stand among the many millions who
> Do hourly wait to pass your pathway down.

In one sonnet he seems to be alluding directly to Rupert Brooke's 'The Dead':

> When you see millions of the mouthless dead
> Across your dreams in pale battalions go,
> Say not soft things as other men have said,
> That you'll remember. For you need not so.
> Give them not praise. For, deaf, how should they know
> It is not curses heaped on each gashed head?
> Nor tears. Their blind eyes see not your tears flow.
> Nor honour. It is easy to be dead.
> Say only this, "They are dead." Then add thereto,

Brooke, Grenfell, Sorley

"Yet many a better one has died before."
Then, scanning all the o'ercrowded mass, should you
Perceive one face that you loved heretofore,
It is a spook. None wears the face you knew.
Great death has made all his for evermore.

Unlike poets who were concerned with some kind of community
linking the dead with the living, Sorley's preoccupation is
with the absolute 'otherness' of death, a totally alien experience which destroys all the distinctions that had been so important to the living:

Such, such is Death: no triumph: no defeat:
Only an empty pail, a slate rubbed clean,
A merciful putting away of what has been.

One of Sorley's best poems, and one of the most often reprinted, is 'All the Hills and Vales Along' (sometimes printed
under the title of 'Route March'), about a company of soldiers
singing on the march (once, not long before, Sorley had been
excited by seeing German soldiers in such a situation; but now
the troops were British and marching, many of them, to death).
It is a good example of Sorley's ability to unify disparate elements of experience: the physical exhilaration of the marching
men and his own underlying absorption in the idea of death.
The opening lines might, at a casual glance, suggest a clear-cut
rousing song by one of the lesser Georgians:

All the hills and vales along
Earth is bursting into song,
And the singers are the chaps
Who are going to die perhaps.

But the third and fourth lines, juxtaposing the Housmanesque
'chaps' with the throwaway casualness of 'going to die perhaps'
to considerable ironic effect, should make it clear that Sorley
was writing with his characteristic subtlety and ambivalence.
The second stanza of the poem seems to demand an indifference in the face of life or death similar to that which Yeats
was to attribute to his Irish airman:

Cast away regret and rue,
Think what you are marching to.
Little live, great pass.

The following lines oddly anticipate the harsh, laconic utterance of Yeats's later style (though the dominant influence on the poem is certainly Housman's):

> Jesus Christ and Barabbas
> Were found the same day.
> This died, that went his way.

In the next, penultimate stanza, Sorley asserts the total indifference of nature to human deeds and aspirations—unlike Grenfell, who saw heroic energy as part of the natural process—in a manner that recalls the modern existentialist stress on the alienation of man from his environment:

> Earth that never doubts nor fears,
> Earth that knows of death, not tears,
> Earth that bore with joyful ease
> Hemlock for Socrates,
> Earth that blossomed and was glad
> 'Neath the cross that Christ had,
> Shall rejoice and blossom too
> When the bullet reaches you.
> Wherefore, men marching
> On the road to death, sing!
> Pour your gladness on earth's head,
> So be merry, so be dead.

With 'so be merry, so be dead' the contradictions in the situation—to some extent already dramatized in the conflict between the poem's lilting form and its reflective content—are brought into deliberate collision.

Dr. Dennis Welland has rightly observed, in his book on Wilfred Owen, that 'a reliable guide to war poetry could be written in terms of changes in poetic attitudes to death'. In this and other poems Sorley seems to me to have adopted a strikingly individual attitude; unlike, on the one hand, the uninformed acceptance of Brooke, or the more informed but still romantic acceptance of Grenfell; or, on the other hand, the angry rejection of Sasson or the burning pity of Owen. Sorley's view of death seems to regard it as an act of existential assertion of human values in the face of an alien universe. One can find something similar in a fine poem written during the Second World War which looks back to the First, Herbert Read's

Brooke, Grenfell, Sorley

'To a Conscript of 1940' (whose epigraph, from Georges Bernanos, reads, *'Qui n'a pas une fois désespéré de l'honneur, ne sera jamais un héros'*):

> But one thing we learned: there is no glory in the deed
> Until the soldier wears a badge of tarnished braid;
> There are heroes who have heard the rally and have seen
> The glitter of a garland round their head.
>
> Theirs is the hollow victory. They are deceived.
> But you, my brother and my ghost, if you can go
> Knowing that there is no reward, no certain use
> In all your sacrifice, then honour is reprieved.

Save in a few lines here and there, Sorley did not achieve uniquely memorable verbal expression; his language was not always adequate for what he wanted to say—but there can be no doubt that it would have become abundantly so had he lived longer. Every death is an absolute loss: but Sorley's, at such an early age and when he had already given evidence both in his verse and in his letters of such remarkable powers of intelligence and feeling, was a tragedy for English letters. One can only quote, in a spirit of seriousness, the possibly ironical concluding lines of one of his sonnets to death:

> But a big blot has hid each yesterday
> So poor, so manifestly incomplete.
> And your bright Promise, withered long and sped,
> Is touched, stirs, rises, opens and grows sweet
> And blossoms and is you, when you are dead.

4

POETS II
Graves, Blunden, Read,
and others

As the months passed, the war, prolonged now far beyond the expectations of most people in August 1914, continued to be commemorated in verse, both at home and amongst the forces overseas. Indeed, for many civilian writers the production of poems with an exhortatory note was a substantial part of their war effort. Most of these efforts, even by quite accomplished poets, are now better forgotten, though they can provide an hour or so of painful diversion for the determinedly inquisitive reader who browses through one of the popular anthologies of the period, such as G. H. Clarke's *A Treasury of War Poetry* (1917). This process perhaps reached its nadir in the unspeakable verses of Sir William Watson. Here is the sestet of his sonnet 'The Three Alfreds', written in honour of Lord Northcliffe:

> Last—neither King nor bard, but just a man
> Who, in the very whirlwind of our woe,
> From midnight till the laggard dawn began,
> Cried ceaseless, 'Give us shells—more shells,' and so
> Saved England; saved her not less truly than
> Her hero of heroes saved her long ago.

One or two civilian poets attempted, unwisely, to reproduce from imagination, or at second-hand, the experiences of the fighting man. Thus W. W. Gibson, though one of the best of the Georgians, essayed a bogus toughness in deplorable passages like this:

> This bloody steel
> Has killed a man.
> I heard him squeal
> As on I ran.
>   ('The Bayonet')

60

The one poem by a civilian that has had more than a passing fame is Laurence Binyon's 'For the Fallen', first published in *The Times* on 21st September 1915. This is a rhetorical piece but with a certain decent gravity; one of its stanzas has become familiar in commemorations of the dead of the Great War:

> They shall grow not old, as we that are left grow old:
> Age shall not weary them, nor the years condemn.
> At the going down of the sun and in the morning
> We will remember them.

By 1916 the alienation of the soldiers in France from the Home Front had become very pronounced: Professor V. de Sola Pinto has referred to a separation between the 'Two Nations', divided by far more than the mere physical expanse of the Channel.[1] And as the soldier poets developed new modes of expression corresponding with their experience of trench warfare, while the civilians continued unthinkingly to uphold traditional attitudes, this alienation was given sharp expression in literature—most notably, in Siegfried Sassoon's satirical verses. But for about a year many young poets in uniform were content to reproduce the attitudes of Rupert Brooke's 1914 sonnets—an elementary sense of dedication and a love of England—and many of them didn't survive to do more. But in those who did survive one can trace an interesting development of sensibility.

Throughout the war, poetry, and in particular poetry from the Front, was in great demand. Douglas Goldring has left a sardonic account of the phenomenon, written from a belligerently pacifist standpoint, in his essay 'The War and the Poets', published in *Reputations* (1920):

> Lying about in every smart London drawing-room you would find the latest little volume, and at every fashionable bookshop the half-crown war poets were among the "best selling lines". . . . An atmosphere was quickly and easily created favourable to the sale of verse, and the always gullible English public, flattered by the remarks in the Press about its "revived interest in poetry", disbursed its shillings with a lavishness only equalled by its lack of discrimination.

These remarks were echoed by Richard Aldington, who wrote in *Death of a Hero* of:

the alleged vogue for 'war poets', which resulted in the parents of the slain being asked to put up fifty pounds for the publication (which probably cost fifteen) of poor little verses which should never have passed the home circle.

Goldring describes the pathetic verse of young men just out of school who (for a time, at least) continued to write what was expected of them:

> Many of these Public Schoolboy soldiers must have gone straight from the cricket-field and the prefect's study to the trenches, in a kind of waking dream. Their mental equipment for withstanding the shock of experience was as useless as the imitation suit of armour, the dummy lance and shield of the actor in a pageant. It was their false conception of life, their inability to look at facts except through tinted glasses of one particular colour, which rendered the poems of so many of these young subalterns so valueless as literature, so tragic and accusing as human documents.

As an example of what he is referring to Goldring quotes these lines (they are from a poem called "Without Shedding of Blood . . ." by Geoffrey Johnson):

> Malvern men must die and kill,
> That wind may blow on Malvern Hill;
> Devonshire blood must fall like dew,
> That Devon's bays may yet be blue;
> London must spill out lives like wine,
> That London's lights may ever shine.

This is not only feeble as poetry but false in sentiment: Sorley had achieved a deeper insight when he posited the indifference of nature to human affairs. Devon's bays would be equally blue in a German-occupied England. Goldring comments on these lines:

> This is precisely the doctrine of the "You-go-first" or "Comb-them-all-out-except-me" press, accepted with a blind and touching credulity, and it is certainly not intended to be the scarifying satire which, in effect, it is.

The most popular English poet during the later years of the war was a figure now little remembered, Robert Nichols, who wholeheartedly accepted the role of a professional 'war poet' after a very brief experience of the Front. Nichols was a conceited and theatrical figure—Wilfred Owen referred to him as 'so self-concerned and *vaniteux* in his verse'—and Robert Graves has left a sharp account of Nichols as he appeared shortly after the war:

> Another poet on Boar's Hill was Robert Nichols, one more neurasthenic ex-soldier, with his flame-opal ring, his wide-brimmed hat, his flapping arms, and a 'mournful grandeur in repose' (the phrase comes from a review by Sir Edmund Gosse). Nichols served only three weeks in France, with the gunners, and got involved in no show; but, being highly strung, he got invalided out of the army and went to lecture on British war-poets in America for the Ministry of Information. He read Siegfried's poetry and mine, and started a legend of Siegfried, himself and me as the new Three Musketeers, though the three of us had never once been together in the same room.

Nichols's first book, *Invocation: War Poems and Others* (1915), consisted largely of the Brooke-pastiche so prevalent in the first year of the war, rendered with more than ordinary mawkishness:

> Begin, O guns, and when ye have begun
> Lift up your voices louder and proclaim
> The sick moon set, arisen the strong sun,
> Filling our skies with new and noble flame.
> The Soldier and the Poet now are one
> And the Heroic more than a mere name.

Nichols's next collection, *Ardours and Endurances,* the product of his brief glimpse of active service, was something of a best-seller in 1917. For this reason, it deserves a moment of attention for its historical interest, though its intrinsic poetic merits are nil. One can see why the book was such a success, for Nichols provided a formula well calculated to appeal to civilian taste, which combined the stirring but ignorant heroics of 1914-15 with a degree of mild realism about the actual fighting, though without anything so embarrassing as Sassoon's and Owen's emphasis on physical horror and the brutalizing effect of combat. One section that was particularly admired was 'The Assault', in which Nichols abandons his customary, sedate formality and launches into an essay in impressionistic free verse in the manner of Vachel Lindsay:

> I hear my whistle shriek,
> Between teeth set;
> I fling an arm up,
> Scramble up the grime
> Over the parapet!
> I'm up. Go on.
> Something meets us.
> Head down into the storm that greets us.
> A wail.
> Lights. Blurr.
> Gone.
> On. On. Lead. Lead. Hail.
> Spatter. Whirr! Whirr!
> *"Toward that patch of brown;*
> *Direction left."* Bullets a stream.
> Devouring thought crying in a dream.
> Men, crumpled, going down. . . .
> Go on. Go.
> Deafness. Numbness. The loudening tornado.
> Bullets. Mud. Stumbling and skating.
> My voice's strangled shout:
> *"Steady pace, boys!"*
> The still light: gladness.
> *"Look sir. Look out!"*
> Ha! Ha! Bunched figures waiting.
> Revolver levelled quick!
> Flick! Flick!
> Red as blood.
> Germans. Germans.
> Good! O good!
> Cool madness.

Once more, Douglas Goldring offers a trenchant comment: 'It was characteristic of our war-time criticism that this masterpiece of drivel, instead of exciting derision, was hailed as a work of genius and read with avidity.' Nichols's most useful contribution to the literature of the Great War is perhaps the long introduction in dialogue form to his *Anthology of War Poetry 1914-18*, published in 1943, in which he takes a retrospective look at the attitudes of 1914 and discusses, from a strongly traditionalist point of view, some of the subsequent works about the war.

There were many better poets than Nichols who fought and wrote about the war as they knew it: the two finest, Isaac Rosenberg and Wilfred Owen, were killed in 1918; they will be discussed subsequently. Of the poets who survived, most returned to their experiences in prose works, often of great distinction, published during the nineteen-twenties: most notably, Robert Graves, Edmund Blunden and Herbert Read. All three came to manhood, if not to artistic maturity, during the war: in 1914, Graves was nineteen, Blunden, eighteen, and Read, twenty-one.

Graves's wartime poems were printed in two small volumes, *Over the Brazier* (1916) and *Fairies and Fusiliers* (1917), both of which he subsequently suppressed in his customary spirit of rigorous self-criticism, though he permitted a selection from them to be reprinted in James Reeves's Penguin anthology, *Georgian Poetry* (1962). In many respects, Graves, in his early work, was a quintessential Georgian, with a taste for ballad-like forms, unpretentious, small-scale subjects with a rural flavour, and a particular inclination to folk-lore and fairy-tale. But Graves's Irish background gave his work a quality that separated him from the more conventional love of rural England of the other Georgians. His attachment to myth has been a constant element in his poetry for fifty years, whether it was the prettified fairy-stories of his earliest poetry, or the powerful myths, dominated (and generated) by the White Goddess, that occur in his mature work. There is a successful example in *Fairies and Fusiliers*, 'Goliath and David', which retells the story of the famous biblical encounter; in this version, David's attempt fails and Goliath moves in for the kill:

> Loud laughs Goliath, and that laugh
> Can scatter chariots like blown chaff
> To rout; but David, calm and brave,
> Holds his ground, for God will save.
> Steel crosses wood, a flash, and oh!
> Shame for beauty's overthrow!
> (God's eyes are dim, His ears are shut.)
> One cruel backhand sabre-cut—

65

E

"I'm hit! I'm killed!" young David cries,
Throws blindly forward, chokes . . . and dies.
And look, spike-helmeted, grey, grim,
Goliath straddles over him.

If it were not for the specific, placing detail in the penultimate line, this could be a poem of generalized nightmare, a pure symbol akin to, say, Edwin Muir's 'The Combat'. As it is, the symbolism and the homely rhythm and down-to-earth diction serve, in a partial way, to hold back the full despairing horror of the situation (the poem was dedicated to a friend of Graves's, killed in action).

Douglas Goldring admired Graves's war poems and wrote of him, 'Mr. Graves has a gentle voice, naturally gay and cheerful, and always his own. He does not probe or question; when the actual becomes unbearable he flies away on the wings of his fancy.' In 1920, this was a fair judgment: Graves was certainly not alone in seeking a retreat from unbearable actuality in a measure of fancy or myth-making. The collapse of the patriotic myth-patterns of 1914-15 left all the best poets of that time disorientated and in search of a more valid frame of reference. In another poem about the war Graves counterpoints 'fancy', remembered or imagined, with the trenches—'It's a Queer Time' (actually written, in a spirit of anticipatory speculation, some weeks before Graves saw any action):

Or you'll be dozing safe in your dug-out—
A great roar—the trench shakes and falls about—
You're struggling, gasping, struggling, then . . . hullo!
Elsie comes tripping gaily down the trench,
Hanky to nose—that lyddite makes a stench—
Getting her pinafore all over grime.
Funny! because she died ten years ago!
          It's a queer time.

The trouble is, things happen much too quick;
Up jump the Bosches, rifles thump and click,
You stagger, and the whole scene fades away:
Even good Christians don't like passing straight
From Tipperary or their Hymn of Hate
To Alleluiah-chanting, and the chime
Of golden harps . . . and . . . I'm not well to-day . . .
          It's a queer time.

The wilful understatement of the refrain, 'It's a queer time', indicates the habitual stance that Graves adopted, or tried to adopt, to the realities of war: basically, an attitude of 'stiff upper-lip' reserve, lightened with gaiety and backed by the always-possible retreat into myth. But this stance was not always successful: in some of Graves's poems we see the visible crack-up of the Brooke-Grenfell attitude, and in recording this with horrified fascination Graves loses some of his customary detachment. As in 'Big Words', a monologue spoken by a young soldier telling himself he is not afraid to die; it ends:

> ". . . I know I'll feel small sorrow,
> Confess no sins and make no weak delays
> If death ends all and I must die to-morrow."
>
> But on the firestep, waiting to attack,
> He cursed, prayed, sweated, wished the proud
> words back.

On those occasions when Graves confronts the horror around him without obliquity, the fascination—which Sassoon refers to in *Memoirs of an Infantry Officer*—is apparent; but Graves is unable to do anything with the experience itself; it doesn't provoke either the anger of Sassoon or the pity of Owen:

> Where, propped against a shattered trunk,
> In a great mass of things unclean,
> Sat a dead Boche; he scowled and stunk
> With clothes and face a sodden green,
> Big-bellied, spectacled, crop-haired,
> Dribbling black blood from nose and beard.
>
> ('Dead Boche')

G. S. Fraser has interestingly compared this poem with another from the Second World War on a similar subject, Keith Douglas's 'Vergissmeinicht', which shows a much greater habituation to the fact of death, and more subtlety in its treatment.[2] Graves spent longer in the front line than most of his contemporaries—on the Somme he was already a veteran of Loos —and miraculously survived until the Armistice, although he was at one point officially reported killed. But the experiences of war obsessed Graves for a long time, and his post-war poetry was romantic, trivial and overtly escapist: not until he had come to terms with his wartime past in *Goodbye to All That* was he able to feel some degree of emotional liberation. Indeed, there is probably much truth in A. Alvarez's assertion that Graves has never wholly recovered from the Great War and the long ensuing period of spiritual shell-shock; a good deal about his poetic personality suggests this: he has a superb technical equipment which is often wasted on marginal subjects or variations on already familiar themes—characteristically the vicissitudes of tormented love, treated with great honesty and narrowness; there is also Graves's physical exile from England and his deliberate alienation from the life and ideas of his age; and the evasive use of mythology.

Edmund Blunden, like Graves, has every claim to be regarded as a Georgian. He, too, was absorbed in country scenes and folk-lore, into which the reality of war made a brutal intrusion; and, like Graves, he precipitated his experience in a memorable prose work, *Undertones of War*. Yet if there is one quality which distinguishes Blunden from the other Georgians it has always been the intensity of his absorption in the countryside. When dealing with Blunden it is hardly appropriate to talk of the 'rural scene' with all that that implies of a background or mere setting: he knows the country with a deep knowledge and a deep love and it pervades the whole structure of his mind and feelings. Reading Blunden, one is reminded of a number of literary antecedents: Richard Jefferies, John Clare and, inevitably Wordsworth; but one is equally aware, I think, of the eighteenth-century proto-Romantics, notably Thomas Gray. Blunden's world of nature is not particularly wild or wayward in a Romantic fashion: it is ordered and in harmony with man, and it offers, above all, an image of civilization, the pattern of a pastoral, pre-industrial society. It goes a good deal deeper than the weekend-cottage view of nature of the typical Georgian. That this was an anachronistic, even primitivistic view to hold in the opening decades of the twentieth century goes without saying: Blunden's poetry, traditional in themes, language and feeling, is entirely naked to any attacks that the embattled modern sensibility cares to make upon it. But I am not now concerned with defending all of Blunden's poetic procedures, merely with pointing out that it was his particular cast of mind and feeling that enabled him to stand up to the experiences of the Front with remarkable firmness.

Blunden, in short, was less fundamentally affected by the trenches—though his experiences there were as harrowing as many others'—than some of his contemporaries. His sensibility was modified, certainly, but it was not entirely shattered and remade. He himself has remarked:

> Among the multitudes of us shipped to the Pas de Calais a few months before the Great Push (or Drive) of the British Army in 1916, I was a verse-writer; my interests were not yet changed from what life had formed before all this chaos. Lurking in the trenches by day or prowling out of them at night, I would perforce know what a bedevilled world is, and yet to make poems about it was a puzzle. In May and June 1916, in my note-books, the grimness of war began to compete as a subject with the pastorals of peace. By the end of the year, when madness seemed totally to rule the hour, I was almost a poet of the shell-holes, of ruin and of mortification. But the stanzas then written were left in the pocket-book: what good were they, who cared, who would agree?'

He is indeed capable of providing a direct description of the mechanical nightmares of war suppressing the ordered world of nature, as in ' "Transport Up" at Ypres', which concludes:

And so they go, night after night, and chance the shrapnel fire,
The sappers' waggons stowed with frames and concertina wire,
The ration-limbers for the line, the lorries for the guns:
While overhead with fleering light stare down those withered suns.

The admirable phrase, 'withered suns', makes its point effectively. But more often Blunden places the destruction and disorder of war within an existing frame of reference rooted in rural values. 'The Unchangeable', dated 1917, offers a good example of this:

> Though I within these two last years of grace
> Have seen bright Ancre scourged to brackish mire,
> And meagre Belgian becks by dale and chace
> Stamped into sloughs of death with battering fire—
> Spite of all this, I sing you high and low,
> My old loves, Waters, be you shoal or deep,

Waters whose lazy and continual flow
Learns at the drizzling weir the tongue of sleep.
For Sussex cries from primrose lags and brakes,
"Why do you leave my woods untrod so long? . . ."

Poems such as this inevitably direct at Blunden the charge of escapism, of retreating ostrich-like from the reality of battle into a pastoral dream-world. Such a charge raises a number of difficult questions. One might say, initially, that in so far as writing poetry under fire was for Blunden to some extent a therapeutic activity, his 'retreat' to the familiar may have been justified in the process of preserving his wholeness of mind. Again, Blunden was very aware of his limitations, and one of the things that he was not often capable of expressing was the sense of scandal, of outrage at the moral enormities of war, that characterized the response of Sassoon and Owen. He simply accepted the war as one of the basic data of experience that could not be evaded, even though it was always fundamentally less 'real' than the sights and sounds of rural England. It is an axiom of the modern literary consciousness that painful experiences are more intrinsically authentic than pleasant ones, that a mutilated man is more 'real' than a sound one, that fighting is more 'real' than taking a country walk: but philosophically, such assumptions would, I think, be hard to justify.

In a perceptive note on Blunden's war poetry Ian Carr has written:

His best poems, with only one or two exceptions, are about the tiny breathing spaces or static moments between one action and the next. His themes are: self-preservation and how to offset madness; the devastation of nature by war; the fears and imaginings of a war-sodden mind; order and chaos.[4]

Unlike Graves, Blunden continued to write poems about the war once it was over: he returned thankfully to the contemplation and celebration of the countryside, its creatures and its lore, but his feelings were played upon, though not distorted, by the memory of war—as, for instance, in '1916 Seen From 1921':

Tired with dull grief, grown old before my day,
I sit in solitude and only hear

Graves, Blunden, Read

Long silent laughters, murmurings of dismay,
The lost intensities of hope and fear;
In those old marshes yet the rifles lie,
On the thin breastwork flutter the grey rags,
The very books I read are there—and I
Dead as the men I loved, wait while life drags

Its wounded length from those sad streets of war
Into green places here, that were my own. . . .

Undertones of War contains a sizeable 'Supplement of Poetical Interpretations and Variations': one of these poems, 'Third Ypres', had previously been published in a collection called *The Shepherd* in 1922: Blunden described it as one of his most comprehensive and particular attempts to render war experience poetically. In it Blunden makes the direct confrontation of violent experience that characterized Rosenberg, Owen and Sassoon; it is, without a doubt, his finest war poem. It is an autobiographical fragment in blank verse; Blunden sticks to the slightly archaic diction and phrasing that he habitually employs, but he nevertheless achieves an impressive strength and starkness; in these lines one notices his use of a pastoral image —the ploughman—stressing the traditional, 'right' use of the land, contrasting with its present occupants who have ploughed it up to no useful end:

The hour is come; come, move to the relief!
Dizzy we pass the mule-strewn track where once
The ploughman whistled as he loosed his team;
And where he turned home-hungry on the road,
The leaning pollard marks us hungrier turning.
We crawl to save the remnant who have torn
Back from the tentacled wire, those whom no shell
Has charred into black carcasses—Relief!
They grate their teeth until we take their room,
And through the churn of moonless night and mud
And flaming burst and sour gas we are huddled
Into the ditches where they bawl sense awake,
And in a frenzy that none could reason calm,
(Whimpering some, and calling on the dead)
They turn away: as in a dream they find
Strength in their feet to bear back that strange whim
Their body.

In a subsequent passage we have a clear example of Blunden's use of the manifestations of nature not as 'escape' or marginal illustration, but in a deliberately sanative way:

> And while I squeak and gibber over you,
> Look, from the wreck a score of field-mice nimble,
> And tame and curious look about them; (these
> Calmed me, on these depended my salvation).

Blunden's major contribution to the literature of the Great War was in prose. Yet his war poems contain the same qualities of mind and feeling that were displayed so brilliantly in *Undertones of War*—above all, the concrete presence of physical environment and awareness of detail. If they are neither traditionally heroic nor radically anti-heroic, they are the products of a gentle mind intent upon preserving its defences; not, in such conditions, an ignoble aim.

Another writer whose finest literary memorial to the war was in prose in Herbert Read: his *In Retreat* is a classic of its kind, worthy to rank with the longer achievements of Graves and Blunden. Possibly as a penalty of having written so much, and in so many different fields, Read's poetry has never been given the attention it deserves. So it is as well to recall that both during the First World War and subsequently Read wrote some of the best poetry about it to be produced by any English writer. Read—an anarchist knight—has always been a paradoxical, even contradictory figure, and the letters from the Front that he recently published in *The Contrary Experience* (1963) show that this was equally true of the young officer of 1915-18. At the outbreak of war Read considered himself a pacifist—though 'politically', not 'ethically'—but he was also, without any great sense of contradiction, a member of the Leeds University O.T.C. At the same time, like many ardent young men of those days, he was a disciple of Nietzsche. In 1915 he was commissioned, and his letters from France reveal an odd mixture of idealism and non-conformism; in one letter written in January 1917 he ranges, in a single short paragraph, through the whole gamut of possible attitudes to the war:

> But war is a tragic paradox: it destroys that which it should preserve. To any right-minded person life is sacred: so that

the question of war becomes a question of values: is such an ideal *which can only be attained by war*, of more value than life? Modern war is largely actuated by economic aggression. And that 'ideal' can hardly be compared with life. But a war for justice, for liberty, he who loses his life in such a war shall find it.

Read was not conventionally patriotic, but he had his own reasons, rooted in Nietzschean individualism, for his commitment. In April 1917 he wrote:

> I don't want to die for my king and country. If I do die, it's for the salvation of my own soul, cleansing it of all its little egotisms by one last supreme egotistic act.

Although Read appreciated the comradeship of army life, he came increasingly to hate the military machine; and yet, at the Armistice, he seriously considered applying to stay on in the army.

As a poet Read is unlike the other writers I have so far discussed, in that his literary affiliations were defiantly modern. If he classed himself with a group it would be with the Imagists, not the Georgians, and the poems in his books *Naked Warriors* and *Eclogues* (both 1919) are *avant-garde* in technique, employing free verse and precise, disjointed images. *Naked Warriors* is starkly realistic in its methods, but Read wrote of it:

> It isn't exactly a joyful book: it is a protest against all the glory camouflage that is written about the war: It means I have to be brutal and even ugly. But the truth should be told, and though I'm not quite conceited enough to imagine that I can do it finally, I think my voice might get a hearing. But I'd rather write one 'pastoral' than a book of this realism. My heart is not in it; it is too objective.

Naked Warriors, which did not appear until the war had ended, is indeed brutal in its realism. One of the poems in it, 'The Happy Warrior', parodies the pious Wordsworthian ideal by showing the soldier reduced to a state of brutish insensibility:

> I saw him stab
> And stab again
> A well-killed Boche.

73

Here and in other pieces in this brief collection Read is striking a note of straightforward protest, in the manner of Sassoon, though his reliance on the imagistic mode of presentation and abstention from overt comment leads to remoteness rather than immediacy. But in some of the poems Read's philosophical interests provide an additional dimension. 'Fear' is an example:

> Fear is a wave
> Beating through the air
> And on taut nerves impinging
> Till there it wins
> Vibrating chords.
>
> All goes well
> So long as you tune the instrument
> To simulate composure.
>
> (So you will become
> A gallant gentleman.)
>
> But when the strings are broken,
> Then you will grovel on the earth
> And your rabbit eyes
> Will fill with the fragments of your
> shatter'd soul.

This has the bleakness and surgical precision of Read's other war poems, and though free in form is unified in imagery: the nerves of the body are seen as the strings of a highly-tuned instrument, played on by fear; then, in the last stanza, they are transformed into the strings of a marionette. When they are broken the toy collapses, and this image works backward to take in the neat, parenthetically enclosed 'gallant gentleman', and suggests that he too is no more than a puppet. The final image becomes concrete with the phrase, 'rabbit eyes', suggesting not only the traditional emblem of cowardice, but also the piteous condition of a wounded, terrified rabbit crawling on the ground. Read is here confronting the ever-present possibility of cowardice in battle—the overthrow of Hotspur by Falstaff —whch is conventionally a crime but which is, often, purely biological, the revolt of the organism against the directives of the ethical intelligence.

He explores this question at greater length in 'The Execution of Cornelius Vane', a narrative poem in clipped, laconic, free verse about a soldier who runs away from battle, is captured and shot for cowardice. The man is presented as a simple manifestation of the desire to live, a desire which underlies the whole of burgeoning nature but which is an insufficient basis for the complexities of human civilization:

> Cornelius perceived with a new joy
> Pale anemones and violets of the wood,
> And wished that he might ever
> Exist in the perception of these woodland flowers
> And the shafts of yellow light that pierced
> The green dusk.
>
> Two days later
> He entered a village and was arrested.
> He was hungry, and the peace of the fields
> Dissipated the terror that had been the strength of his
>   will.

Condemned to death for desertion, he continues to the end to proclaim the biological virtue of cowardice, the desire to be part of the natural rather than the human order:

> He saw a party of his own regiment,
> With rifles, looking very sad.
> The morning was bright, and as they tied
> The cloth over his eyes, he said to the assembly:
> 'What wrong have I done that I should leave these:
> The bright sun rising
> And the birds that sing?'

Read's finest contribution to the poetry of the Great War was not written until several years afterwards; this is *The End of a War*, published in 1933, which Allen Tate has described as 'not only a great war poem but a great poem on a great subject: the impact upon the contemplative mind of universal violence, whether the violence be natural or man-made'. In this magnificent poem Read uses a bizarre incident from the closing hours of the war: on 10th November 1918, a battalion of British soldiers was advancing in pursuit of the retreating German army, harrassed by machine-gun fire. Towards dusk they find a wounded German officer lying on the outskirts of a village; he tells them that the Germans have evacuated the place. The British march into the village and are ambushed by concealed Germans with machine-guns and many of them are shot down. The enraged survivors seek out the hidden German soldiers and bayonet them, and the wounded officer who had betrayed them is similarly treated. Later the mutilated body of a murdered girl is discovered in a cottage; the British officer in charge of the unit can do nothing at that hour, and, exhausted, he retires to bed. The next day when he wakes the Armistice has been declared and the war is over.

Read does not attempt to articulate these incidents into a dramatic unity; the poem is a triptych whose separate sections are headed, 'Meditation of the Dying German Officer', 'Dialogue Between the Body and the Soul of the Murdered Girl', and 'Meditation of the Waking English Officer'. Read's intentions are contemplative, not dramatic or narrative; his verse is subtle and austere, low-pitched and muscular. By a remarkable feat of imaginative sympathy Read, who had previously shown such a deep understanding of the nature of cowardice, presents in the dying German's monologue a fervent statement of the case for traditional patriotism and militarism:

> Faith in self comes first, from self we build
> the web of friendship, from friends to confederates
> and so to the State. This web has a weft
> in that land we live in, a town, a hill
> all that the living eyes traverse. There are lights
> given by the tongue we speak, the songs we sing,
> the music and the magic of our Fatherland.
> This is a tangible trust. To make it secure
> against the tempests of inferior minds
> to build it in our blood, to make our lives
> a tribute to its beauty—there is no higher aim.
> This good achieved, then to God we turn
> for a crown on our perfection: God we create
> in the end of action, not in dreams.

He accepts his imminent death as inevitable:

> I die, but death was destined. My life was given
> my death ordained when first my hand
> held naked weapons in this war. The rest

76

has been a waiting for this final hour.
In such a glory I could not always live.

My brow falls like a shutter of lead, clashes
on the clench'd jaw. The curtain of flesh
is wreathed about these rigid lines
in folds that have the easy notion of a smile.
So let them kiss earth and acid corruption:
extinction of the clod. The bubble is free
to expand to the world's confines or to break
against the pricking stars. The last lights shine
across its perfect crystal: rare ethereal glimmer
of mind's own intensity.

As so often in Read's verse, the isolated images are all the more
effective for the apparent flatness of their context; and the verse
movement has a remarkable distinction.

In the second section the two voices of soul and body alter-
nate with an imagistic concentration that is not easy to paraphrase; there are hints of Marvell's 'Dialogue between Body and
Soul', but the opposition is less absolute. The murdered girl
is seen as an embodiment of the life-principle, but her spiritual
aspirations are stuff from which the passions which lead to
war may spring; once more the insufficiency of the purely
'natural' is cruelly underlined:

SOUL
War has victims beyond the bands
bonded to slaughter. War moves with armoured wheels
across the quivering flesh and patient limbs
of all life's labile fronds.

BODY
France was the garden I lived in.
Amid these trees, these fields, petals fell
flesh to flesh; I was a wilder flower.

SOUL
Open and innocent. So is the heart
laid virgin to my choice. I filled
your vacant ventricles with dreams
with immortal hopes and aspirations that exalt
the flesh to passion, to love and hate.

77

> Child-radiance then is clouded, the light
> that floods the mind is hot with blood
> pulse beats to the vibrant battle-cry
> the limbs are burnt with action.

The Wordsworthian theme of the obscuring of early innocence has always been fundamental to Read and has inspired some of his most beautiful writing in prose and verse.

The third section sets against the hard certainties and assertions of the dying German officer the hesitations and confusions of the Englishman, which echo the sentiments of many British war poets and which may be seen as typifying the educated young Englishman's response to the war once the exaltation of 1914 had passed. As against the German's belief in an immanent God revealing himself in action, the Englishman clings to a belief, despite the horror around him, in a God who is love, who is, in fact, the Christian God:

> Now I see, either the world is mechanic force
> and this the last tragic act, portending
> endless hate and blind reversion
> back to the tents and healthy lusts
> of animal men: or we act
> God's purpose in an obscure way.

There is no reason to suppose that Read endorses any one of the views he imaginatively enacts and juxtaposes: they are attempts at completeness of contemplation. Read is not a moralist in the ordinary sense; in this poem, at least, he is attempting to unfold the possible diversities of human response to a tragic event. In a note at the end of the poem he has written:

> It is not my business as a poet to condemn war (or, to be more exact, modern warfare). I only wish to present the universal aspects of a particular event. Judgment may follow, but should never precede or become embroiled with the act of poetry.

Such a view of poetry seems, at first glance, to be quite contradictory to that of someone like Owen, but it is probably truer to say that it complements it. Like Owen, Read wrote poems of protest during the war; but after it, when enough years had passed, he was able to replace the poetry of protest with a poetry of contemplation whose sympathies were impartially distributed and which did not contain directives for action. Owen was denied such an opportunity. *The End of a War* is Read's major poetic statement about the Great War, and, as Allen Tate has said, it is one of the greatest poems about it that anyone has written. But it is not quite Read's final word: he returned to the topic, very movingly, in the context of the Second World War when he wrote 'To a Conscript of 1940'.

There were a number of other writers whose principal contribution to the literature of the Great War was made in prose some years after it ended, but who also wrote poems which recorded their immediate reactions and impressions and which, though not of outstanding merit, can be given some attention. Perhaps the most prominent was Ford Madox Ford—known until 1919 as Ford Madox Hueffer—whose *Parade's End*, published in 1924-8, is the greatest English novel to come out of the war. In 1914 Ford was forty-one and already an established writer, though much of his output had been of a journalistic and pot-boiling kind: his brilliant novel *The Good Soldier* —not a war story—appeared in 1915. Despite his partly German origins, and the fact that a few years earlier he had made an attempt to claim German nationality in order to obtain a divorce in Germany, Ford responded to the war in a wholeheartedly patriotic fashion; indeed, there may have been an element of compensation for his previous inclinations towards Germany. Under the auspices of a Government propaganda scheme Ford produced two books of a somewhat didactic kind, one attacking Prussia and the other praising France. He also wrote a poem called 'Antwerp' about the wretched plight of the Belgian refugees arriving in London in the autumn of 1914. Ford had written a substantial amount of poetry since his youth, but not very much of it has proved to be of enduring merit; he himself did not take the business of writing poetry seriously— he always considered prose to be his proper element, and in this he was surely right—but Ezra Pound said some generous things about Ford's *Collected Poems* in 1914. 'Antwerp' is clearly the product of intense and laudable feelings, but it exhibits the characteristic faults of most of Ford's poetry: it is rhythmically inert, with lax, intermittently rhyming lines, and little interest in the verbal texture. There are one or two passages, however, that are superior to the rest of the poem, and achieve a certain power:

> This is Charing Cross;
> It is midnight;
> There is a great crowd
> And no light.
> A great crowd, all black that hardly whispers aloud.
> Surely, that is a dead woman—a dead mother!
> She has a dead face;
> She is dressed all in black;
> She wanders to the bookstall and back,
> At the back of the crowd;
> And back again and again back,
> She sways and wanders.

In 1915, Ford, though over military age, volunteered for the Army and was commissioned as a subaltern in the Welch Regiment. He had a simple patrotic motive in doing so, but, as his biographer, Douglas Goldring, admits, Ford may have also had a secondary motive in wishing to get away from his entanglement with the novelist, Violet Hunt. Although he was not long in the front lines, he suffered from gas and shell-shock and endured a good deal of ill health, as well as the further provocation of getting on badly with his superior officers (who considered him too old for his duties). He spent most of the war on semi-administrative duties, first in France and then in England; but his experience of the fighting was reflected in a number of poems which were published in *On Heaven* in 1918. Most of them are written in the semi-free verse which Ford favoured, with lines of irregular length and emphatic rhymes, often feminine. It is a maddening vehicle, but Ford was strangely attached to it. The poems are loosely meditative, tending to be sentimental, reflecting a seemingly anachronistic —for 1917-18—mood of simple devotion to England, recalling the aspirations of 1914; or commemorating dead comrades:

> Poor little Arnott—poor little lad . . .
> And poor old Knapp,
> Of whom once I borrowed a map—and never returned it,
> And Morris and Jones and all the rest of the Welch,
> So many gone in the twenty-four hours of a day. . . .

In some places Ford attempts to write about the actualities of

battle in a ballad-measure which, in effect, prevents them being
realized at all; unlike Sorley's poems of a superficially similar
kind, which set up an ironic tension between form and content:

> Dust and corpses in the thistles
> Where the gas-shells burst like snow,
> And the shrapnel screams and whistles
> On the Bécourt road below. . . .

Not until he wrote *Parade's End* was Ford able to confront
such experiences without evasion. But in places he catches
something of the sardonic note that characterizes the war
poetry of his younger comrades, as in the flat, ironic reflections of 'That Exploit of Yours', which anticipates some images
in Wilfred Owen's 'Strange Meeting':

> I meet two soldiers sometimes here in Hell
> The one, with a tear in the seat of his red pantaloons
> Was stuck by a pitchfork,
> Climbing a wall to steal apples.
>
> The second has a seeming silver helmet,
> Having died from the fall of his horse on some tram-lines
> In Dortmund.
>
> These two
> Meeting in the vaulted and vaporous caverns of Hell
> Exclaim always in identical tones:
> 'I at least have done my duty to Society and the Fatherland!'
> It is strange how the cliché prevails . . .
> For I will bet my hat that you who sent me here to Hell
> Are saying the selfsame words at this very moment
> Concerning that exploit of yours.

Like Ford, Richard Aldington was better known as a novelist
than as a poet; his *Death of a Hero* was one of the most discussed war novels of 1929. But he was also a prolific poet who
wrote a good many poems on active service, collected in *Images
of War* in 1919. Also like Ford, Aldington had been a friend and
associate of Ezra Pound in the years before 1914; they had
both appeared in Pound's *Des Imagistes* anthology and had
contributed to *Blast*. But Aldington, as a much younger man
—he was born in 1893—was more actively a protégé of Pound's,
who claimed Aldington and Hilda Doolittle (subsequently Al-

dington's wife) as the original members of the Imagist school in 1912. Aldington's pre-war Imagist poems were graceful but slight, and very literary in their orientations; he had had a classical education, and inclined towards the recreation of classical legend rather than the precise delineation of the physical world around him.

Aldington's war poems are still Imagist in form, and they move uneasily between retreats into Greek legend and idealized Mediterranean imagery, and determined attempts to face the present facts of mass slaughter. Aldington was at best a loose, casual versifier, and his Imagist war poems lack the concentration and tautness of those by Herbert Read. But here and there he effectively pinned down a moment of experience:

> Dusk and deep silence . . .
>
> Three soldiers huddled on a bench
> Over a red-hot brazier,
> And a fourth who stands apart
> Watching the cold rainy dawn.
>
> Then the familiar sounds of birds—
> Clear cock-crow, caw of rooks,
> Frail pipe of linnet, the "ting! ting!" of chaffinches,
>
> And over all the lark
> Outpiercing even the robin . . .
>
> Wearily the sentry moves
> Muttering the one word: "Peace."
>
> ('Picket')

The two-way movement in Aldington's verse between brutal realism and aestheticism is evident in the following pair of poems:

> 'Soliloquy—1'
>
> No, I'm not afraid of death
> (Not very much afraid, that is)
> Either for others or myself;
> Can watch them coming from the line
> On the wheeled silent stretchers
> And not shrink,

But munch my sandwich stoically
And make a joke, when "it" has passed.

But—the way they wobble!—
God! that makes one sick.
Dead men should be so still, austere,
And beautiful,
Not wobbling carrion roped upon a cart . . .

Well, thank God for rum.

'Soliloquy—2'

I was wrong, quite wrong;
The dead men are not always carrion.
After the advance,
As we went through the shattered trenches
Which the enemy had left,
We found, lying upon the fire-step,
A dead English soldier,
His head bloodily bandaged
And his closed left hand touching the earth,

More beautiful than one can tell,
More subtly coloured than a perfect Goya,
And more austere and lovely in repose
Than Angelo's hand could ever carve in stone.

In a rather longer poem, 'The Blood of the Young Men',
Aldington expresses the feeling, which is central to Owen and
Sassoon, that young men are being uselessly sacrificed in
large numbers for the good of those at home—women and old
men—and emphasizes the division between the Two Nations
which had become so marked by the middle of the war:

Old men, you will grow stronger and healthier
With broad red cheeks and clear hard eyes—
Are not your meat and drink the choicest?
Blood of the young, dear flesh of the young men.

In dealing with such a pressing but intractable theme, Aldington
has little of Owen's delicacy and control and tends to collapse
into bathos and hysteria, with unwanted overtones of *fin de
siècle* vampirism, though the poem does have a certain harsh
force. In general, Aldington is revealed in his war poems as

an extremely self-regarding writer, with a purely personal re-
vulsion from the scenes of war, concerned solely with registering his sensations, whether of disgust or aesthetic revery: he is
scarcely capable of transcending his personal situation and achieving the generalized states of feeling of his better contemporaries.

In 1930 (a few weeks after *Death of a Hero*) Frederic
Manning's novel of trench life, *Her Privates We*, was also
acclaimed; both books were part of the wave of war books,
whether memoirs or novels, published in 1928-30, which I
shall discuss in a later chapter. Manning was not, in fact, acknowledged as the author of *Her Privates We*, which was published under the pseudonym of 'Private 19022', but by the
time of his death in 1935 the fact of his authorship was fairly
well known. Nothing in Manning's previously literary career
would have prepared one for the tough colloquial realism of this
novel. Like Ford and Aldington, he had been a friend—or perhaps only an acquaintance—of Pound in pre-war days; he
was a rather shadowy figure, born in Australia, who had been
something of a cultivated wanderer between London and the
Continent. In 1910 he published a collection of elegant essays
on historical and mythological topics, *Scenes and Portraits*, and,
in the same year, *Poems*, which had a strongly 'ninetyish
flavour. In his second collection of poems, *Eidola* (1917), which
were mostly in precisely written free verse and classical and
literary in inspiration, Manning makes some reference to his
war experiences:

> These are the damned circles Dante trod,
> Terrible in hopelessness,
> But even skulls have their humour.
> An eyeless and sardonic mockery:
> And we,
> Sitting with streaming eyes in the acrid smoke,
> That murks our foul, damp billet,
> Chant bitterly, with raucous voices
> As a choir of frogs
> In hideous irony, our patriotic songs.
>
> ('Grotesque')

And in 'The Face' Manning writes about death with a delicacy
that shows up the comparative crudeness of Aldington's treatment:

Out of the smoke of men's wrath,
The red mist of anger,
Suddenly,
As a wraith of sleep,
A boy's face, white and tense,
Convulsed with terror and hate,
The lips trembling. . . .
Then a red smear, falling. . . .
I thrust aside the cloud, as it were tangible,
Blinded with a mist of blood.
The face cometh again
As a wraith of sleep:
A boy's face delicate and blonde,
The very mask of God,
Broken.

Although unquestionably minor, Manning's verse deserves something a little better than its present total obscurity.

All the poets I have so far discussed in this chapter survived the war, and three of them—Graves, Blunden and Read—are still very much alive. But there were others—apart from Rosenberg and Owen—who died in action, and of these the finest was Edward Thomas. As C. K. Stead has remarked,[5] Thomas demonstrates the Georgian virtues at their best (though he was never one of the official Georgian group): patient accuracy of observation before the facts of nature, unpretentiousness, a plain and decent affection for the everyday, and unemphatic sensitivity of language. Thomas was killed in 1917; under the stress of war his poetry—which he began writing only in his thirties—had flowered remarkably: like Blunden he found a therapeutic and sanative value in contemplating nature, or remembering rural England, in the midst of violence and destruction. Yet very few of Thomas's poems are actually about the war, even obliquely: in his loving concentration on the unchanging order of nature and rural society, the war exists only as a brooding but deliberately excluded presence. Thomas did, however, reveal a commitment to the national cause in 'No Case of Petty Right or Wrong'—not one of his best poems— which asserts both a love of country and a loathing of the jingoistic:

> Beside my hate for one fat patriot
> My hatred of the Kaiser is love true. . . .

As with the other Georgians, his commitment is to an idea of England and English traditions:

> She is all we know and live by, and we trust
> She is good and must endure, loving her so:
> And as we love ourselves we hate her foe.

Thomas's treatment of the effects of war is better seen in 'A Private', where the stress is on the continuity of natural processes rather than in making any assertion about the fact of war itself:

> This ploughman dead in battle slept out of doors
> Many a frozen night, and merrily
> Answered staid drinkers, good bedmen, and all bores:
> "At Mrs. Greenland's Hawthorn Bush," said he,
> "I slept." None knew which bush. Above the town,
> Beyond "The Drover," a hundred spot the down
> In Wiltshire. And where now at last he sleeps
> More sound in France—that, too, he secret keeps.

Thomas resembles Blunden in placing war and its effects within an English rural context; there is, however, a certain coyness about the tone of this poem, a worrying feeling that the idea of the dead ploughman sleeping more soundly in France than in Wiltshire has come somewhat too easily.

A writer who can be more straightforwardly called a war poet, though he wrote few poems, and they are not well known, is Arthur Graeme West: his literary remains were published in 1919 as *The Diary of a Dead Officer*. He was born in 1891, was a Balliol graduate, and was killed in April 1917. West's diary is a singularly melancholy book; no one, after the initial stage of exaltation, enjoyed the war very much, but West seems to have been less resilient than most, and he has little of the tough-mindedness of Graves or Blunden or Read, who were, one imagines, men of equally acute sensibilities. His diary contains some cloudy Paterian philosophizing about death, and various rather threadbare reflections: 'What midges we all are, what brief phantoms in a dream—a dream within a dream, this truly is my life, and how gladly would I end it now.' West came to reject all traditional values, comradeship, patriotism, religion, and aspired first towards stoicism and then towards nihilism. He was haunted by an impulse to desert and commit suicide, but was unable to bring himself to the point of action: he saw himself as a Hamlet-figure:

> I do ill to go. I ought to fight no more. But death, I suppose, is the penalty, and public opinion and possible misunderstanding. . . . You see how complicated it gets. . . . I am *almost* certain I do wrong to go—not quite certain, and anyhow, I question if I am of martyr stuff.

Like Sassoon, he became convinced that the war was being unnecessarily prolonged, but his response to this realization had nothing of Sassoon's moral clarity and courage. He was unable to transcend a purely personal despair and irascibility.

Nevertheless, some of West's poems are impressive. 'God! How I hate you, you young cheerful men' shows a savage reaction against the heroics of the early phase of war poetry:

> Hark how one chants—
> 'Oh happy to have lived these epic days'—
> 'These epic days'! And *he'd* been to France,
> And seen the trenches, glimpsed the huddled dead
> In the periscope, hung on the rusty wire:
> Choked by their sickly foetor, day and night
> Blown down his throat: stumbled through ruined hearths,
> Proved all that muddy brown monotony
> Where blood's the only coloured thing.

West's best poem is certainly 'The Night Patrol', a piece of bleak, faithful description in blank verse which shows the early dominance—it is dated March 1916—of the mode of extreme realism, and conveys an anti-heroic attitude all the more effectively for being implicit:

> And we placed
> Our hands on the topmost sand-bags, leapt and stood
> A second with curved backs, then crept to the wire,
> Wormed ourselves tinkling through, glanced back
> and dropped.
> The sodden ground was splashed with shallow pools,
> And tufts of crackling cornstalks, two years old,
> No man had reaped, and patches of spring grass,
> Half-seen, as rose and sank the flares, were strewn

With the wrecks of our attacks: the bandoliers,
Packs, rifles, bayonets, belts, and haversacks,
Shell fragments, and the huge whole forms of shells
Shot fruitlessly—and everywhere the dead.
Only the dead were always present—present
As a vile sickly smell of rottenness;
The rustling stubble and the early grass,
The slimy pools—the dead men stank through all,
Pungent and sharp; as bodies loomed before,
And as we passed, they stank; then dulled away
To that vague factor, all encompassing,
Infecting earth and air.

This is admirable, for its expressive rhythms and syntax, and the firm but unhysterical insistence of its realistic detail. In the best of his poems, West seems to have achieved the control that is missing in the more directly personal writing of his letters and diary entries; certainly 'The Night Patrol' deserves a prominent place in any collection of the poetry of the Great War.

There are a number of other poets who survived the war and who contributed something worthy of note to its literary records: not least amongst them is Edgell Rickword. His fine *Collected Poems* appeared in 1947 and aroused little interest either at the time or subsequently; at the beginning of the book there are a few excellent poems written as a result of Rickword's wartime experience, amongst them, 'The Soldier Addresses His Body' and 'Trench Poets', showing Rickword's early dedication to Donne; and 'Winter Warfare', in which he uses an ironically jaunty ballad-measure and a delicate, exact fancy to capture the quality of winter in the Line:

> Those who watched with hoary eyes
>   saw two figures gleaming there;
> Hauptman Kalte, Colonel Cold,
>   gaunt in the grey air.
>
> Stiffly, tinkling spurs they moved,
>   glassy eyed, with glinting heel
> stabbing those who lingered there
>   torn by screaming steel.

A less sophisticated writer was Ivor Gurney, poet and musician, who was one of the saddest casualties of the war; he survived the Western Front, but went mad a few years after the war ended, and from 1922 until his death in 1937 he was confined in a mental home. Gurney's wartime poems were published in two small collections, *Severn and Somme* (1917) and *War's Embers* (1919), which show a conventional but accomplished talent. In particular, one is aware of a deft handling of rhythm and a feeling for the musical potentialities of language; as one might expect, for Gurney was well known as a composer of songs. His poems have a limited range and deal, like the verse of many other soldiers, with the poignant contrast between the sights and the sounds of home and the brutalities of the present: the contrast is underlined in the title of Gurney's first book, *Severn and Somme* (there is a similar opposition in Graves's title, *Fairies and Fusiliers*). 'Home' for Gurney was the Gloucestershire countryside, and he celebrated it in a mood of subdued but authentic patriotism. He never attempted the extremes of savage realism or anti-heroic revolt; he saw the war as a puzzle rather than a crime. This mood could, however, produce some successful poems, as in 'The Target', from *War's Embers*:

> I shot him, and it had to be
> One of us! 'Twas him or me.
> "Couldn't be helped," and none can blame
> Me, for you would do the same.
>
> My mother, she can't sleep for fear
> Of what might be a-happening here
> To me. Perhaps it might be best
> To die, and set her fears at rest.
>
> For worst is worst, and worry's done.
> Perhaps he was the only son . . .
> Yet God keeps still, and does not say
> A word of guidance any way.
>
> Well, if they get me, first I'll find
> That boy, and tell him all my mind,
> And see who felt the bullet worst,
> And ask his pardon, if I durst.
>
> All's a tangle. Here's my job.
> A man might rave, or shout, or sob;

And God He takes no sort of heed.
This is a bloody mess indeed.

Gurney's theme of the two dead enemies encountering each other after death was most fully treated in Owen's 'Strange Meeting'. In this poem, as elsewhere, Gurney, like Sorley, showed himself aware of the ironic potentialities in Housman's terse manner.

A selection of Gurney's later work, written after his mental collapse, was edited by Edmund Blunden and published in 1954 under the title of *Poems*. It is not difficult to see in these poems, crude and fragmentary as so many of them are, evidence of their author's mental disorder, but there is a strength about them which is, on the whole, lacking in Gurney's early work. In the poems of his later years he frequently returned to his wartime experiences, puzzling over them in retrospect, angry at his own fate, and his contemporaries'. One of them, called 'War Books', begins:

What did they expect of our toil and extreme
Hunger—the perfect drawing of a heart's dream?
Did they look for a book of wrought art's perfection,
Who promised no reading, nor praise, nor publication?
Out of the heart's sickness the spirit wrote
For delight, or to escape hunger, or of war's worst anger,
When the guns died to silence and men would gather sense
Somehow together, and find this was life indeed,
And praise another's nobleness, or to Cotswold get hence.

Closely associated with Gurney was his friend, F. W. Harvey, another Goucestershire poet: his wartime poems are slight and traditional in style and attitude, usually melodious, though without much profundity. In 'The Soldier Speaks' Harvey presents yet one more Brooke-pastiche, though in 'To the Devil on His Appalling Decadence' he brings off a neatly turned piece of sardonic light verse:

But you were called familiarly "Old Nick"—
The Devil, yet a gentleman you know!
Relentless—true, yet courteous to a foe.
Man's soul your traffic was. You would not kick
His bloody entrails flying in the air.
Oh, "Krieg ist Krieg," we know, and "C'est la guerre!"
But Satan, don't you feel a trifle sick?

The poets I have discussed in this chapter, all of them writing after the initial phase of war poetry represented by the dead of 1915—Brooke, Grenfell, and Sorley—show marked differences in talent and seriousness. But most of them, apart from Robert Nichols, represent one of two possible attitudes: either the poetry, traditionalist in its orientations, which found strength when confronting the realities of battle in the idea and the images of rural England, amongs whose practitioners one can class Blunden, Thomas, Gurney, Harvey, and to some extent Ford; or the poetry of anti-heroic protest, using rather than evading the conditions of the Front and applying a deliberate technique of realism; here one would include Read, Aldington, and West. Robert Graves moves, in his wartime poems, rather uncertainly between the two. Most of these poets were very young and not well known at the time (Ford and Thomas were, of course, older and more established) though *Severn and Somme* went into a second edition, and Wilfred Owen said in a letter, 'I have ordered several copies of *Fairies and Fusiliers,* but shall not buy all, in order to leave the book exposed on the Shrewsbury counters'. Owen's letter was addressed to Siegfried Sassoon, his friend and mentor of 1917-18, and it is in Sassoon's poetry that we discover the most radical progress from early patriotic idealism through to ironic realism and then to the angry extremes of anti-heroic protest.

POSTSCRIPT

On page 85 above I imply that Edward Thomas was writing poetry while at the Front; in fact, all his poetry was written before he left for France.

5

POETS III
Sassoon

APART from the transiently popular Nichols, Sassoon was the one soldier poet to be widely read during the course of the war. In 1917 *The Old Huntsman* made an impact on civilians because of the originality of its themes, and on soldiers because of their authenticity; Owen said of it, 'Nothing like his trench-life sketches has ever been written or ever will be written'. And in the following year, the searing poetic manifesto of *Counter-Attack* attracted a large number of admiring readers, among them —rather disconcertingly for Sassoon—Winston Churchill.

There was nothing in Sassoon's early life and background to suggest a potential rebel and a defier both of public opinion and military authority. In *The Memoirs of a Fox-Hunting Man*, the first of the volumes of fictionalized autobiography that make up the 'Sherston' trilogy, and in two books of straight auto-biography, *The Old Century* (1938) and *The Weald of Youth* (1942), Sassoon has left a full and evocative account of his pre-war life (he was older than most of the other poets of the war, being already twenty-eight in 1914), which can, not unfairly, be described as one of cultivated idleness: his energies were largely taken up with hunting and cricket, with collecting old books (rather more for their bindings than their contents), and with the composition of exquisite countrified verses that denoted a poetic talent minor to the point of debility. Sassoon typified an *echt*-Georgian state of mind: whatever radicalism he manifested during the war was forced upon him by events, not temperamental; and in his moments of most bitter anger his poetic methods remained traditional, however startling his sentiments. Like so many poets who were caught up in the war, Sassoon began with an exercise in the Brookian mode, 'Absolution':

Sassoon

The anguish of the earth absolves our eyes
Till beauty shines in all that we can see.
War is our scourge; yet war has made us wise,
And, fighting for our freedom, we are free.

Sassoon himself commented, in *Siegfried's Journey*,

The significance of my too nobly worded lines was that they
expressed the typical self-glorifying feelings of a young man
about to go to the Front for the first time. The poem subsequently found favour with middle-aged reviewers, but the
more I saw of war the less noble-minded I felt about it.

In *Goodbye to All That* Robert Graves has left a spirited account of his first meeting in France with Sassoon:

At this time I was getting my first book of poems, *Over
the Brazier,* ready for the press; I had one or two drafts in
my pocket-book and showed them to Siegfried. He frowned
and said that war should not be written about in such a
realistic way. In return, he showed me some of his own
poems. One of them began:

Return to greet me, colours that were my joy,
Not in the woeful crimson of men slain . . .

Siegfried had not yet been in the trenches. I told him, in
my old-soldier manner, that he would soon change his style.

(The wartime friendship of Graves and Sassoon has been
entertainingly documented in their respective autobiographies;
Graves appears in *Memoirs of an Infantry Officer* as 'David
Cromlech', a provocatively opinionated and argumentative
young man, who, though several years younger than Sassoon,
seems to have been the dominant personality.) Sassoon's statement continues with an account of his change of style and
attitude:

This gradual process began, in the first months of 1916,
with a few genuine trench poems, dictated by my resolve
to record my surroundings, and usually based on the notes
I was making whenever I could do so with detachment. These
poems aimed at impersonal description of front-line conditions, and could at least claim to be the first things of their
kind.

One of Sassoon's early war poems is 'The Kiss':

> To these I turn, in these I trust—
> Brother Lead and Sister Steel.
> To his blind power I make appeal,
> I guard her beauty clean from rust.
>
> He spins and burns and loves the air,
> And splits a skull to win my praise;
> But up the nobly marching days
> She glitters naked, cold and fair.
>
> Sweet Sister, grant your soldier this:
> That in good fury he may feel
> The body where he sets his heel
> Quail from your downward darting kiss.

According to Graves, Sassoon, having originally written this poem in a state of genuine bellicose fervour, later offered it as a satire. If one compares the states of mind that would enable one to read the poem as, respectively, serious and satirical, one finds not merely a contrast between two traditional attitudes to fighting, but a vivid indication of the radical way in which attitudes to the Great War shifted during the course of it. In order to read the poem seriously one would need to see the horror of stabbing and shooting men (whether intensely realized or not) as [a] necessary, and [b] strictly subsidiary to the end of achieving victory—which represented the absolute value underlying the poem. When one reads the poem satirically these values are reversed: the absolute value is seen as *not* stabbing and shooting men in any circumstances—and the notion of doing so is exposed as self-evidently wicked—and to this all other questions, including that of achieving victory, are strictly subsidiary. This was, of course, a matter of emotional rather than narrowly intellectual conviction; it remained an axiom among the best poets of the final phase of the Great War, and, again, in the wave of anti-war literature that swept through Britain and other countries in 1928-30, that to expose with sufficient fidelity the nature of death and mutilation in battle was a sufficient argument against war; the life-ethic which T. E. Hulme had condemned became dominant. (But this was not universally so; for instance, the memoirs of Ernst Jünger,

The Storm of Steel, contain passages as grim as anything in Barbusse or Owen, and yet Jünger wrote as a convinced militarist.)

As Sassoon indicated, the impulse behind the more mature war poems in *The Old Huntsman* was strictly realistic, even naturalistic, a desire to show things as they were without any haze of patriotic sentiment. In some ways Sassoon was not particularly well equipped for the role of ruthless realist; his basic, strongly Georgian sensibility and background were very inclined to see man and his surroundings in some kind of harmony, no matter how precarious. In such a poem as 'At Carnoy', for instance, he traces this harmony on the very edge of its imminent dissolution.

> Down in the hollow there's the whole Brigade
> Camped in four groups: through twilight falling slow
> I hear a sound of mouth-organs, ill-played,
> And murmur of voices, gruff, confused, and low.
> Crouched among thistle-tufts I've watched the glow
> Of a blurred orange sunset flare and fade;
> And I'm content. To-morrow we must go
> To take some cursèd Wood . . . O world God made!

July 3rd, 1916.

Here the subjoined date—two days after the opening of the Somme offensive—is an intrinsic part of the poem's meaning. It was circumstances rather than temperament that made Sassoon a realist; unlike some of his fellow soldier poets he could not be content with using scenes of rural English life as a compensation and balance for the brutality of life at the Front: in 'The One-Legged Man' Sassoon thrusts the two together in angry and shocking juxtaposition. The poem begins as a deceptive pastoral piece:

> Propped on a stick he viewed the August weald;
> Squat orchard trees and oasts with painted cowls;
> A homely, tangled hedge, a corn-stooked field,
> With sound of barking dogs and farmyard fowls.

But in the final couplet the unexpected point is hammered home with unsubtle force.

> He hobbled blithely through the garden gate,
> And thought: "Thank God they had to amputate!"

In other, similarly epigrammatic poems Sassoon directs an impulse of pure anger across the constantly growing gulf that separated the unthinking civilian world of the Nation at Home with its jingoistic slogans from the embattled Nation overseas. One example is 'They' with its devastating thrust at a platitudinous bishop—as D. J. Enright has remarked, rather a sitting bird; another is ' "Blighters" ':

> I'd like to see a Tank come down the stalls,
> Lurching to rag-time tunes, or "Home, sweet Home,"—
> And there'd be no more jokes in Music-halls
> To mock the riddled corpses round Bapaume.

Sassoon recalls in *Siegfried's Journey* how this poem was written after a visit to the Liverpool Hippodrome: 'it was my farewell to England, and as such it was the sort of thing I particularly wanted to say.'

Elsewhere in *The Old Huntsman* collection Sassoon made a more radical onslaught on traditional attitudes than he may have realized; as in 'The Hero', summed up in his original notes as: 'Brother officer giving white-haired mother fictitious account of her cold-footed son's death at the front. "He'd told the poor old dear some gallant lies which she would nourish all her days, no doubt".' In this poem—based all too probably on authentic happenings—the image of the hero is undermined with the energy of a Thersites. Sassoon has observed of this poem and 'The One-Legged Man': 'These performances had the quality of satirical drawings. They were deliberately written to disturb complacency.' This sums up very well the quality of Sassoon's war poetry; it has a deliberate simplicity and hard outline that recalls the impact of good poster art. He is usually regarded as a smaller, because less compassionate and universal, poet than Owen; and this is certainly true. Satire does not reach the heights achieved by Owen's generalized lyric pity; but the comparison is not an easy one, and within the limitations of his satirical mode Sassoon is a brilliant performer. In those poems, however, in which he attempts something closer to Owen's manner, Sassoon's treatment is less assured. One example is 'Died of Wounds':

> His wet, white face and miserable eyes
> Brought nurses to him more than groans and sighs:

But hoarse and low and rapid rose and fell
His troubled voice: he did the business well.

The ward grew dark; but he was still complaining,
And calling out for "Dickie". "Curse the Wood!
"It's time to go. O Christ, and what's the good?—
"We'll never take it; and it's always raining."

I wondered where he'd been; then heard him shout,
"They snipe like hell! O Dickie, don't go out" . . .
I fell asleep . . . next morning he was dead;
And some Slight Wound lay smiling on his bed.

The desperate pathos of the first two stanzas is effectively maintained; but Sassoon seems to flinch away from too direct a confrontation of the actual death, and the assertive irony of the final line looks like something of a retreat.

In *The Old Huntsman* one can follow the transformation of Sassoon's war poetry from early conventional idealism to the severe realism of the poems based on his note-book entries; and here the tone is often didactic rather than realistic in any detached documentary fashion: Sassoon was increasingly dominated by the desire to use poetry as a means of forcibly impressing on the civilian world some notion of the realities of front-line life. In his next collection, *Counter-Attack*, which appeared in the summer of 1918, we find Sassoon's most powerful and memorable war poetry. But between the publication of the two books Sassoon underwent the experience that he has described in detail in *Memoirs of an Infantry Officer*, and of which Graves has given his own account in *Goodbye to All That*: his revolt against military authority, his one-man campaign against the continuation of the war.

Sassoon had joined up at the beginning of the war, been commissioned, fought in France with exceptional bravery, even ferocity—he was known to his company as 'Mad Jack'—and had been awarded the M.C. and recommended for the D.S.O. But in the summer of 1917 he decided that the war was being unjustifiably prolonged when there was a possibility of a negotiated peace, and that the sufferings of the troops in France were correspondingly betrayed. He made a statement to his commanding officer which was reproduced in the press; it began:

G

I am making this statement as an act of wilful defiance of military authority, because I believe that the war is being deliberately prolonged by those who have the power to end it.

I am a soldier, convinced that I am acting on behalf of soldiers. I believe that this war, upon which I entered as a war of defence and liberation, has now become a war of aggression and conquest. I believe that the purposes for which I and my fellow-soldiers entered upon this war should have been so clearly stated as to make it impossible to change them, and that, had this been done, the objects which actuated us would now be attainable by negotiation.

I have seen and endured the sufferings of the troops, and I can no longer be a party to prolong these sufferings for ends which I believe to be evil and unjust.

Sassoon had hoped that he would be court-martialled, and that his protest would receive publicity and have a certain propaganda value; but the outcome was rather different, mainly, it appears, because of Graves's energetic intervention. Graves describes in his autobiography how shocked he was by Sassoon's pronouncement; not because he disagreed with the sentiments but because he felt that it would do no good and might have a disastrous result for Sassoon personally. So he made use of such influential friends as he could muster to get the authorities to play down the protest and treat Sassoon gently; Sassoon was invited to appear before a medical board who would enquire into his state of mind. He declined to do so, but Graves finally persuaded him to appear before a second board: in Sassoon's account the 'persuasion' took the form of a flat lie, in which Graves assured Sassoon that even if he refused to attend the second medical board the military authorities would still refuse to court-martial him; instead he would be confined in a lunatic asylum for the remainder of the war. Sassoon wrote, in *Memoirs of an Infantry Officer*: 'I was unaware that David had, probably, saved me from being sent to prison by telling a very successful lie. No doubt I should have done the same for him if our positions had been reversed.' Graves, in his account, merely states, 'At last, unable to deny how ill he was, Siegfried consented to appear before the medical board.'

The board agreed that he should be treated as a shell-shock case, and Sassoon was sent as a patient to Craiglockhart military hospital near Edinburgh, where he was a patient of the neurologist and anthropologist, W. H. R. Rivers, and where he formed a crucial friendship with a young fellow-patient—Wilfred Owen. Sassoon had been disposed of tactfully enough; in his own later writings his accounts of the episode are a little ambiguous. Writing as 'Sherston' in *Memoirs of an Infantry Officer* (1931), he gives the impression of an unsophisticated figure, bitterly affected by his experiences at the Front and a little out of his depth in the intellectual pacifist circles that he began to frequent, whose protest was a rational act, even though 'Sherston' seems to have been not wholly single-minded in his convictions. In a later account, written in his own person, *Siegfried's Journey* (1945), Sassoon does not contradict his earlier narrative but seems to imply that his own mental condition played a larger part in forcing his protest than he had previously suggested. He denies, however, the bland official contention that he had been suffering from a nervous breakdown: 'people in such a condition don't usually do things requiring moral courage.'

Whatever his precise motives, there can be no doubt about Sassoon's courage; and many other young officers would have shared his sentiments even though they might have doubted the wisdom and efficacy of making his kind of gesture. By 1917 there was a spreading mood of revolt against the war; Graves refers in *Goodbye to All That* to 'Osbert and Sacheverell Sitwell, Herbert Read, Siegfried, Wilfred Owen, myself, and most other young writers of the time, none of whom believed in the war'. Some of Osbert Sitwell's poems savagely expressed a feeling of protest akin to Sassoon's, though in a less concise and memorable form. One of the best of them, 'The Trap', uses the symbolism of a rabbit caught and bleeding in a trap to refer to the habit of the press in dismissing all suggestions for a negotiated peace—such as the Pope's and Lord Lansdowne's—as 'traps'. In 'Hymn to Moloch' Sitwell dramatizes the familiar alienation between the generations: the young men at the Front and their seniors safely at home.

Eternal Moloch, strong to slay,
Do not seek to heal or save.
Lord, it is the better way
Swift to send them to the grave.
Those of us too old to go
Send our sons to face the foe,
But, O lord! *we* must remain
Here, to pray and sort the slain.

In *Siegfried's Journey*, Sassoon continued to uphold his protest, referring to it as 'a course of action that I have never
regretted and for which there was no apparent alternative'.
But a page or so later he disconcertingly states:

> I must add that in the light of subsequent events it is difficult
> to believe that a Peace negotiated in 1917 would have been
> permanent. I share the general opinion that nothing on earth
> would have prevented a recurrence of Teutonic aggressiveness.

This, it seems to me, is a rather astonishing volte-face (though
doubtless conditioned by the fact that Sassoon was writing
during the Second World War): if a negotiated peace in 1917
would not have been worthwhile, then, in retrospect, the generals and politicians who urged a fight to the finish regardless
of the cost were right; and all those lonely voices, the Pope's
and Lord Lansdowne's as well as Second-Lieutenant Sassoon's,
who urged a truce, were objectively wrong; and Sassoon's brave
gesture of protest had no point.

Whether a negotiated peace was ever a possibility is a matter
for historians to decide upon. Perhaps it was not, but it was
widely believed by the soldiers that it was and that the Government was criminal in not following up the possibility. This,
certainly, is still the opinion of Robert Graves, who has written
in a recent newspaper article[1]:

> All the political and military blunders of the past forty
> years derive from a single one. It was the abandonment in
> the first world war of a well-tried British rule: namely never
> to fight beyond the point where victory will cost more than
> defeat.

The truth of this seems hard to resist: presumably it was
the entanglement with France that made it impossible for Britain

to extricate herself from the war when continued participation in it was no longer serving any kind of British interest. What would have happened if the more radical elements in the Liberal Government had succeeded in preserving British neutrality in August 1914 so that we had never become involved in a catastrophic Continental conflict is, again, a matter for fruitless speculation: but no one now, after fifty years, can doubt that we lost infinitely more than we gained by going in, just as we did later by insisting on a fight to the bitter end. Undoubtedly, the psychological pressures in favour of going to the defence of Belgium against a clear act of German aggression were immensely strong: though Bertrand Russell was to make himself very unpopular by coolly pointing out that the treaty guaranteeing Belgian neutrality was a rather loosely-phrased document and did not seem very rigidly binding on Britain. He showed that in the eighteen-eighties, when Britain was more friendly towards Germany than towards France, the idea was freely put forward in Britain that the Belgian guarantee did not require British intervention if the Germans entered Belgium simply in order to secure a passage for their troops to invade France (this, of course, was precisely the German claim in August 1914). In fact, Russell argued, the Belgian guarantee was invoked as an excuse for war rather than the other way round. But as we have seen, in August 1914 no one had any notion of the duration or the consequences of the struggle that was so enthusiastically embarked on. But by 1917 people knew only too well. Graves has written:

> Our rulers blundered criminally by not accepting that German peace offer as a basis for negotiation. Once an armistice had been arranged, nothing would have prevented the rival forces from fraternising, and nothing could have made them fight again. Many millions of lives would have been saved. The balance of power would have been kept in a Europe returned to sanity. Germany would have been spared the savage Versailles Treaty and her subsequent nervous breakdown, which induced the Hitler war.

There is surely more truth here than in Sassoon's remarks in 1945 about the inevitability of 'a recurrence of Teutonic aggressiveness'.

After these large reflections we may return to Sassoon's poetry, and in particular to *Counter-Attack*. In these poems Sassoon completes the transformation of documentary realism into an angry didactic outcry. Although he was never a poetic modernist or even, like Owen, a conscious experimenter, Sassoon was forced by the need for exactness in registering front-line experience into a degree of colloquial language and a conversational tone that was still a novelty in contemporary verse. The quality of his realism, in language and subject-matter, is evident in the first stanza of the title-poem:

> We'd gained our first objective hours before
> While dawn broke like a face with blinking eyes,
> Pallid, unshaved and thirsty, blind with smoke.
> Things seemed all right at first. We held their line,
> With bombers posted, Lewis guns well placed,
> And clink of shovels deepening the shallow trench.
> The place was rotten with dead; green clumsy legs
> High-booted, sprawled and grovelled along the saps
> And trunks, face downward, in the sucking mud,
> Wallowed like trodden sand-bags loosely filled;
> And naked sodden buttocks, mats of hair,
> Bulged, clotted heads slept in the plastering slime.
> And then the rain began,—the jolly old rain!

There is an immediate contrast between the two parts of the stanza: in the opening lines the stress is on action; the attacking troops, though possibly exhausted, are alert and prepared:

> We held their line,
> With bombers posted, Lewis guns well placed.

Tone and diction have a marked colloquial bareness: 'Things seemed all right at first.' But this patch of local military activity is seen to be literally resting on the dead; the larger point emerges that the war is being fought on a foundation of corpses. In the opening phrase of the second part, 'The place was rotten with dead', the colloquial tone is continued, with a suggestion that the dead are now equated with infesting vermin or some form of loathsome corruption. But then the manner changes, and the remaining extended description of the accumulated corpses is written in a complex, almost Miltonic syntax which creates a tension with the continued brutal realism of the diction and subject: the dead, the literal foundation of the activity of the living, are described with a kind of gruesome ritualism that sets them apart from the modest, brisk activity of the still-living. There is a sharp return to the colloquial in the final phrase, 'the jolly old rain!' Jon Silkin has commented on this phrase:

> One cannot speak the phrase 'jolly old rain' without evoking the hearty, almost lunatic, back-slapping camaraderie endemic in a society insensible to human pain, insensible therefore to the grotesque dead here. And thus, characteristically, Sassoon makes one of his lunges at the establishment he held responsible for the prolonged suffering of the soldiers.[2]

This is a plausible interpretation, though it is possible that Silkin is making these words bear too large a weight of meaning: the larger context is not satirical, and a phrase like 'the jolly old rain' may be no more than an instance of the soldier's inevitable tendency to reduce the phenomena of front-line life to something like acceptable proportions by the use of familiar and contemptuous terms; one can compare the song about corpses 'hanging on the old barbed wire'.

The description of the huddled corpses is also reminiscent of a work that must have had a certain influence on the poems in *Counter-Attack*—Henri Barbusse's *Le Feu*. This novel appeared in France in 1916, and the English translation, *Under Fire*, came out the following year. Barbusse is a realist in the tradition of Zola; his novel is a series of loosely connected sketches of trench life, based, it appears, on his own diaries; it is a work of violent protest against the war and the destruction of values that it involved, and it is marked by a harrowing and emphatic stress on death, mutilation and corruption, both moral and physical. Like the English war poets, Barbusse is concerned to shatter the traditional image of the hero:

> "How will they regard this slaughter, they who'll live after us, to whom progress—which comes as sure as fate—will at last restore the poise of their conscience? How will they regard these exploits which even we who perform them don't know whether one should compare them with those of Plutarch's and Corneille's heroes or with those of hooligans and apaches?"

Le Feu, being written so close to the experiences which inspired it, is a novel of violent feeling and no detachment. In
many respects, it is a work of intensive documentary realism;
but in some ways Barbusse seems to have distorted, or at least
formalized, his narrative in order to construct significant and
didactic patterns. Unlike his English contemporaries, he betrays
a strong political commitment; he was well to the Left, and in
later years became an active Communist. One should also mention here that a French critic, Jean Cru, subsequently ques-
tioned much of the accuracy of Barbusse's detail, and was very
critical of the authenticity of the total picture conveyed by the
novel (see Cru's *Témoins,* Paris, 1929). Nevertheless, Sassoon
and Owen both responded very favourably to *Le Feu* when they
read it at Craiglockhart in 1917, and herein lies its significance
for a study of English war poetry. Sassoon lent *Le Feu* to
Owen, 'which set him alight as no other war book had done',
and a paragraph from the novel about the brutalizing effect of
war appears as an epigraph to *Counter-Attack.*

In this collection Sassoon brought to perfection the hard,
punchy, epigrammatic style that had already served him as an
apt instrument for satire. We also see a certain extension of his
range, as in the bitter pathos of 'Does it Matter?'

> Does it matter?—losing your sight? . . .
> There's such splendid work for the blind;
> And people will always be kind,
> As you sit on the terrace remembering
> And turning your face to the light.
>
> Do they matter?—those dreams from the pit? . . .
> You can drink and forget and be glad,
> And people won't say that you're mad;
> For they'll know that you've fought for your country,
> And no one will worry a bit.

Or consider, again, the blend of complex feelings in 'To Any
Dead Officer':

> Good-bye, old lad! Remember me to God,
>   And tell Him that our Politicians swear
> They won't give in till Prussian Rule's been trod
>   Under the Heel of England . . . Are you there? . . .
> Yes . . . and the War won't end for at least two years;

Sassoon

But we've got stacks of men . . . I'm blind with tears,
    Staring into the dark. Cheero!
I wish they'd killed you in a decent show.

Here Sassoon makes a compelling use of colloquialism and the
relaxed understatements of casual conversation. One might
mention, again, 'Repression of War Experience', where the
movement of the verse enacts a collapse from precarious seren-
ity to shell-shocked nightmare; or 'Suicide in the Trenches',
in which Sassoon, like other war poets, discovers the possibilities for ironical effect in a Housmanesque vehicle:

> You smug-faced crowds with kindling eye
> Who cheer when soldier lads march by,
> Sneak home and pray you'll never know
> The hell where youth and laughter go.

Yet despite the extended range in *Counter-Attack*, Sassoon
remains fundamentally a poet of narrow but direct effects: his
language is hard, clear, sharply defined, rather than suggestive
or capable of the associative effects of a poet of larger resources.
On the whole, Sassoon remained aware of his limitations and did
not attempt a profundity that was beyond him: his gifts
were, pre-eminently, those of a satirist, and it was in satire that
he excelled; some of his epigrams have achieved a permanent
status, like 'The General'—' "He's a cheery old card," grunted
Harry to Jack. . . . But he did for them both by his plan of
attack.' The principal target for Sassoon's satire was the civilian
population, and, in particular, figures like politicians and jour-
nalists, who issued exhortations or encouragements to the troops
without having any real conception of what they were enduring. And in one harsh poem, 'Glory of Women', Sassoon seems
to attack the female sex in general: 'You love us when we're
heroes, home on leave, Or wounded in a mentionable place. . . .'
The feeling of being alienated from the women at home, who
were fixated in civilian ignorance and conventional heroic responses, was expressed by a number of writers who went
through the war; they felt themselves thrown back on the
deeper and more authentic camaraderie of their fellows in arms.
Sassoon's animus was given horrifying, crisp expression in
'Fight to a Finish':

The boys came back. Bands played and flags were flying,
    And Yellow-Pressmen thronged the sunlit street
To cheer the soliders who'd refrained from dying,
    And hear the music of returning feet.
"Of all the thrills and ardours War has brought,
This moment is the finest." (So they thought.)

Snapping their bayonets on to charge the mob,
    Grim Fusiliers broke ranks with glint of steel,
At last the boys had found a cushy job.

.   .   .   .

I heard the Yellow-Pressmen grunt and squeal;
And with my trusty bombers turned and went
To clear those Junkers out of Parliament.

In such a poem as this—whose verbal accomplishment seems
to me admirable—one is, I think, made aware of the inherent
limits of Sassoon's (and perhaps of any) satirical approach:
the complexities of actual experience are reduced to a single
satisfying gesture (and a phrase like 'the soldiers who'd refrained from dying' suggests that the anti-heroic mode, just as
much as the heroic, can achieve its effects too easily). In fact,
although Sassoon's political sympathies at this time were
vaguely on the Left (but not in the committed manner of Barbusse), this poem gives a revealing indication of a state of mind
that could lead to fascism in its early, idealistic phase: the
Italian *fascisti*, after all, were disillusioned ex-servicemen who
considered that they had been betrayed by the corrupt institu-
tions of a decadent parliamentary society (their anti-proletarian
bias had been anticipated by the feelings of the English Tommy
that munition-workers were 'shirkers'; Graves remarked to a
shocked Bertrand Russell during the war that his men loathed
munition-workers and would be only too glad of the chance to
shoot a few). Fortunately there was to be no native growth of
ex-service fascism, save in the Black-and-Tans and the mythology of the Bulldog Drummond stories.

Counter-Attack secured Sassoon's reputation as a poet. By
1918 the public mood was ready for what he had to say, and
his attacks on the Nation at Home were accepted with a possibly
masochistic fervour. It found admirers in unexpectedly high

places; Winston Churchill, at that time Minister of Munitions, was one: he learnt by heart some of the poems in *Counter-Attack*, and approved of them because, he claimed, they would finally bring home to the civilian population what the troops at the Front had to endure. Thus, Sassoon's anti-war outcry had been transformed, by a more agile mind than he could have foreseen, into a subtler form of pro-war propaganda. The Establishment has always been adept at incorporating rebels, and Sassoon—now once more a serving officer—saw something of the process when he was invited to meet Churchill and good-humouredly treated to a set speech on the militaristic virtues.

There is a significant passage in Henry Williamson's novel, *A Test to Destruction*: the hero, Phillip Maddison, has heard *Counter-Attack* discussed by some other young officers whilst he was in hospital, and later he asks his Colonel about it:

"Have you read, by any chance, the poems called *Counter Attack*, sir?"

"Oh yes. I read them in course of duty. I'm Intelligence at the War House, for my sins."

"What do you think of them, sir?"

"Oh, I think we've all felt like that, at one time or another. I'm no judge of poetry, but I heard Winston Churchill at White's talkin' about them the other day. 'Cries of pain wrung from soldiers during a test to destruction', were his words."

If the poems in *Counter-Attack* were, in fact, regarded as inspired shell-shock symptoms, as psychological evidence rather than moral statements, then it seems as if Sassoon's public protest was blunted, just as his attempt at a personal protest had been. Nevertheless these poems, expressing a mood of anti-heroic revolt with such fervour and harsh wit, strike a new and incisive note in the literature of war.

Throughout the 'twenties, when he continued to have left-wing leanings, Sassoon wrote sharp, epigrammatic verses that sniped at authority and conventional attitudes. In this respect he was at one with his age (one can compare the more concentrated satirical observations of Edgell Rickword), and sometimes these poems rise to an unusual level of poetic intensity, as in 'On Passing the New Menin Gate':

Here was the world's worst wound. And here with pride
'Their name liveth for ever,' the Gateway claims.
Was ever an immolation so belied
As these intolerably nameless names?
Well might the Dead who struggled in the slime
Rise and deride this sepulchre of crime.

As with other writers who narrowly survived the Great War, it was to remain Sassoon's one authentic subject; it, or the emotions stemming from it, inspired his best poems, and his admirable prose works. When Sassoon attempted to write straightforward poems on subjects remote from the war, he dwindled to the stature of a minor Georgian survival: the bulk of his later poetry, sententious or laxly pastoral, is carefully written and overpoweringly dull. He continued to write pungently satirical poems into the 'thirties, but in 1940 he commemorated the feelings of the time in one or two flatly conventional patriotic poems. 'Silent Service', for instance, begins,

Now, multifold, let Britain's patient power
Be proven within us for the world to see.
None are exempt from service in this hour;
And vanquished in ourselves we dare not be.

This has been aptly described by D. J. Enright as 'a dash of Winston Churchill in an ocean of water'; he suggests the necessarily damaging comparison with Herbert Read's 'To a Conscript of 1940'.[3] (There were more reasons for *feeling* like this in 1940 than in 1914, but less excuse for writing like it.) In such pieces the mood is close to that of Sassoon's early exalted war poems of 1915; the wheel has swung full circle. But it is the poems of 1916-18 that count, and that represent Sassoon's ineradicable contribution both to English poetry and the records of the Great War.

6

POETS IV
Rosenberg and Owen

MOST of the poets I have written about so far shared a number of attributes: the British soldier-poet of 1914-18 was, in all probability, a young junior officer from a middle-class home and with a public school education, whose imagination and sensibility had been nurtured by English rural life. Isaac Rosenberg, killed in action on 1st April 1918, was none of these things; but he was undoubtedly one of the finest poets that the Great War produced. Rosenberg, the child of a poor Jewish family, was born in 1890 in Bristol but grew up in the East End of London. He left school at fourteen, but soon displayed unusual talents both as a writer and painter, and in 1910 some wealthy friends paid for him to attend the Slade School. In 1912 he published at his own expense a small pamphlet of poems, *Night and Day*. When the war broke out Rosenberg was in South Africa—like, as it happens, another poet of very different temperament, Julian Grenfell—where his sister was living and where he had gone in search of an improvement in his health. In 1915 Rosenberg returned to England and joined the army, though not for the most obvious motives. He remarked in a letter:

> I never joined the army from patriotic reasons. Nothing can justify war. I suppose we must all fight to get the trouble over. Anyhow before the war I helped at home when I could and I did other things which helped to keep things going. I thought if I'd join there would be the separation allowance for my mother.[1]

Rosenberg never rose above the rank of private, and for physical and temperamental reasons he found army life more difficult than most; in his letters he speaks of being frequently punished for forgetfulness. But he was still able to find time for writing: in 1915 he published a second pamphlet of poems, *Youth*, and in 1916, a verse play, *Moses*; his remaining poems written in the army were not published until after his death.

Rosenberg was distinguished from the other war poets, first, by his Jewish origins, and then by his urban and working-class background, which meant that he had no English pastoral nostalgia to set against front-line experience. And since he went through the war as a private he saw that experience in a different perspective from the junior officer. But above all, Rosenberg is distinguished by the nature of his poetic talent. Most of his contemporaries had been formed in the Georgian mould, and had to adapt their basically conventional verse forms to sustain a weight of new experience: one sees the process very clearly in Sassoon; but Rosenberg was from the beginning an experimenter, or perhaps an explorer, in his use of poetic language. His pre-war poems are numerous enough to show his originality of approach, and even if the war had not intervened there is every reason to suppose that he would have continued his explorations. Unlike some of his slightly younger contemporaries, Rosenberg was not made into a poet by the war, but it both brought his gifts to a sudden maturity and cut them short.

Siegfried Sassoon has spoken of the biblical and prophetic quality of Rosenberg's work—Hebrew history and legend were one of his prime sources of inspiration—and has summed it up in this way:

> His experiments were a strenuous effort for impassioned expressions; his imagination had a sinewy and muscular aliveness; often he saw things in terms of sculpture, but he did not carve or chisel; he *modelled* words with fierce energy and aspiration, finding ecstasy in form, dreaming in grandeurs of superb light and deep shadow; his poetic visions are mostly in sombre colours and looming sculptural masses, molten and amply wrought.[2]

One central aspect of Rosenberg's exploratory habit of language has been more precisely defined by D. W. Harding, in a valuable essay on Rosenberg:

Rosenberg and Owen

Rosenberg allowed his words to emerge from the pressure of a very wide context of feeling and only a very general direction of thought. The result is that he seems to leave every idea partly embedded in the undifferentiated mass of related ideas from which it has emerged.[3]

One might, perhaps, gloss this by saying that rather often Rosenberg wasn't at all sure what he wanted to say when he was writing a poem: the comparison of a sculptor plastically working on his statue and letting the conception grow accordingly isn't altogether exact, since clay and words are, of course, very different media. Certainly, one is much more aware of *process*, of composition as something continuous rather than a single act, in reading Rosenberg's poetry than with any of his contemporaries. But taking a less favourable view than Professor Harding's, I would be inclined to say that a great deal —perhaps most—of Rosenberg's earlier work is marred by a quality that could be called groping as much as exploration. A lot of this work seems to me incoherent and often desperately obscure. But this is no more than to say that it was the apprentice work of a dedicated and potentially powerful talent.

The impact of the war had an immediately sharpening effect on Rosenberg's poetry: his poem, 'On Receiving News of the War', written in Cape Town in 1914, offers a good example of Rosenberg's capacity for linguistic compression and for conveying meaning non-discursively through symbolic images:

Snow is a strange white word.
No ice or frost
Has asked of bud or bird
For Winter's cost.

Yet ice and frost and snow
From earth to sky
This Summer land doth know.
No man knows why.

In all men's hearts it is.
Some spirit old
Hath turned with malign kiss
Our lives to mould.

Red fangs have torn His face.
God's blood is shed.
He mourns from His lone place
His children dead.

O! ancient crimson curse!
Corrode, consume.
Give back this universe
Its pristine bloom.

The rather cryptic final stanza suggests that Rosenberg, though
seeing the catastrophic nature of war much more clearly than
most of his contemporaries, was also inclined to regard it as a
possibly regenerative disaster; as Rilke, for instance, had in
the *Fünf Gesang*. One recalls Rilke's image, 'Hot, an iron-clad
heart from an iron-clad universe' (see page 43) in the final
stanza of another of Rosenberg's poems, 'August 1914':

Iron are our lives
Molten right through our youth.
A burnt space through ripe fields
A fair mouth's broken tooth.

Here Rosenberg manipulates very skilfully the multiple associations of his images; each of them can be construed both
literally and figuratively. War has transformed 'our lives'
to iron by the imposition of a cruel and inexorable pattern;
but the first two lines also suggest the slaughter by iron—
shell-splinters, say—of 'our youth', namely the young soldiers
engaged in fighting. Similarly, the 'burnt space through ripe
fields' is both a literal picture of what must have been a common sight in France in the late summer of 1914, and a com-
pressed image of the destruction wrought by war on the ameni-
ties and traditions of normal human behaviour. Again, 'a fair
mouth's broken tooth' can be a slight but disfiguring physical
mutilation resulting from battle, or more extensively a symbol
of the brutalizing effect of war on any manifestations of human
beauty.

Rosenberg is set apart from other poets of the Great War,
in the first place, by a certain detachment and impersonality;
in D. W. Harding's words, 'he tried to feel in the war a significance for life as such, rather than seeing only its convulsion

of the human life he knew'. One might go further and say that there was always an element of aestheticism in Rosenberg's vision; whereas Owen aimed at fusing the poetry and the pity, Rosenberg kept them separate. There is a significant passage in one of his pre-war essays:

> It is a vain belief that Art and Life go hand in hand. Art is as it were another planet, which does indeed reflect the ways of life, but is, nevertheless, a distinct and separate planet.

The symbolist notion of a separate and self-contained world of art could not have been phrased more concisely.

There is a good example of Rosenberg's aestheticism in a poem called 'Louse Hunting', in which the stress is not on the misery of the lice-infested soldiers but rather on the grotesque visual patterns they make in trying to kill the lice (Rosenberg also treated this theme in a wryly ironical fashion in 'The Immortals'). Undoubtedly the fact that he was also a painter influenced Rosenberg's development as a poet.

Rosenberg had, above all, a two-fold vision of the war: he was aware both of the human suffering it involved, and the unsurpassed human effort, which he regarded as a kind of absolute value, which it called forth. And this set him apart from traditional patriots and from the poets of anti-war protest. Although, as his letters show, Rosenberg could not regard the war as in any way justifiable, he accepted it imaginatively as a totally embracing way of life. There was nothing in his previous existence that could serve him as a sanative norm in the way that rural England did for many of his contemporaries (if anything, it was Jewish history and tradition that filled this role for Rosenberg); and as a private soldier he was more deeply immersed in the war than the officer-poets. At the same time, his detachment was unimpaired by the appalling sense of responsibility for others that they had to bear, and which is one of the dominant motives of Owen's poetry. The contrast is clearly brought out if one compares Rosenberg's 'Marching' with Sorley's 'All the Hills and Vales Along': in the latter there is an implicit separation between the speaker and the marching men—'the chaps Who are going to die perhaps'—who are enjoined, in a blend of compassion and irony, 'So be merry, so

H

be dead'. Rosenberg's poem, on the other hand, is written from
the standpoint of one of the marching men:

> My eyes catch ruddy necks
> Sturdily pressed back—
> All a red brick moving glint.
> Like flaming pendulums, hands
> Swing across the khaki—
> Mustard-coloured khaki—
> To the automatic feet.
>
> We husband the ancient glory
> In these bared necks and hands.
> Not broke is the forge of Mars;
> But a subtler brain beats iron
> To shoe the hoofs of death
> (Who paws dynamic air now).
> Blind fingers loose an iron cloud
> To rain immortal darkness
> On strong eyes.

The precisely observed and isolated visual detail of the opening
lines indicates the painter's eye. Then, in the second part, we
have the packed, rapidly succeeding metaphors that character-
ize much of Rosenberg's verse. The poem allows for the viability
of the heroic mode, inasmuch as the men 'husband the ancient
glory'; the mythological forge of Mars continues to function,
but the changed nature of modern war seems to be recognized,
and the hovering impatient presence of death is also acknowledged. In the richly complex closing lines, which resist
complete explication, Rosenberg combines a number of diverse
strands. The 'blind fingers' are blind because they are Fate's;
but also because of the muddle directing the course of the war
which is constantly sending men to death. The 'iron cloud',
incorporating one of Rosenberg's favourite eipthets, is both a
generalized symbol for war and a more exact indication of some
specific phenomenon, perhaps an artillery bombardment, which
rains 'immortal darkness'. This last phrase is deliberately ambiguous: it may mean that death can bestow immortality; but
also that the darkness of death is itself 'immortal' (i.e. un-
ending). In conjunction with the 'strong eyes' of the final line,
one has both an idea of the unseeing but defiant eyes of some

heroic statue secure in its immortal reputation, and of the 'strong' (that is, vigorous and active) eyes of men prematurely closed by death: one may compare Ezra Pound's 'Quick eyes gone under earth's lid'. And 'blind' in the antepenultimate line adds force to the juxtaposition of 'darkness' and 'eyes', and suggests a further possibility, namely that the 'immortal darkness' fallen on the 'strong eyes' is not that of death but of blindness. D. W. Harding has referred to the way in which Rosenberg fuses two apparently disparate attitudes, which as he puts it, 'express a stage of consciousness appearing before either simple attitude has become differentiated'. Certainly Rosenberg's imagination seems to have functioned dialectically, and this may have been both cause and effect of his great attachment to the poetry of Donne, of whom he wrote before the war, 'I have certainly never come across anything so choke-full of profound meaningful ideas. It would have been very difficult for him to express something commonplace if he had to.' The dialectical habit of mind, and the specific influence of Donne, are very apparent in one of Rosenberg's best, and best-known, poems, 'Break of Day in the Trenches', in which the dialectical movement is objectified by the figure of the rat, moving freely between the British and German trenches. The basic structure of the poem recalls Donne's 'The Flea'. The soldier in the trench is juxtaposed between two modest natural objects:

> The darkness crumbles away—
> It is the same old druid Time as ever.
> Only a live thing leaps my hand—
> A queer sardonic rat—
> As I pull the parapet's poppy
> To stick behind my ear.

Yet he does not employ them primarily for solace, as a means of escape from the destructive presence of war in the manner of, say, Blunden. The rat's function is to emphasize by his very freedom the arbitrary separation between the two front lines, and by his low, ugly vitality to point up the fact of human death:

> It seems you inwardly grin as you pass
> Strong eyes, fine limbs, haughty athletes
> Less chanced than you for life. . . .

115

(The carrying over of 'strong eyes' from 'Marching' is an instance of Rosenberg's rather frugal device of repeating his favourite phrases.) The poem returns to the poppy in the final lines:

> Poppies whose roots are in man's veins
> Drop, and are ever dropping;
> But mine in my ear is safe,
> Just a little white with the dust.

The poppies were, of course, to become a celebrated emblem of the British war dead following the popularity of John McCrae's 'In Flanders Fields':

> If ye break faith with us who die
> We shall not sleep, though poppies grow
> In Flanders fields.

Here, Rosenberg is emphasizing their intimate connection with the dead; the magnificent image, 'Poppies whose roots are in man's veins', refers to the way in which the poppies are, as it were, growing out of the innumerable bodies of the dead, whose red blood seems to have flown out of their veins and into the flowers. The poppies are a short-lived flower—they 'drop, and are ever dropping'—but their transience is scarcely more than that of the men who are constantly dropping in their midst. Nevertheless, the one poppy singled out for attention at the beginning of the poem is, for the moment, 'safe', in the precarious haven of the soldiers ear: they are, perhaps, destined to drop together. This is an unusual but effective alignment of man and nature, and shows Rosenberg's originality of insight. The poem ends with all the multiple associations of the pregnant word, 'dust'; the dust that whitens the poppy is the same dust that covers the dead and to which they will, in the end, turn.

Rosenberg's finest poem, and his most complete crystallization of war experience, is without doubt 'Dead Man's Dump'; A. Alvarez has described it as the greatest poem by an Englishman to have been produced by the war, and I am inclined to agree. Rosenberg left an account of the genesis of this poem in a letter to Edward Marsh, dated 8th May 1917:

> Ive written some lines suggested by going out wiring, or rather carrying wire up the line on limbers and running over

dead bodies lying about. I don't think what I've written is
very good but I think the substance is, and when I work on
it Ill make it fine. . . .

Read without reference to the poem itself, this outline might
indicate a piece of brutal realism, worked up from personal
experience, rather in the manner of Sassoon's front-line
sketches. But the finished achievement of 'Dead Man's Dump'
is something very different: realism is transformed into symbolism and, as in his other trench poems, Rosenberg does not
dwell on the details of violent death and mutilation. In D. W.
Harding's words, 'he thinks only in terms of death which comes
quickly enough to be regarded as a single living experience'.
'Dead Man's Dump' is indeed an exploration of death as an
absolute experience, which at the same time has something of
the complexity and gradations of life. One notices from the beginning how Rosenberg's language fuses realism and symbolism:

> The plunging limbers over the shattered track
> Racketed with their rusty freight,
> Stuck out like many crowns of thorns,
> And the rusty stakes like sceptres old
> To stay the flood of brutish men
> Upon our brothers dear.

The bleak phrase from his letter, 'carrying wire up the line on
limbers', has been thoroughly transformed: the first two lines
are direct, realistic observation, but in the third line, the comparison of the coils of barbed wire to 'crowns of thorns' is both
visually apt and richly associative. In the reference to stakes
'like sceptres' which are supposed to stay the enemy flood
one is, I think, meant to recall Canute, and no doubt, too, the
fact that his attempt to stay the actual flood of the sea was
fruitless: so too the wire may fail in its protective function.
One sees at this point how Rosenberg has already moved farther
away from the particular and the concrete, towards a generalized significance; it is, however, part of his strength that his
perceptions are always rooted in the concrete, and he always
returns to it:

> The wheels lurched over sprawled dead
> But pained them not, though their bones crunched,
> Their shut mouths made no moan.

> They lie there huddled, friend and foeman,
> Man born of man, and born of woman,
> And shells go crying over them
> From night till night and now.

If one compares this with the huddled corpses in the opening stanza of Sassoon's 'Counter-Attack', one can gauge how
very different Rosenberg's intentions were. In the third stanza
we find a remarkable statement of the idea glanced at in 'Break
of Day in the Trenches', that there is a relation between man
and nature which is brought to fruition when the dead return
to the soil:

> Earth has waited for them,
> All the time of their growth
> Fretting for their decay:
> Now she has them at last!
> In the strength of their strength
> Suspended—stopped and held.

In the fifth stanza there is a kind of awe at the absoluteness
of the experience of death fused with a sense of loss and pity;
the last two lines recall some of the dominant images of 'August
1914', here used with greater freedom:

> None saw their spirits' shadow shake the grass,
> Or stood aside for the half used life to pass
> Out of those doomed nostrils and the doomed mouth,
> When the swift iron burning bee
> Drained the wild honey of their youth.

Professor Harding has said of this stanza, 'It is noteworthy here
that Rosenberg is able and content to present contrasted aspects
of the one happening without having to resort to the bitterness
or irony which are the easier attitudes to such a contrast.' To
those who are accustomed to think of the best war poetry as
essentially a poetry of protest and revolt, Rosenberg's detachment and impersonality may seem disturbing, even a little inhuman. Whilst recognizing this, one must also point out that
he moves to a degree of transcendence that takes him far away
from his starting point in the realities of front-line activity; in
such poetry we have a profound exploration of the concept of
death, startling in its imaginative intensity, which goes beyond

simple description, no matter how deeply felt, of the casualties
of battle:

> They left this dead with the older dead,
> Stretched at the cross roads.
>
> Burnt black by strange decay
> Their sinister faces lie,
> The lid over each eye,
> The grass and coloured clay
> More motion have than they,
> Joined to the great sunk silences.
>
> Here is one not long dead;
> His dark hearing caught our far wheels. . . .

In the middle stanza, Rosenberg shows both a painter's eye and
an ontological insight: if one were looking for an Arnoldian
touchstone, the inexplicable but moving phrase, 'Joined to the
great sunk silences', would surely qualify as an index of poetic
authenticity. The poem moves towards the sombre paradox of
its conclusion when the just-dead try to cry out to the living—
and succeed:

> We heard his weak scream,
> We heard his very last sound,
> And our wheels grazed his dead face.

The last word, in the dialectical development of Rosenberg's
poem, rests with the anguish of both the living and the dead.
   There is another poem in which Rosenberg attempts to pene-
trate death as a self-contained and absolute way of life, transcending that of the living—'Daughters of War'. Here he abandons any attempt at realism, and builds his poem on a symbolic
structure which shows the fallen swept up by the 'Daughters of
War', who are seen as both Amazons and Valkyries:

> Even these must leap to the love-heat of these maidens
> From the flame of terrene days,
> Leaving grey ashes to the wind—to the wind.

Rosenberg believed this to be his best poem, and it contains
some characteristically fine lines and images; but it seems
to me to lack both the unity and the exactness of 'Dead Man's

Dump'. Above all, it suffers from being wholly in a symbolic mode, instead of displaying the strength which comes from counterpointing the symbolic against the realistic.

Rosenberg's war poems are not numerous, and I think that those I have referred to are the best of them, though there are others that would require mention in a more extended discussion, such as 'In War' and 'A Worm Fed on the Heart of Corinth'. Some critics, notably Jon Silkin,[4] have seen signs of a major achievement in Rosenberg's verse plays, *Moses* and the fragmentary *The Unicorn*. This is something I find hard to accept; it is certainly true that he may have been feeling his way in these compositions towards larger themes than he had so far attempted, but their language seems to me obscure and clotted, typical of the groping effect that Rosenberg's poetry manifested when he was in less than perfect control of his medium. Some of the individual speeches are impressive, but the plays themselves fail to convince, above all, as drama. Because of the nature of his approach to composition, which produced something of a hit-or-miss effect, Rosenberg's successes are scattered, and his failures to move into meaning and coherence are rather numerous. But the superb quality of his successes is a sufficient sign of the talent that the war destroyed. Above all, Rosenberg is distinguished from most of his contemporaries who wrote about their experiences as combatants by seeming to have already mastered the war in poetic terms, instead of being mastered by it. For most of the poets who survived, the war remained the central experience of their lives, exercising profoundly traumatic effects and continuing to influence their attitudes in later years. This is true, above all, of Sassoon, and to a considerable extent of Graves and Blunden; and, among novelists, of Henry Williamson. If Rosenberg had survived, in all probability the war would have been only one potential subject, and perhaps not the most important, in his activity as a poet; I do not think it would have had the same dominating effect on his imagination as it had on some of his contemporaries.

But to prophesy that Rosenberg might have achieved a degree of literary greatness had he survived is idle. His imperfections were large and must be recognized, but for all that he seems to me to have had the most interesting potentialities, as opposed to realized achievements, of any of the war's victims. And it is time his stature was recognized, for he has been shabbily treated in the past: he was excluded from Robert Nichols's 1943 anthology of poets of the Great War, and received only a contemptuously fleeting mention in Edmund Blunden's British Council pamphlet, *War Poets 1914-18* (1958). The point must be insisted on: his only peer is Wilfred Owen.

Owen and Rosenberg, both casualties of the final year of the war, though very different as personalities, were complementary rather than antithetical as poets. Rosenberg, despite his working-class origins, was the heir to Jewish culture and was responsive to the intellectual currents of the metropolis; though self-educated, he was widely read. Owen, on the other hand, though the son of middle-class parents, and destined to become an officer, was provincial both in origins and attitudes, and despite his adequate formal schooling seems to have had a narrower range of literary interests than Rosenberg. It is significant that whilst Rosenberg read and absorbed Donne at an early age, Owen's principal poetic idols and influences were Keats and Shelley. Owen grew up in much greater intellectual isolation than Rosenberg. Both of them wrote their finest poems about the war; Rosenberg treating it intensely but impersonally as a complex manifestation of values: Owen, with greater personal engagement, in which compassion, anger and a desire to inform all played a part: as he wrote in the fragmentary preface to the projected book of poems that was never published in his lifetime: 'All a poet can do today is warn.'

Owen's reputation has grown slowly but surely since the first selection of his work appeared under Siegfried Sassoon's editorship in 1920. It has been marked by two subsequent editions, Edmund Blunden's in 1931, and C. Day Lewis's complete and definitive text of the poems in 1963; there have been biographical studies of Owen by Siegfried Sassoon, Sir Osbert Sitwell, and the poet's brother, Harold Owen; and a detailed critical and textual examination of his poems by Dennis Welland. Since the fiftieth anniversary of 1914 and the appearance of the complete edition, interest in Owen has grown still more marked. He is, by common consent, the greatest poet of

the First World War, and Professor Kenneth Muir has recently
suggested that Owen deserves to rank as the most impressive
English poet of this century (excepting, on grounds of nationality, Eliot and Yeats).[9] In the face of such an assured status, it
can do Owen no harm, and may be critically illuminating, to
consider one or two unfavourable judgments that were passed
on him during the years when his reputation was becoming
established. In 1924 the Drake-boosting Edwardian Imperialist,
Sir Henry Newbolt, made some significant comments in a letter
about Owen's poetry. One is struck, immediately, by the monu-
mental wrongness of Newbolt's prognostication about Owen's
future fame: 'I don't think these shell-shocked war poems will
move our grandchildren greatly—there's nothing fundamental
or final about them.' In fact, after forty years, the generation
of Newbolt's grandchildren is finding Owen's poems far more
moving than he could have imagined. But some of Newbolt's
other comments offer more scope for fruitful speculation:

> [Sassoon] has sent me Wilfred Owen's poems, with an Intro-
> duction by himself. The best of them I knew already—they
> are terribly good, but of course limited, almost all on one
> note. I like better Sassoon's two-sided collection—there are
> more than two sides to this question of war, and a man is
> hardly normal any longer if he comes down to one. S.S. says
> that Owen pitied others but never himself: I'm afraid that
> isn't quite true—or at any rate not quite fair. To be a man
> one must be willing that others as well as yourself should
> bear the burden that must be borne. When I looked into
> Douglas Haig I saw what is really great,—perfect accept-
> ance, which means perfect faith. Owen and the rest of
> the broken men rail at the Old Men who sent the young to
> die: they have suffered cruelly, but in the nerves and not the
> heart—they haven't the experience or the imagination to
> know the extreme human agony—'Who giveth me to die for
> thee, Absalom my son, my son'. Paternity apart, what
> Englishman of fifty wouldn't far rather stop the shot himself
> than see the boys do it for him?[6]

One's immediate reaction is that this is an intolerably smug
piece of writing, with its presumption to distinguish between
degrees of suffering: Newbolt fails to realize that for many

young officers the ultimate agony was precisely the sense of paternal responsibility they felt for their men, forced prematurely on them when they themselves were scarcely more than youths. Nevertheless, his honesty and sincerity are unmistakable. Newbolt expresses the pain and bafflement of those older civilians who were a regular target for the wrath of the soldier-poets. Undoubtedly, many older men would have taken part in the fight if they could; and the death of a son can hardly be anything other than a personal tragedy. Yet underlying Newbolt's remarks is the implicit and unexamined premise that the civilians accepted without question, and which the spokesmen of the Nation Overseas came increasingly to reject: namely, that the military continuation of the struggle was absolutely necessary and unavoidable; the war had to be fought to a finish and any suggestion of a negotiated peace was a 'trap'. As we have seen, Sassoon, and those who felt like him, were convinced that the slaughter could be arrested and an attempt at negotiations made. By insisting on a fight to the finish the older generation were, in effect, prolonging the mass destruction of young men, no matter how keenly they were aware of the personal tragedy involved. The sense of alienation between Home Front and Army was most painfully felt when it divided the generations; when young soldiers were faced with the blank incomprehension of their fathers, secure in civilian ignorance, brain-washed by official propaganda and filled with Hun-hating hysteria. This alienation has been vividly rendered by Henry Williamson in the wartime volumes of *A Chronicle of Ancient Sunlight*, in which young Phillip Maddison, on leave from the Front, is constantly at odds with his smug though well-meaning father. And from this feeling there stemmed the conviction that the young men at the Front were being offered as a blood sacrifice by the older civilians at home, which inspired such poems as Richard Aldington's 'The Blood of the Young Men', and Osbert Sitwell's 'Hymn to Moloch', and which was given passionate expression by Owen in 'The Parable of the Old Man and the Young':

> When lo! an angel called him out of heaven,
> Saying, Lay not thy hand upon the lad,
> Neither do anything to him. Behold,
> A ram, caught in a thicket by its horns;

Offer the Ram of Pride instead of him.
But the old man would not so, but slew his son,—
And half the seed of Europe, one by one.

(The final line makes the point rather too explicit; it is omitted in one of the surviving manuscripts of the poem.)

In the face of such feelings, Newbolt and others of his generation could only reply that the charge was unfair, and return accusations of 'loss of nerve' or 'shell-shock'. For them, the Hotspurian categories of 'heroism' and 'honour' had become hardened, indeed fossilized, into unshakeable rigidities of mind. By contrast, the front-line fighters, for all their anguish of mind and body, were uttering a rational and traditional conviction: if war is the continuation of politics by other means, as Clausewitz had claimed, then it should be conducted for precise and limited aims, which should be clearly defined; and when the struggle for victory is costing more than defeat then some other means of achieving those ends should be sought. In fact, the British war aims were not clearly defined, and punishing Germany became an end in itself, as the Treaty of Versailles made evident. In the conviction that everything must be subjugated to the war, which had to be continued at whatever cost, we see the origins of the totalitarian state of mind which subjects all human activity to the overriding needs of the State.

But considered more narrowly as literary criticism, some of Newbolt's objections do have a degree of validity. In particular, it *is* true that Owen's range is narrow, in some ways 'all on one note': his concern is with suffering, and he directs his energies to rendering it with as much power and fidelity as he can muster. This, of course, is deliberate—'Above all I am not concerned with Poetry. . . . My subject is War, and the pity of War'—but his conscious restriction of range does, I think, count against him if he is being considered as a claimant for absolute greatness. Rosenberg, though he wrote fewer war poems than Owen, was able, in the best of them, to master a larger area of experience. Another, more celebrated criticism of Owen was levelled by W. B. Yeats in his last years: he had excluded Owen from the *Oxford Book of Modern Verse* (1936) on the grounds that 'passive suffering was not a proper subject for poetry', and he defended the exclusion in a letter to Dorothy Wellesley of 21st December 1936:

Rosenberg and Owen

When I excluded Wilfred Owen, whom I consider unworthy of the poets' corner of a country newspaper, I did not know I was excluding a revered sandwich-board man of the revolution, and that somebody has put his worst and most famous poem in a glass-case in the British Museum—however, if I had known it, I would have excluded him just the same. He is all blood, dirt and sucked sugar-stick (look at the selection in *Faber's Anthology*—he calls poets 'bards', a girl a 'maid', and talks about 'Titanic wars'). There is every excuse for him, but none for those who like him.

The venomous tone of Yeats's remarks is inexcusable, denoting a degree of senile rancour and, perhaps, of jealousy. He was also using Owen as a stick to beat the Leftist 'pylon poets' of the 'thirties, who had lately adopted Owen as a progenitor of their own attitudes. Yet however grotesque Yeats's assertions are as literary criticism, they contain a seed of truth (just as the harsh and unfair criticisms made of Keats by Arnold and Hopkins do, in fact, isolate and spotlight one aspect of Keats's poetic personality). In particular, I think, they underline the extreme rapidity of Owen's development, and the unevenness of his finally achieved maturity. It is well to remember that Owen, despite his early interest in poetic experiment and his technical curiosity, began as a manufacturer of sub-Keatsian poetic confectionery, and that traces of mawkishness can be found even in the work produced in the final great creative phase of his Keatsian *annus mirabilis*, 1917-18. This is particularly true in those occasional poems in which Owen's imagination is not involved with its major subject, the war; as, for instance, 'The Kind Ghosts' (dated as late as 30th July 1918):

> She sleeps on soft, last breaths; but no ghost looms
> Out of the stillness of her palace wall,
> Her wall of boys on boys and dooms on dooms.

Owen was brought to a cruelly premature flowering in the hothouse of the Western Front, and his work shows something of the fragility as well as the brilliance of the forced product. Yeats's criticism of Owen's diction does point to the undeniable fact that his language was slower to develop than his sensibility, and wasn't always equal to Owen's demands on it.

Having acknowledged these limitations, one can go on to point to the magnitude of Owen's achievement. Within a few months he gave the poetry of the anti-heroic attitude—prefigured by Byron and Stendhal, and, more immediately, in the verse of Sassoon and the prose of Barbusse—as absolute an expression as the traditional heroic attitude had received in countless epics and dramas of the Western tradition. And this reflected a basic change in human sensibility. It was the inability to realize that such a change had taken place that caused the bafflement of Newbolt. War was no longer the same; modern technology had seen to that; and Owen ensured that it could no longer be *seen* as the same. In theory, no doubt, to die in agony from a gas attack was no different from dying 'cleanly' by the sword or a bullet in the traditional manner; in practice, however, the discrepancy between ends and means became too great, and the horror of the means discredited the end:

> If you could hear, at every jolt, the blood
> Come gargling from the froth-corrupted lungs,
> Obscene as cancer, bitter as the cud
> Of vile, incurable sores on innocent tongues,—
> My friend, you would not tell with such high zest
> To children ardent for some desperate glory,
> The old Lie: Dulce et decorum est
> Pro patria mori.

Owen's first poetic treatment of the war is a sonnet called '1914' which is, in Mr. Day Lewis's words, 'of interest both for its resemblances and its unlikenesses to the state of mind expressed in Rupert Brooke's *1914*':

> War broke: and now the Winter of the world
> With perishing great darkness closes in.
> The foul tornado, centred at Berlin,
> Is over all the width of Europe whirled,
> Rending the sails of progress. Rent or furled
> Are all Art's ensigns. Verse wails. Now begin
> Famines of thought and feeling. Love's wine's thin
> The grain of human Autumn rots, down-hurled.
>
> For after Spring had bloomed in early Greece,
> And Summer blazed her glory out with Rome,
> An Autumn softly fell, a harvest home,

A slow grand age, and rich with all increase.
But now, for us, wild Winter, and the need
Of sowings for new Spring, and blood for seed.

Basically, this sonnet is no more than a rhetorical exercise (the
Keatsian strain is evident in the closing lines of the octet), but
it is thematically interesting inasmuch as there is a deflection
from personal excitement and idealism to the generalized apocalyptic note sounded by a number of European poets in 1914
(and which was detectable in Rosenberg).

The poems by which Owen will be remembered were written
later, the majority of them between August 1917 and September 1918. It was in July 1917 that Owen had his crucial
encounter with Siegfried Sassoon at Craiglockhart. Meeting
Sassoon did not transform Owen's poetry, for he had already
embarked on his mature poetic manner—'Exposure', for instance, was written early in 1917—but the older poet's en-
couragement and example were of immense help to Owen in
confirming him in his path. In Sassoon he found the intellectual
stimulus that he had so far lacked. Owen left an account of
their friendship in a number of letters, and Sassoon has described it in *Siegfried's Journey* and in an article—originally a
broadcast given in 1948—called 'Wilfred Owen: A Personal
Appreciation',[7] in which he has this to say:

I could see that this was the sort of poetry I liked. But at that
time my critical perceptions were undeveloped, and I was
slow in realising that his imagination worked on a larger scale
than mine, and that in technical accomplishment and intellectual approach he was on a higher plane. My trench-
sketches were like rockets, sent up to illuminate the darkness.
They were the first thing of their kind, and could claim
to be opportune. It was Owen who revealed how, out of
realistic horror and scorn, poetry might be made. My judgment was to some extent affected by his attitude of devoted
discipleship. I knew that I could write epigrammatic satires
better than he could, and he was attempting, in a few of his
pieces, to imitate them. This has sometimes caused my
influence on him to be exaggerated. The truth of the matter
was that I arrived just when he needed my stimulation and
advice. It was my privilege to be in close contact with him

while he was attaining a clear view of what he wanted to say and deploying his technical resources to a matured utterance.

In a few poems, such as 'The Chances' and 'The Letter', we see Owen attempting Sassoon's bitterly epigrammatic vein, and achieving a modest success; but it is equally evident that his real talents were best expressed in other kinds of writing.

Some idea of the assistance Owen received from Sassoon is evident from the discussion of the various drafts of 'Anthem for Doomed Youth' in C. Day Lewis's edition. He substitutes 'patient minds' in the penultimate line for Edmund Blunden's former reading of 'silent minds', and shows from the manuscript that 'patient' was inserted in the final version at Sassoon's suggestion.

Unlike other war poets, Owen rarely attempts a contrast, nostalgic or ironic, between the trenches and remembered English scenes. His absorption in the concrete realities of the Front is complete, and the only authentic England is in France:

> (This is the thing they know and never speak,
> That England one by one had fled to France,
> Not many elsewhere now, save under France.)
> ('Smile, Smile, Smile')

His poetry is also rooted in the despair springing from an awareness that the war might go on for an indefinite number of years, with no possible end in sight: the final German collapse in 1918 caught many people by surprise. Owen's dominant theme is the slaughter, or maiming, apparently endless, of young men; and it is marked by a concentration on 'The thousand several doors where men may take their exits': gassing, in 'Dulce Et Decorum Est'; blinding, in 'The Sentry' and 'A Terre'; mutilation, in 'Disabled'; madness, in 'Mental Cases' and 'The Chances'; shell-shock, in 'The Dead-Beat'; and suicide, in S.I.W.'. Owen is distinguished from Rosenberg by his stress on the details of death and mutilation, and by his predominantly realistic manner of description. But in one of his most terrifying poems, 'The Show', he moves into symbolism, in a nightmare vision where the battlefield is seen as a mass of writhing caterpillars:

I saw their bitten backs curve, loop and straighten,
I watched those agonies curl, lift, and flatten,
Whereat, in terror what that sight might mean,
I reeled and shivered earthward like a feather.

And Death fell with me, like a deepening moan.
And He, picking a manner of worm, which half had hid
Its bruises in the earth, but crawled no further,
Showed me its feet, the feet of many men.
And the fresh-severed head of it, my head.

But this kind of obliquity is not Owen's characteristic manner, which usually stays closer to the human end of the spectrum. One of his finest and most typical poems is 'Futility':

Move him into the sun—
Gently its touch awoke him once,
At home, whispering of fields unsown,
Always it woke him, even in France,
Until this morning and this snow.
If anything might rouse him now
The kind old sun will know.

Think how it wakes the seeds,—
Woke, once, the clays of a cold star.
Are limbs, so dear-achieved, are sides,
Full-nerved—still warm—too hard to stir?
Was it for this the clay grew tall?
—O what made fatuous sunbeams toil
To break earth's sleep at all?

With considerable economy of means, Owen places the tragedy of an individual death on a plane of cosmic significance; or rather, this death, so futile in its finality, points to an ultimate futility in the whole order of things. The 'sowing' of the first stanza, with the multiple associations of rural activity, of a young man's unrealized potentialities, and of unachieved sexual fulfilment, is transformed in the second to an image of life itself, the germ awakened in the nascent earth by the action of light, leading, ultimately, to the emergence of human life—epitomized in the fine image, 'Was it for this the clay grew tall?' This poem, so satisfactory in its movement and over-all structure, does nevertheless show signs of the fumbling that Owen's

inexperience manifested even in his mature phase: the last two
lines of the first stanza are rather weak, and the phrase, 'Are
limbs, so dear-achieved', though worked over a good deal (as
the manuscripts indicate), is still clumsy.

The poem illustrates the constant preoccupation of Owen's
major phase: the destruction of youth. The note here is mutedly
sensuous; it is more overtly so in other poems. 'Greater Love' is
a key example, in which Owen explores the ultimate sacrifice
made by the dead; their devotion both resembles and transcends
sexual love. I have already mentioned, in discussing Sassoon,
the attitude which rejected women and feminine values, seeing
in them manifestations of the uncomprehending civilian ethos;
Sassoon gave it angry expression in 'Glory of Women'. Owen
clearly shared this feeling, stressing the masculine self-suffi-
ciency of the companionship of the trenches, as in 'Apologia
Pro Poemate Meo':

> I have made fellowships—
>> Untold of happy lovers in old song.
>> For love is not the binding of fair lips
>> With the soft silk of eyes that look and long,
>
> By Joy, whose ribbon slips,—
>> But wound with war's hard wire whose stakes
>>> are strong;
>> Bound with the bandage of the arm that drips;
>> Knit in the webbing of the rifle-thong.

In 'Greater Love' Owen writes:

> Red lips are not so red
>> As the stained stones kissed by the English dead.
> Kindness of wooed and wooer
> Seems shame to their love pure.
> O Love, your eyes lose lure
>> When I behold eyes blinded in my stead!

The rejected 'red lips' are an emblem both of women and of
normal sexuality; and in subsequent stanzas there are successive rejections, supposedly addressed to the personified
'Love' but in fact recalling various attributes of femininity:

> Your slender attitude
>> Trembles not exquisite like limbs knife-skewed. . . .

> Your dear voice is not dear,
> Gentle, and evening clear,
> As theirs whom none now hear. . . .

Or consider these lines from 'The Send-Off':

> So secretly, like wrongs hushed-up, they went.
> They were not ours:
> We never heard to which front these were sent.
>
> Nor there if they yet mock what women meant
> Who gave them flowers.

As Day Lewis remarks, 'Owen had no pity to spare for the suffering of bereaved women'; there is, admittedly, the beautiful line in 'Anthem for Doomed Youth', 'the pallor of girls' brows shall be their pall', but this is a visual detail rather than a profoundly compassionate note. Male fellowship and self-sacrifice is an absolute value, and Owen celebrates it in a manner that fuses the paternal with the erotic (not that one would overestimate the latter quality, but its implicit presence will surely be apparent to any open-minded reader): Owen's attitude to the 'boys' or 'lads' destined for sacrifice has some affinities with Housman's.

One uses the word sacrifice advisedly: Owen had early on abandoned orthodox Christianity, and marked his abandonment in the poem, 'At a Calvary near the Ancre', which ends:

> But they who love the greater love
> Lay down their life; they do not hate.

But at the same time he identified the sufferings of his men with the passion of Christ: in a letter of 1917 he wrote:

Already I have comprehended a light which never will filter into the dogma of any national church: namely, that one of Christ's essential commands was: Passivity at any price! Suffer dishonour and disgrace, but never resort to arms. Be bullied, be outraged, be killed; but do not kill. It may be a chimerical and an ignominious principle, but there it is. It can only be ignored; and I think pulpit professionals are ignoring it very skilfully and successfully indeed. . . . And am I not myself a conscientious objector with a very seared conscience? . . . Christ is literally in 'no man's land'. There men often hear His voice: Greater love hath no man than this, that a man lay down his life for a friend. Is it spoken in English only and French? I do not believe so. Thus you see how pure Christianity will not fit in with pure patriotism.

The aesthetic passivity of Owen's admired Keats was transformed into an attitude of religious quietism. And in 1918 Owen wrote in a letter to Osbert Sitwell:

> For 14 hours yesterday I was at work—teaching Christ to lift his cross by numbers, and how to adjust his crown; and not to imagine he thirst till after the last halt; I attended his Supper to see that there were no complaints; and inspected his feet that they should be worthy of the nails. I see to it that he is dumb and stands at attention before his accusers. With a piece of silver I buy him every day, and with maps I make him familiar with the topography of Golgotha.

It is the sense of the war as a ritual sacrifice, in which he was involved as both priest and victim, that gives Owen's finest poems their particular quality, far transcending the simple protest and rebellion of Sassoon (or some of his own less ambitious pieces).

Among Owen's finest poems is 'Strange Meeting': Mr. T. S. Eliot has lately described it as a poem 'which is of permanent value and, I think, will never be forgotten, and which is not only one of the most moving pieces of verse inspired by the war of 1914-18, but also a technical achievement of great originality.'[8] The technical achievement, of course, lay in Owen's use of pararhyme, of which Edmund Blunden has said, 'What he made of it is felt at its fullest, perhaps, in the solemn music of "Strange Meeting", but again and again by means of it he creates remoteness, darkness, shock, emptiness, the last word.' 'Strange Meeting' has been given very adequate critical discussion by Dennis Welland, in his book on Owen, and in a recent article by Jon Silkin.[9] Welland describes Owen's debt to Canto v of Shelley's *Revolt of Islam*, and, to a lesser extent, to some lines from *Endymion;* he sees the poem as a treatment of the *Doppelgänger* myth, already familiar in Romantic iconography, in which the poet kills his own *alter ego*: 'I am the enemy you killed, my friend.' Silkin prefers an approach which stresses the poem's origins in the concrete realities of battle and mutual killing. To a large extent, of course, these two approaches are complementary. The poem does, in fact, impose a double vision on the reader:

> It seemed that out of battle I escaped
> Down some profound dull tunnel, long since scooped
> Through granites which titanic wars had groined.
> Yet also there encumbered sleepers groaned,
> Too fast in thought or death to be bestirred.
> Then, as I probed them, one sprang up, and stared
> With piteous recognition in fixed eyes,
> Lifting distressful hands as if to bless.

The poet is caught up in a dream vision in which his surroundings—the dug-out and his sleeping comrades—are transformed into something very different—a tunnel through granite —and yet still dimly recognizable. The scene is Hell, and he meets the enemy he has lately killed (one of Owen's drafts reads, 'I was a German conscript, and your friend').

The opening is magnificently dramatic, but later passages seem to me needlessly obscure: Owen has created a powerful myth, but does not seem at all sure what, in detail, he wishes to do with it. Admittedly, one admires the proleptic insight of lines like:

> Now men will go content with what we spoiled,
> Or, discontent, boil bloody and be spilled.
> They will be swift with swiftness of the tigress.
> None will break ranks, though nations trek from progress.

Yet in the immediately following lines one has free-wheeling eloquence rather than the poetic concentration of other parts of the poem:

> Courage was mine, and I had mystery,
> Wisdom was mine, and I had mastery:
> To miss the march of this retreating world
> Into vain citadels that are not walled.

'Strange Meeting' is, I suggest, a slightly overrated poem, which has many splendid lines but is not entirely thought through. And Geoffrey Hill's recent criticism of the poem's diction is worth referring to: he quotes the line, 'With a thousand pains that vision's face was grained', and asks, 'is this the agony of the trenches transcended, or is it a half-reluctant acknowledgment of the overpowering music of *Hyperion?'*[10]

One of Owen's best poems, in which he is wholly absorbed in the physical and moral desperation of the troops' condition, and is not deflected from realism, is 'Exposure'. And in 'Anthem for Doomed Youth' he gave a memorable form to his sense of the war as a prolonged ritual oblation. I would also agree with Jon Silkin's high valuation of 'Insensibility', which might be called Owen's 'Hollow Men': in this poem he achieved an unusual hardness of tone and a highly expressive verse movement:

> Happy are men who yet before they are killed
> Can let their veins run cold.
> Whom no compassion fleers
> Or makes their feet
> Sore on the alleys cobbled with their brothers.
> The front line withers,
> But they are troops who fade, not flowers
> For poets' tearful fooling:
> Men, gaps for filling:
> Losses who might have fought
> Longer; but no one bothers.

(Is there, perhaps, in the opening of this and subsequent sections an ironic glance at Joachim Du Bellay's sonnet, 'Heureux qui, comme Ulysse, a fait un beau voyage'?) The harsh reference to 'Poets' tearful fooling' points directly to the 'Preface': 'Above all I am not concerned with Poetry. My subject is War, and the pity of War.'

In one sense, however, Owen's poems need to be read together: they mutually illuminate each other and have a cumulative power. In their totality, as I have suggested, they have done more than any other work in English to form a sensibility that can grasp the nature of technological war. If Brooke and Binyon seem irrecoverably anachronistic, then that is largely because of what we have learnt from Owen. And he achieved this change in our perceptions by hammering hard at limited but intense areas of experience: for all his power, his emotional range is restricted. He wished it to be, as his 'Preface' makes clear. (It also raises an odd problem: why should the officer-pacifist, the opponent of the war, say of his book: 'if the spirit of it survives—survives Prussia'? Was Owen, after all, less single-minded than his poems suggest?[11]) I find it hard to imagine how Owen might have developed had he survived: the war was his overwhelming subject, and the work of his great final year was, in more than one sense, a consummation. It seems to me that a total cessation of creative activity would have been as likely a result of the anti-climax of peace as the vein of Catullan love-poetry that Mr. Day Lewis tentatively suggests he might have gone on to produce.

In this chapter I have juxtaposed Isaac Rosenberg and Wilfred Owen, but without attempting a detailed comparison between them: they were complementary figures, and the contrast should indicate something of their respective strengths and limitations. If Owen had the larger and more impressive achievement, Rosenberg, it seems to me, had the greater potentialities.

7

Civilian Responses

ALTHOUGH my main concern is with the literary records of the Great War that were left by those who fought in it, I should like to glance briefly at the work of a few civilian writers, which may illuminate or establish a context for the poetry and prose of the combatants.

Without any doubt, the most celebrated novel to describe reactions to the war on the Home Front was H. G. Wells's *Mr. Britling Sees it Through*; published in September 1916, it quickly ran into many editions. As we have seen, Wells, although a socialist and a pacifist, accepted the war as a means of extirpating Prussian militarism and the militaristic spirit generally, and so helping to establish universal peace. The early facile optimism of his pamphlet, *The War That Will End War*, was soon dissipated by events, although Wells continued to believe to the end that the war was a basically just conflict between the peace-loving powers—Britain and France—and the forces of militarism. *Mr. Britling Sees it Through* is a work of inspired journalism rather than of marked literary distinction, but it provides an absorbing account of the impact of war in August 1914 on a liberal, prosperous, professional family living in a comfortable house in Essex. Mr. Britling is a scarcely disguised projection of Wells himself (seen, perhaps, as a modest representative of national attitudes, since 'Britling' can be interpreted as 'little Briton'). The novel is a product of the reflective mood that succeeded Wells's early optimism, when it became apparent that the war was certain to be prolonged and the toll of casualties grew continually higher. Much of the novel is no more than a vehicle for Wells's own reflections, but, as the huge success of the book indicated, these were very much in tune with public feeling at the end of 1916, when the Somme disaster had had a chastening effect on even the most ebullient patriots. Wells, in the person of Mr. Britling, whilst still accept-

Civilian Responses

ing the rightness of the Allied cause and insisting on the guilt
of Germany both in starting the war and in perpetrating the
Belgian atrocities, tries to get beyond narrow patriotism, to form
a vision of a post-war world when war itself shall be abolished,
and when a purged Germany, professing the traditional German
virtues, is once more a member of the family of nations. In
fact, there is a certain conflict in the book, which Wells exemplifies in the tormented puzzling of Mr. Britling, between the
aspirations of the patriot and those of the visionary inter-
nationalist: whilst sternly denouncing German war crimes, he
recalls that comparable offences have been committed by the
British and French in the establishing of their colonial empires.
He even insists that the Germans did not have a monopoly of
cruelty in the conduct of the war—a remarkably frank admis-
sion for 1916.

In the final chapters Wells succumbed to the curious spirit
of religious sentiment that temporarily possessed him during
the war years; he imagines the fallen as somehow caught up
by God, though a Finite God who is very unlike the Almighty of
Christian orthodoxy. (Wells adumbrated this notion further in
such works as *God the Invisible King* (1917) and *The Soul of a
Bishop* (1917), though he soon abandoned it, and in later years
regarded this 'religious' phase with some embarrassment.)

Mr. Britling Sees it Through had an intense but transient
vogue—comparable in some ways to Robert Nichols' *Ardours
and Endurances*—but it still has a certain documentary and
historical interest. Douglas Goldring described it as 'a brilliant
exposition of that first awakening from intellectual numbness
which took place in England after the first year of the War.
The book did not bring about this awakening, it recorded it.
It was published at precisely the right moment and was an
immense success.'[1]

Another eminent writer whom the war provoked into a
characteristic literary response was Rudyard Kipling: the conflict came as no surprise to Kipling, who had long foreseen
it, but it brought him personal tragedy with the death of his
only son, and much of his wartime writing is marked by savage
bitterness. From the publication of 'For All We Have and
Are' Kipling continued to address a succession of exhortatory
poems to the nation (in May 1918 a bogus Kipling poem called

'The Old Volunteer' appeared in *The Times*, the work of an unknown hoaxer). And under the stress of war Kipling also produced some remarkably cruel short stories, of which the most famous is perhaps 'Mary Postgate': in literary terms, it is certainly one of his most brilliant compositions. In this story, the faded spinster, Mary Postgate, hears of the death in the Flying Corps of the boy, Wynn, she had helped to bring up; a little later a child is killed in her presence by a bomb from a German plane. Soon afterwards when she is burning Wynn's toys and books in an incinerator, she discovers a German airman lying wounded in a near-by shrubbery; she refuses to help him and threatens him with a pistol, repeating: '*Ich haben der todt Kinder gesehn.*' She waits for his death, in fact urging him to die, and when the end comes she experiences a clearly orgiastic satisfaction. In a penetrating analysis of this story,[2] Mr. W. W. Robson has shown that it is far more than a crude anti-German tract, being, in essentials, a study in the warped psychology of Mary Postgate, who is placed and distanced throughout as a pathetically unattractive figure. Nevertheless, whilst accepting the truth of this interpretation, one may doubt if it was read with such sensitive understanding when it first appeared in 1915: for many readers, in the pressures of a wartime context, the story must have seemed an object-lesson in hating the child-killing Hun. And 'Mary Postgate' was, after all, published together with a poem called 'The Beginnings':

> It was not part of their blood,
> It came to them very late
> With long arrears to make good,
> When the English began to hate.

One of the things that had disturbed Mr. Britling was the anti-English 'Hymn of Hate', sung by the Germans with such enthusiasm: it seemed to him the product of a pathological state of mind. But 'The Beginnings', though possibly more controlled in its sentiments, is a not dissimilar phenomenon.

Bernard Shaw was one of that small radical minority who adopted a less partisan and more openly sceptical attitude to the war. He saw with greater clarity than the assertive patriots just how far the war was causing the break-up of the pattern of civilization that had seemed so inviolable in 1914, and he embodied something of this vision in *Heartbreak House* (1919), which he subtitled 'A Fantasia in the Russian manner on English themes'. In his preface Shaw wrote: 'HEARTBREAK HOUSE is not merely the name of the play which follows this preface. It is cultured, leisured Europe before the war.' In fact, the play offers a microcosm of cultivated English society, futile, elegant, mildly eccentric, which is shattered at the end by bombs from a Zeppelin.

There were two other civilian writers who registered with extreme clarity their conviction that a phase of British civilization was in dissolution: they shared with the Georgian soldier-poets a feeling for traditional England, an England which they doubted could survive the war. I am referring to Ezra Pound and D. H. Lawrence. Both were in different ways somewhat detached spectators of the national effort: Pound because he was an American citizen (though he had lived in London since 1908), and Lawrence because of the working-class origins which made him feel an alien in Establishment circles (by the outbreak of war he had become *déclassé*, and his pacifist convictions, together with the influence of a German wife, meant that he spent the war years as what would now be termed an 'internal *émigré*').

Pound crystallized his response to the war in two of his major poems: *Homage to Sextus Propertius* (1917) and *Hugh Selwyn Mauberley* (1920). In the first he deals with the contemporary situation by indirection: the crisis of the British Empire is described in terms of Propertius' Rome: like London, a great metropolis and the centre of a great Empire. In 1931 Pound wrote of this poem: 'it presents certain emotions as vital to me in 1917, faced with the infinite and ineffable imbecility of the British Empire, as they were to Propertius some centuries earlier, when faced with the infinite and ineffable imbecility of the Roman Empire.'[3] But it was in *Mauberley* that Pound, who had once delighted in the theatrical belligerence of 'Altaforte', made his most direct and poignant confrontation of the war:

> These fought in any case,
> and some believing,
>   pro domo, in any case . . .

Some quick to arm,
some for adventure,
some from fear of weakness,
some from fear of censure,
some for love of slaughter, in imagination,
learning later . . .
some in fear, learning love of slaughter;

Died some, pro patria,
            non 'dulce' non 'et decor' . . .
walked eye-deep in hell
believing in old men's lies, then unbelieving
came home, home to a lie,
home to many deceits,
home to old lies and new infamy;
usury age-old and age-thick
and liars in public places.

Daring as never before, wastage as never before.
Young blood and high blood,
fair cheeks, and fine bodies;

fortitude as never before

frankness as never before,
disillusions as never told in the old days,
hysterias, trench confessions,
laughter out of dead bellies.

                .   .   .

There died a myriad,
And of the best, among them,
For an old bitch gone in the teeth,
For a botched civilization,

Charm, smiling at the good mouth,
Quick eyes gone under earth's lid,

For two gross of broken statues,
For a few thousand battered books.

The high civilization for which men had died, and which
should have been a constant living source of value, has been

contemptuously reduced to a heap of disparate objects, broken statues and battered books.

In the very beautiful 'Envoi' of the sequence, Pound seems to be addressing himself, as Donald Davie has suggested,[4] to the England he had come to know and love, and which seemed increasingly indifferent to her cultural riches:

> *Tell her that goes*
> *With song upon her lips*
> *But sings not out the song, nor knows*
> *The maker of it, some other mouth,*
> *May be as fair as hers,*
> *Might, in new ages, gain her worshippers. . . .*

When the war ended, Pound found that the quality of English life had deteriorated so much that he could no longer bear to live in London, the city that had once seemed to him the supreme literary and intellectual metropolis. He departed for the Continent, living first in France and then in Italy, until he was returned to the United States by the American army in 1945, charged with treason. Yet, twenty-five years after his departure, picking over his memories of the pre-1914 world in the prison camp at Pisa, he was able to look back at the old, vanished England with a nostalgic concern (and something of a Yeatsian feeling for the passing of aristocratic tradition):

> or is it all rust, ruin, death duties and mortgages
> and the great carriage yard empty
>   and more pictures gone to pay taxes. . . .
>
> Tudor indeed is gone and every rose,
> Blood-red, blanch-white that in the sunset glows
> Cries: 'Blood, Blood, Blood!' against the gothic stone
> Of England, as the Howard or Boleyn knows.
>
> (*Canto* LXXX)

As an American, and one who thought instinctively in literary and aesthetic categories, Pound had a somewhat external concept of English tradition. D. H. Lawrence, who was inalienably English by birth and upbringing, had similar but more intimate feelings. As his letters record, the war was an unbroken torment for him, and he was quite specific in saying that he considered a German victory a lesser evil than a continuation of the war. His pacifism was of the uncompromising kind that would face a foreign occupation with equanimity:

> I know that, for me, the war is wrong. I know that if the Germans wanted my little house, I would rather give it them than fight for it: because my little house is not important enough to me. If another man must fight for his house, the more's the pity. But it is his affair. To fight for possessions, goods, is what my soul *will not* do. Therefore it will not fight for the neighbour who fights for his own goods.[5]

Lawrence's conviction that the war was destroying traditional England was expressed in some superbly poignant passages in his wartime letters, as in the following paragraph from a letter to Lady Cynthia Asquith written in November 1915:

> When I drive across this country, with autumn falling and rustling to pieces, I am so sad, for my country, for this great wave of civilisation, 2000 years, which is now collapsing, that it is hard to live. So much beauty and pathos of old things passing away and no new things coming: this house of the Ottoline's—it is England—my God, it breaks my soul —their England, these shafted windows, the elm-trees, the blue distance—the past, the great past, crumbling down, breaking down, not under the force of the coming birds, but under the weight of many exhausted lovely yellow leaves, that drift over the lawn, and over the pond, like the soldiers, passing away, into winter and the darkness of winter —no, I can't bear it. For the winter stretches ahead, where all vision is lost and all memory dies out.

Lawrence conveyed a similar, though even more intense, epiphany in a letter to Lady Ottoline Morrell, dated 1st December 1915, in which he described his vision as being like that of a drowning man in which he sees 'all his past crystallised into one jewel of recollection':

> The window-shafts, like pillars, like bars, the shallow Tudor arch looping over between them, looping the darkness in a pure edge, in front of the far-off reluctance of the dawn.
> Shafted, looped windows between the without and the within, the old house, the perfect old intervention of fitted

stone, fitted perfectly about a silent soul, the soul that in drowning under this last wave of time looks out clear through the shafted windows to see the dawn of all dawns taking place, the England of all recollection rousing into being.

The wet lawn drizzled with brown, sodden leaves; the feathery heap of the ilex tree; the garden-seat all wet and reminiscent.

Between the ilex tree and the bare, purplish elms, a gleaming segment of all England, the dark plough-land and wan grass, and the blue, hazy heap of the distance, under the accomplished morning.

Lawrence's vision of England, of a traditional, rural-centred order, had affinities with the nostalgia for England of the poets in uniform, though it was far more intense than theirs, and was made tragic by the conviction that this order was collapsing (Lawrence had also, one recalls, been a regular contributor to the Georgian anthologies). Writing in December 1916, Lawrence said of the then Prime Minister, Asquith: 'He is too much the old, stable, measured, *decent* England. Alas and alack, that such an England must collapse and be trodden under the feet of swine and dogs.' And a few days later, when Lloyd George, whom Lawrence loathed, had taken over the premiership, he commented with the savagery that became increasingly marked as the war continued: 'It is what the countryful of swine wanted, now let them have it. All we have to do is to wait for the debauch.' Like Pound, Lawrence found England insupportable when the war ended, and in 1919 he left this country for good and embarked on the years of restless wandering that ended with his death in 1930.

He returned to his wartime experiences in his Australian novel, *Kangaroo* (1923), in which he devotes a fifty-page chapter called 'The Nightmare' to an avowedly autobiographical recapitulation of his life in wartime England. It is a pure digression in the otherwise tedious narrative of *Kangaroo*, and it has the almost hallucinatory power and intensity of those passages in Lawrence's writing in which he describes his most searing personal experiences (the account of Ursula's first day as a schoolteacher in *The Rainbow* (1915) is a comparable example). 'From 1916 to 1919,' he wrote, 'a wave of criminal lust rose and possessed England, there was a reign of terror, under a set of indecent bullies like Bottomley of *John Bull* and other bottom-dog members of the House of Commons.' Lawrence's account of the tribulations he endured during the war frequently rises to the level of hysteria, but even after discounting the excesses of his tone, one is left with a vivid impression of the coarsening and corrupting effect that the war had in its later years on English life. Ford Madox Ford, in *Parade's End*, was to make, from another point of view, a comparable analysis and indictment.

At the end of the chapter Lawrence describes his final departure from what he had now come to see as a corpse-like England:

> There was snow on the Downs like a shroud. And as he looked back from the boat, when they had left Folkestone behind and only England was there, England looked like a grey, dreary-grey coffin sinking in the sea behind, with her dead grey cliffs and the white, worn-out cloth of snow above.

(Lawrence was evidently attached to the image of England as a coffin, for he had already used it in *The Lost Girl* (1920): 'England, like a long, ash-grey coffin slowly submerging'.)

For Lawrence and Pound and other expatriates, such as Ford and Richard Aldington, the England they had known may well have seemed dead. But the life of a community must, inevitably, continue in one form or another, no matter how radical the transmutations it has undergone. The literature of the early nineteen-twenties offers various reflections of the efforts to continue living made by those on whom the memories of the war weighed most painfully: the denizens of *The Waste Land* (1922), for instance; or the exquisite Mrs. Viveash in Aldous Huxley's *Antic Hay* (1923), incapable of feeling but still obsessed with the memory of her lover, Tony Lamb, killed in 1917; or, in Virginia Woolf's *Mrs. Dalloway* (1925), the shell-shocked Septimus Warren Smith. If the war could not be forgotten, the refurbished post-war London, whose superficially relaxed atmosphere is evoked by the descriptions of Huxley and Virginia Woolf and by such works as Galsworthy's *A Modern Comedy* (1929), offered a variety of competing distractions. For a few years, there was to be no great public demand for books about the war.

K

8

RETROSPECT I
Autobiography

FOR those actively involved in the struggle, the immediate literary response to war had been necessarily confined to such compact forms as the private letter or diary entry, and, above all, to brief lyric poems. But many of the poets who survived returned to their experiences in longer, retrospective prose works written ten or more years after the Armistice. The years 1928-30 witnessed a remarkable return to public favour of books about the war, which coincided with the further stage of war literature represented by autobiographical works such as Blunden's *Undertones of War*, Sassoon's *Memoirs of a Fox-Hunting Man* and *Memoirs of an Infantry Officer*, and Graves's *Goodbye to All That*; and by novels like Aldington's *Death of a Hero* and Manning's *Her Privates We*. Nor was this resurgence of interest confined to British writers: *A Farewell to Arms* in America, and *All Quiet on the Western Front* in Germany, showed its international nature.

Yet there had been a steady trickle of war books appearing from 1919 onwards, ranging from artless personal narratives to official histories of regiments or campaigns, which had attracted dedicated readers. One of the best of these earlier books is C. E. Montague's *Disenchantment*, published in 1922, which anticipates the temper of the retrospective studies of the end of the decade. It is a highly personal work, which offers, not sustained description or narrative, but a loosely linked series of studies, belle-lettrist in manner and occasionally rising to stylistic distinction, of the changes in front-line morale during the course of the war. Montague writes as an ardent over-age volunteeer for the New Army of 1915, filled, like so many others, with idealism, zeal and high-spirits: his sense of dedication was sorely tried by the corruption and minor stupidities of the minor military bureaucracy, and by the graver in-competences of the Staff: he expressed the common feeling that the New Army consisted of 'lions led by donkeys'. In some respects, an idealism as fine as Montague's was bound to be badly bruised in any form of organized military life; parts of his book do no more than express the perennial human resentment of 'The insolence of office, and the spurns/That patient merit of the unworthy takes'. Yet in other ways Montague provides an index of the attitudes and concerns that were manifested by all the writers who experienced the life of the trenches: in a positive sense, the camaraderie of active service life and the almost cosy domesticity of the quieter sections of the Front; and, on the negative side, the increasing alienation of the troops from the empty jingoism of the Home Front, and, something which Montague passionately deplored, the loss of traditional standards of chivalry in the conduct of the war: he shows that the hate-mongering of the civilians affected some of the Staff, but the front-line soldiers largely rejected it and continued to respect their German opponents. Above all, Montague conveys the sense of waste and futility produced by the seemingly endless prolongation of the war, which proved so demoralizing to those who had once shown such ardour. One of his most moving passages describes his feelings on witnessing the final break-through of the British Army in August 1918: a sense of incredulity that this longed-for event was actually happening, combined with the sad realization that it was taking place *too late*: in 1916, even in 1917, it might have aroused the authentic exhilaration of victory, but it had been too long deferred and too much had been lost in the intervening years.

Prose accounts of the war can be divided between those which were avowedly subjective in their approach, like Montague's, offering the author's own reflections and showing the war as it affected his own development; and those which concentrated on objective narrative, suppressing the author's direct feelings and allowing emotion to be expressed only by implication in the descriptive process. A magnificent example of the latter mode is Herbert Read's brief study, *In Retreat*; this was first published in 1925, but was written as early as 1919, with all the detachment and objectivity of the narratives of ten years later, and is a classic of modern English prose. It deals with a few days in the retreat of the British Army following the German break-through in March 1918. Read divides his narrative into tiny units of experience, expressed by terse, compact sentences, and provides a sense of the rapid passage of time by frequently stating the time of day at which a particular event took place. The opening paragraphs show the narrative method in action; after the briefly informative opening sentences, the focus narrows to provide a succession of isolated sense data (recalling Read's apprenticeship as an Imagist poet):

> We received the warning order just before dinner, and for a while talked excitedly round the mess fire, some scoffing at the idea of an imminent battle, others gravely saying that this time at any rate the warning was justified. Two deserters, with tales of massing guns and the night-movements of innumerable troops, had reached our lines the previous day. Of course, deserters usually had some such tale designed to tempt a captor's leniency, but this time it was likely to be the truth. What else could the enemy's long silence mean? To that question we had no answer. We went early to bed, expecting an early awakening. The harnessed horses stood in lowered shafts.
>
> There was scarcely a wall standing in Fluquières: everywhere demolition and bombardment had reduced the village to irregular cairns of brick and plaster. Winding among these cairns were the cleared roadways. Men and horses rested in patched sheds and an occasional cellar. S—— and I were in a small repaired stable, each with a bed-frame in a manger. I had livened the cleanly whitewashed walls of the place with illustrations from a coloured magazine. That evening all save our trench-kit had been sent to the transport-wagons, and we were lying on the bare netting with only our trench coats thrown over us.

In the hands of a less accomplished writer such baldness of narrative style could easily diminish into flatness and banality; and it is true that much of *In Retreat* recalls the simple and unadorned manner of an official report. But Read is always fully in control of his language, consciously selecting and placing significant details, though the total effect is one of transparency, as though we were actively sharing in the author's experiences without the intervention of the verbal medium. Read's ability to convey the tension and the sheer physical effect of rapidly ensuing action is apparent in the following paragraph, describing a later stage in the retreat:

> At 8 a.m. we began to observe troops retreating in front of us. They came in little groups down the road, or straggled singly over the landscape. The mist gradually lifted. We heard machine-gun fire fairly near, somewhere on the right. The stragglers informed us that the enemy had crossed the canal in the early dawn, and was advancing in considerable force. We waited patiently. At 9 a.m. the enemy came into touch with our fellows on the left, and here we rebutted him successfully. At 9.30 the troops on our right were reported to be withdrawing. About ten o'clock, there happened one of those sudden episodes, which would be almost comic with their ludicrous *bouleversement* were they not so tragic in their results. Seemingly straight from the misty sky itself, but in reality from our own guns, descended round after round of shrapnel bursting terrifically just above our heads, and spraying leaden showers upon us. Simultaneously, from the woods on our right, there burst a fierce volley of machine-gun fire, hissing and spluttering among us. We just turned and fled into the shelter of the village buildings. I shouted to my men to make for the position of the quarry. We scuttled through gardens and over walls. By the time we reached the quarry we had recovered our nerve. We extended and faced the enemy, who were advancing skilfully over the plain on our left. We on our part were a scrap lot composed of various units. We hastily reorganized into sections. Retreat was inevitable. Then followed a magnificent effort of discipline. A major took charge of the situation, and we began to retire with covering fire, section by section, in perfect alternation.

The narrative detachment stops short of the passive impersonality of the camera-eye: there is sufficient human involvement for the final 'magnificent effort of discipline', preserving both life and order, to be praised. Again, on a later page, Read makes evident the famished troops' pleasure in finding food and hot coffee. But in general, *In Retreat* conveys a sense of the war as a large machine that transcends the separate humanity of those caught up in it; Read's prose provides, as it were, a track of its movements over a short stretch of time as recorded by one individual consciousness.

Whereas *In Retreat* is in a dominantly objective mode, another, shorter prose piece, 'The Raid', is closer to the subjective end of the scale: it describes a trench raid that Read led in the summer of 1917, and contains the reflections on cowardice and the account of capturing a German officer that had already provided material for some of his poems. It is a fine piece of writing, even though it falls short of the distinction of *In Retreat*. (Both pieces have been reprinted several times, most recently in Read's autobiographical volume, *The Contrary Experience*, which also contains his war diary.) Read's literary records of the war are not extensive: the few poems of *Naked Warriors, The End of a War*, and these brief prose narratives. Yet together they form a response unsurpassed in sensitivity and penetration by his more prolific contemporaries.

Another consciously objective writer is Edmund Blunden, whose *Undertones of War*, published in 1928, caught the rising tide of popular interest and went into several editions. Blunden, like the other retrospective writers of the late 'twenties, whether in autobiography or fiction, was writing in an attempt to make sense of his own experiences, to trace a pattern in the scarifying events that had impinged on his formative years. To some extent, this endeavour is true of all writers of autobiography, and still more of autobiographic fiction—as Proust so amply demonstrated. But the survivors of the Great War had possibly more urgent motives: in making an extended confrontation of their wartime lives they were engaging in a therapeutic activity. Significantly, both Blunden and Graves confess that they had made previous attempts at describing their wartime experiences but had failed: not until a decade had elapsed could they write about them as they wished.

Undertones of War is much less than a full autobiography: it is a severely selective account of Blunden's experiences as a very young subaltern, on the Somme and at the Third Battle of Ypres. In reading this book we recognize the presence of the same persona that speaks through Blunden's poetry—he describes himself in the final sentence as 'a harmless young shepherd in a soldier's coat'—with a characteristic sweetness and gentleness of disposition, an intensely observant love of nature and a thorough immersion in the traditions of literary pastoral. And yet we are given very little of the substance of the young Blunden's personality, merely a pronounced flavour of his mind and sensibility: this flavour is imparted by the quality of Blunden's prose, with its carefully composed sentences, sometimes idiosyncratic in their structure and out-of-the-way in their choice of words, conveying a sense of mellow, almost middle-aged reminiscence (though Blunden was only in his early thirties when writing this book). Throughout *Undertones of War* the author subdues himself to the succession of events, arranged in chapters each grouped round a separate narrative focus, and doesn't intervene with his reflections and opinions; though here and there we find some uncharacteristically direct comments, as when Blunden refers to his sympathy for Siegfried Sassoon's anti-war stand, and speaks of his 'convictions that the war was useless and inhuman'. But for the most part he maintains a studied reticence.

There is a marked austerity in the planning of *Undertones of War*, in so far as its scenes are confined to life at the Front: when the author goes home on leave we do not follow him. The world of the troops in France is seen as forming a self-contained though bizarre civilization, with its own values, and even its own peculiar time-scheme. In 1916 the remnants of the early campaigns of 1914 seemed immensely ancient, relics of a far-off world:

> The joyful path away from the line, on that glittering summer morning, was full of pictures for my infant war-mind. History and nature were beginning to harmonize in the quiet of that sector. In the orchard through which we passed immediately, waggons had been dragged together once with casks and farm gear to form barricades; I felt that they should never be disturbed again, and the memorial raised near them to the dead of 1915 implied a closed chapter. The empty farm houses were not yet effigies of agony or mounds of punished, atomized material; they could still shelter, and they did. Their hearths could still boil the pot.

Acres of self-sown wheat glistened and sighed as we wound our way between, where rough scattered pits recorded a hurried firing-line of long ago. Life, life abundant sang here and smiled; the lizard ran warless in the warm dust; and the ditches were trembling quick with odd tiny fish, in worlds as remote as Saturn.

Blunden does not draw any sharp, sardonic contrast between the Two Nations, though in Chapter XXII he allows himself a sad comment on the universally attested decline in the quality of civilian life that had come about by 1917: 'During my leave, I remember principally observing the large decay of lively bright love of country, the crystallization of dull civilian hatred on the basis of "the last drop of blood".' The texture of his prose is, however, permeated by a contrast between the brutal realities of war and the remembered or imagined beauties and harmonies of nature and the rural order. As we have seen, this contrast was a dominant element in Blunden's war poems; but in his prose he manipulates it with particular delicacy. The contrast is not bitter or ironical; rather it forms a balance of opposites that go to make up a unified picture:

> Waiting there in the gashed hillsides for Lewis, who had gone below for instructions, we looked over the befouled fragments of Ypres, the solitary sheet of water, Zillebeke Lake, the completed hopelessness. The denuded scene had acquired a strange abruptness of outline; the lake and the ashy city lay unprotected, isolated, dominated finally. But farther off against the sunset one saw the hills beyond Mount Kemmel, and the simple message of nature's health and human worthiness again beckoned in the windmills resting there. There—and here!

Even when he is describing scenes of destruction, Blunden's choice of phrases and images is such that the sense of disorder is blended with a feeling for the continuity of what has been, for the time being, disturbed:

> The heart of the village is masked with its hedges and orchards from almost all ground observation. That heart nevertheless bleeds. The old homes are razed to the ground: all but one or two, which play involuntary tricks upon

probability, balancing themselves like mad acrobats. One has been knocked out in such a way that its thatched roof, almost uninjured, has dropped over its broken body like a tea-cosy. The church maintains a kind of conceptional shape, and has a cliff-like beauty in the sunlight; but as at this ecclesiastical corner visitors are sometimes killed we may, in general, allow distance to lend enchantment. Up that naked road is the stern eye of Beaumont Hamel—turn, Amarylis, turn—this way the tourist's privacy is preserved by ruins and fruitful branches.

Constantly Blunden displays a sharpness and exactness of observation, whether of natural objects or the phenomena of war, or both, that reminds one of the notes of Ruskin or Hopkins:

It is true that steel helmets now became the rule, their ugly useful discomfort supplanting our old friendly soft caps; and the parachute flares winding down from the cloud of night glistened here and there on those curious green mushrooms, or domes, where listening-posts perhaps listened, probably dozed among the weeds and rustlings of No Man's Land.

Blunden continues the description, somewhat changing its tone and allowing himself a moment of overt reflection: this, the end of Chapter VII, is one of the slight climaxes of the book:

The dethronment of the soft cap clearly symbolized the change that was coming over the war, the induration from a personal crusade into a vast machine of violence, that had come in the south, where vague victory seemed to be happening. The south! what use thinking about it? If we were doomed to go, we thought, we were, and we pressed no further. No one seemed to have any mental sight or smell of that vast battle.

Many other writers were aware of the change in the character of the war that occurred after the Somme battles (on the German side it was noticed by Ernst Jünger), the transformation of the conflict into a 'vast machine of violence'. But Blunden does not dwell on the point. *Undertones of War*, as its title implies, is an undramatic book. Although Blunden does not shirk from describing the violence of battle when he was directly involved (displaying, on occasion, great courage and enterprise), and gives a faithful account of death and mutilation and the physical horrors of the Passchendaele front, he does so in a quiet, unemphatic fashion that is at the opposite extreme from the methods of a writer like Barbusse. If one compares the poem 'Third Ypres', with Blunden's later prose account of the same events in *Undertones of War*, one notices the greater detachment of the prose narrative. *Undertones of War* might, perhaps, be criticized, not for not telling the truth about war, for its authenticity is patent, but for presenting only a narrow segment of the truth. Unlike most of the other retrospective works of 1928-30 it does not attempt either an implicit or an explicit criticism of the war, or the manner of its conduct. Blunden's book is marked by its quality of quiet acceptance of all experience, even the most violent. As I have already remarked, in discussing his poetry, Blunden has always been aware of his own intellectual and artistic limitations, and it is this realization that led to the severe selectivity of *Undertones of War*. Yet, within these deliberate limits, the book is a masterpiece. And one can assume that for Blunden, and for many others of his generation who had been haunted for a decade by the memories of the trenches, it provided a means of living more readily with their memories: its gentle, exact, observant prose preserved those experiences and at the same time removed their cruelty.

The other undoubted English autobiographical masterpiece of the war is Robert Graves's *Goodbye to All That*, published in 1929, which is already a classic in the exacting art of autobiography. The differences between Graves's and Blunden's books are instructive: the former is a full-scale autobiography, moving from Graves's childhood and schooldays at Charterhouse through to his period as a Professor in Egypt in the mid-'twenties. But the central chapters of the book are those in which Graves describes his four years of wartime service in the Royal Welch Fusiliers. Any autobiographical writer must project some kind of persona whose experiences and attitudes he is attempting to trace; the real, ultimate 'me' may be an unknowable metaphysical abstraction, but the autobiographer must write about someone who remains recognizable to the reader in different situations, even though he may embody only a fraction of all the writer's possible attributes. Blunden's narrator, as we have seen, was the reticent but observant 'harmless young shepherd in a soldier's coat'. Graves, on the other hand, appears in *Goodbye to All That* as a vigorously eccentric personality, almost insufferably knowledgeable and opinionated, ironically self-possessed, and, like Blunden, a keen observer, though of human foibles rather than of natural phenomena. His prose is lucid, economical, and continually alive with anecdotes, which are always entertaining though, in many cases, disconcertingly without feeling. Graves gives away far more of his own personality than Blunden, but only, one feels, as much as he wishes to: the attitudes that governed his literary persona and which were expressed in his stylistic devices were undoubtedly part of a technique for psychological survival. He made a conscious effort to appear before the world as an embodiment of the 'stiff upper-lip' attitude without its customary inflexibility of mind, just as he learned whilst at Charterhouse to become an accomplished boxer as a defence against bullying. Graves describes very frankly the shattering effect that four years of war, combined with the repression of feeling, had upon him: the writing of *Goodbye to All That* was preeminently a means to the recovery of psychological stability and wholeness.

Graves was never an enthusiast for the war, although he regarded Sassoon's anti-war gesture as a mistake. For the most part, he felt that 'the only way out was the way through', and stoically resigned himself to being as good a soldier as possible: this was very much Sassoon's attitude when he returned to the Front for his final spell of duty in 1918. One of the unexpected things about Graves's attitude, as compared with other war poets, is his concern with regimental tradition and the minor rituals of service life. Although he had joined the Royal Welch Fusiliers quite by chance, he soon became intensely proud of the regiment and its history, and reflected sagely on the difference in morale between one battalion and another in the manner of a seasoned regular officer. Indeed, Graves sometimes gives the regular's impression of regarding the actual fighting as rather an interruption to the real business of soldiering. There has always been an element in Graves's make-up that responds to ritual, and in his later years he came to see the poetic vocation as a ritual service of the White Goddess. During the Great War his devotion to regimental tradition may well have been a device for the preservation of psychic equilibrium, akin to Blunden's loving observation of nature.

The following two paragraphs from Chapter xiv of *Goodbye to All That* give some idea of Graves's literary method, and underlying attitudes. The dry, detached tone, the mathematical precision, the calculated toughness, do not entirely conceal the hints of an underlying humanity, though they are an effective means of distancing and controlling experiences that might otherwise be overwhelmingly painful.

Like everyone else, I had a carefully worked out formula for taking risks. In principle, we would all take any risk, even the certainty of death, to save life or maintain an important position. To take life we would run, say, a one-in-five risk, particularly if there was some wider object than merely reducing the enemy's manpower; for instance, picking off a well-known sniper, or getting fire ascendancy in trenches where the lines came dangerously close. I only once refrained from shooting a German I saw, and that was at Cuinchy, some three weeks after this. While sniping from a knoll in the support line, where we had a concealed loophole, I saw a German, perhaps seven hundred yards away, through my telescopic sights. He was taking a bath in the German third line. I disliked the idea of shooting a naked man, so I handed the rifle to the sergeant with me. 'Here take this. You're a better shot than I am.' He got him; but I had not stayed to watch.

About saving the lives of enemy wounded there was disagreement; the convention varied with the division. Some divisions, like the Canadians and a division of Lowland territorials, who claimed that they had atrocities to avenge, would not only avoid taking risks to rescue enemy wounded, but go out of their way to finish them off. The Royal Welch were gentlemanly: perhaps a one-in-twenty risk to get a wounded German to safety would be considered justifiable. An important factor in calculating risks was our own physical condition. When exhausted and wanting to get quickly from one point in the trenches to another without collapse, we would sometimes take a short cut over the top, if the enemy were not nearer than four or five hundred yards. In a hurry, we would take a one-in-two-hundred risk; when dead tired, a one-in-fifty risk. In battalions where morale was low, one-in-fifty risks were often taken in laziness or despair. The Munsters of the First Division were said by the Welsh to 'waste men wicked', by not keeping properly under cover while in the reserve lines. The Royal Welch never allowed wastage of this sort. At no time in the war did any of us believe that hostilities could possibly continue more than another nine months or a year, so it seemed almost worthwhile taking care; there might even be a chance of lasting until the end absolutely unhurt.

Such phrases as 'it seemed almost worthwhile taking care' and 'there might even be a chance' are indicative of the non-chalance that, on the surface at least, took the place of traditional heroics on the part of many front-line fighters.

Graves's autobiography contains a wealth of anecdote, of which a representative example is the one concerning the soldier charged with murdering a French civilian in an *estaminet*:

It seems that a good deal of cognac had been going round, and the French civilian, who bore a grudge against the British because of his faithless wife, began to insult the private. He was reported, somewhat improbably, as having said: '*Anglais no bon, Allmand très bon. War fineesh, napoo les Anglais. Allmand win.*' The private had thereupon drawn his bayonet and run the man through. At the court-martial the private was exonerated; the French civil representative commending him for having 'energetically repressed local defeatism'.

But the most extraordinary of all Graves's anecdotes, which forms the imaginative centre of his wartime chapters, is the account of his own 'death' from wounds. During the Somme battle an eight-inch shell burst three paces behind him, severely wounding him; he lay unconscious in a dressing-station for more than twenty-four hours and was assumed to be dead; his commanding officer duly wrote a letter of condolence to

Graves's mother. Then it was discovered that he was still alive and he was taken to hospital (he had in the meantime been included on an official casualty list as 'died of wounds').

> I was semi-conscious now, and aware of my lung-wound through a shortness of breath. It amused me to watch the little bubbles of blood, like scarlet soap-bubbles, which my breath made in escaping through the opening of the wound. The doctor came over to my bed. I felt sorry for him; he looked as though he had not slept for days.

He was sent back to a hospital in London where he made a good recovery: 'I heard here for the first time of my supposed death; the joke contributed greatly to my recovery. People with whom I had been on the worst terms in my life, wrote the most enthusiastic condolences to my mother.' Following such an experience, Graves felt more than usually isolated from the civilian population; he described his repulsion from the prevalent hysteria of the Home Front and commented, 'I found serious conversations with my parents all but impossible.'

Much of the hard brilliance in Graves's writing may be directly attributable to the effects of having lived through this Lazarus-like experience; one might expect it to make a permanent and incalculable modification of the sensibility. Graves's early poems show a clear division between harsh realism and the pursuit of bucolic fantasy; for several years after the war his verse was all in the latter mode. With the composition of *Goodbye to All That* Graves returned to a new and deeper realism: physical in the accounts of battle (partly based on a wartime diary) and psychological in the frank analysis of his own attitudes and motives. Above all, this is a magnificently inclusive book, comic as well as harrowing. Graves's reputation as a literary figure rests principally on his poems; but *Goodbye to All That* has played a scarcely less significant part in establishing it.

Blunden and Graves were both survivors of the Somme—the supreme crisis of British arms—and so, too, was Siegfried Sassoon, whose prose reminiscences of the war, as contained in the Sherston trilogy, deserve a place alongside *Undertones of War* and *Goodbye to All That;* though in a literary sense they are, it seems to me, of somewhat smaller interest. In some respects the Sherston volumes fall rather unhappily between the separate forms of strict autobiography and the autobiographical novel. 'George Sherston' is not Siegfried Sassoon: it is evident that various of his personal and family circumstances are different. And yet the underlying assumption seems to be that the events of Sherston's wartime life can be identified with Sassoon's own experience (Sassoon states as much in his later and purely autobiographical volume, *Siegfried's Journey* [1945]). The major difference between Sassoon and Sherston is that the latter is not a poet: he is made to appear a simpler and somewhat less sophisticated figure than his creator. The account of his act of anti-war rebellion in *Memoirs of an Infantry Officer* (1930) may well have corresponded exactly to Sassoon's own behaviour in the summer of 1917, but it would have acquired greater resonance if we had been told that this was the action of the author of *The Old Huntsman* and *Counter-Attack*. In fact, Sassoon seems himself to have felt a certain unease on this point, for *Siegfried's Journey* overlaps untidily with *Memoirs of an Infantry Officer* and *Sherston's Progress* (1936). Reading the trilogy in the light of the later volume one has a sense of muffling and diminution: one's knowledge of what is left out prevents a straightforward response (and some of the devices seem merely irritating, such as the transparent disguises for characters who clearly stand for living people). But no doubt in 1928, when he embarked on the trilogy, Sassoon did not feel ready to present his experience to the world without some attempt at fictional concealment.

Despite its considerable length, the Sherston trilogy provides on an extended scale the basic paradigm on which so many wartime poems were based: a poignant contrast between rural England and the brutalities of trench warfare; here exemplified in Sherston's pre-war life (which seems to have corresponded with Sassoon's very closely) as a country gentleman of leisure, devoting his time to hunting and cricket, and his subsequent transformation into an infantry officer at the Front.

For Sassoon, writing in 1928, the greater part of *Memoirs of a Fox-Hunting Man* would have represented a deliberate thrusting-back of memory and imagination to the idyllic pursuits of pre-war days. The sense of innocence is well preserved: there is no sense in these chapters that the carefree scene is already overshadowed by the prospect of war, although there is an odd proleptic hint of the future in Chapter v when the local Master of Hounds asks the members of the Hunt 'to do everything in their power to eliminate the most dangerous enemy of the hunting man—he meant barbed wire'. Here and there we are aware of Sassoon's deliberate attempts, in an almost Proustian fashion, to recover the vanished past:

> Yet I find it easy enough to recover a few minutes of that grey south-westerly morning, with its horsemen hustling on in scattered groups, the December air alive with the excitement of the chase, and the dull green landscape seeming to respond to the rousing cheer of the huntsman's voice when the hounds hit off the line again after a brief check. Away they stream, throwing up little splashes of water as they race across a half-flooded meadow. Cockbird flies a fence with a watery ditch on the take-off side. "How topping," I think, "to be alive and well up in the hunt"; and I spurt along the sound turf of a green park and past the front of a square pink Queen Anne house with blank windows and smokeless chimneys, and a formal garden with lawns and clipped yew hedges sloping to a sunk fence. A stone statue stares at me, and I wonder who lived there when the house was first built. "I am riding past the past", I think, never dreaming that I shall one day write that moment down on paper; never dreaming that I shall be clarifying and condensing that chronicle of simple things through which I blundered so diffidently.

The scene is vividly evoked. The sense of being a living part of English rural tradition is one with which we are by now familiar; one recalls the passages from D. H. Lawrence's letters quoted in the previous chapter. Yet the choice of words raises once more the problem of the relation between Sherston and the Sassoon of 1928: Sassoon has not merely clarified and condensed his memories, he has simplified them, and Sherston has been given a remarkably simple consciousness. The phrase 'through which I blundered so diffidently' is significant, for a diffident blundering describes very well one's impression of Sherston's progress through the world.

Autobiography

In August 1914 Sherston joins up, is commissioned, and goes to the Front. Home on leave in 1916 he reflects, 'Looking round the room at the enlarged photographs of my hunters, I began to realize that my past was wearing a bit thin. The War seemed to have made up its mind to obliterate all those early adventures of mine.' Sherston's army experiences are continued in *Memoirs of an Infantry Officer;* this book covers many of the same experiences as Sassoon's wartime poems, and sometimes describes the same events, but the mode of presentation is significantly different. Instead of the bitterness and hard outlines of the poems, the prose accounts are gently reflective and curiously undramatic. Sassoon is not coolly detached in the manner of Graves: he is constantly aware of his own involvement in the scenes around him, but manifests an attitude of uncertainty and diffidence: 'Anyhow, I hadn't expected the Battle of the Somme to be quite like this,' he reflects, on seeing the body of a young German soldier. His prose is always effective, and at its best has an excellent if rather casual lucidity. A good example is Sherston's account of capturing a trench single-handed:

Just before I arrived at the top I slowed up and threw my two bombs. Then I rushed at the bank, vaguely expecting some sort of scuffle with my imagined enemy. I had lost my temper with the man who had shot Kendle; quite unexpectedly, I found myself looking down into a well-conducted trench with a great many Germans in it. Fortunately for me, they were already retreating. It had not occurred to them that they were being attacked by a single fool; and Fernby, with presence of mind which probably saved me, had covered my advance by traversing the top of the trench with his Lewis gun. I slung a few more bombs, but they fell short of the clumsy field-grey figures, some of whom half turned to fire their rifles over the left shoulder as they ran across the open toward the wood, while a crowd of jostling helmets vanished along the trench. Idiotically elated, I stood there with my finger in my right ear and emitted a series of 'view-holloas' (a gesture which ought to win the approval of people who still regard war as a form of outdoor sport). Having thus failed to commit suicide, I proceeded to

161

occupy the trench—that is to say, I sat down on the fire-
step, very much out of breath, and hoped to God the Germans wouldn't come back again.

One need not doubt the authenticity of this incident as part of
Sassoon's own experience—Graves has attested to his reckless-
ness as a front-line fighter—but there is a strangely artless
manner in the description, almost as if Sassoon wants us to
see Sherston as something of a Wodehousian silly ass, blundering blindly about the battle-field. It is, perhaps, as good a way
as any of suppressing the embarrassment that must inevitably
attend a first-person account of heroic behaviour. Graves
would have treated the incident with greater sardonic emphasis,
bringing out the anecdotal possibilities.

Some of Sassoon's best prose is to be found in the later
chapters that describe the fighting before the Hindenburg Line
in April 1917, when Sherston is wounded. Sherston's sense of
humour is evident when, lying in a London hospital, he reflects
on the various types of visitor he gets and his differing approaches to them:

> *Some Senior Officer under whom I'd served*: Modest, po-
> litely subordinate, strongly imbued with the 'spirit of the
> Regiment' and quite ready to go out again. 'Awfully nice of
> you to come and see me, sir.' Feeling that I ought to
> jump out of bed and salute, and that it would be appropriate
> and pleasant to introduce him to 'some of my people' (pref-
> erably of impeccable social status). Willingness to discuss ac-
> tive service technicalities and revive memories of shared
> front-line experience.
> *Middle-aged or elderly Male Civilian*: Tendency (in res-
> ponse to sympathetic gratitude for services rendered to King
> and Country) to assume haggard facial aspect of one who had
> 'been through hell'. Inclination to wish that my wound was a
> bit worse than it actually was, and have nurses hovering
> round with discreet reminders that my strength mustn't be
> overtaxed. Inability to reveal anything crudely horrifying to
> civilian sensibilities. 'Oh yes, I'll be out there again by the
> autumn.' (Grimly wan reply to suggestions that I was now
> honourably qualified for a home service job.) Secret antagon-
> ism to all uncomplimentary references to the German Army.

Charming Sister of Brother Officer: Jocular, talkative, debonair, and diffidently heroic. Wishful to be wearing all possible medal-ribbons on pyjama jacket. Able to furnish a bright account of her brother (if still at the front) and suppressing all unpalatable facts about the War. 'Jolly decent of you to blow in and see me.'

Hunting Friend (a few years above Military Service Age): Deprecatory about sufferings endured at the front. Tersely desirous of hearing all about last season's sport. 'By Jingo, that must have been a nailing good gallop!' Jokes about the Germans, as if throwing bombs at them was a tolerable substitute for fox-hunting. A good deal of guffawing (mitigated by remembrance that I'd got a bullet hole through my lung). Optimistic anticipations of next season's Opening Meet and an early termination of hostilities on all fronts.

It was during the subsequent period of convalescence that Sherston-Sassoon decided to make his gesture of protest against the continuation of the war. The remainder of *Memoirs of an Infantry Officer* describes his ensuing experiences, and ends with his arrival at Craiglockhart Hospital, here called 'Slateford'. In the final volume of the trilogy, *Sherston's Progress* we hear about Sherston's period at 'Slateford', his admiring acquaintance with the neurologist, W. H. R. Rivers (though there is nothing about Wilfred Owen); his subsequent service in Ireland and Palestine, and his final return to the Western Front in the spring of 1918. He is again wounded, and the book ends with Sherston once more in a London hospital, being visited by Rivers. This volume is the least satisfactory of the three; it attempts to compress too large and varied a range of experiences in a small compass, and lacks unity of feeling, having neither the poignancy of the remembered rural pleasures of the *Fox-Hunting Man* or the concentration of the battle scenes in the *Infantry Officer*.

The trilogy is, as I have suggested, an incomplete success: Sassoon fails to achieve the limited but intense clarity of observation of Blunden's memoirs, or Graves's sharp, highly controlled focus. In his use of a quasi-fictional persona Sassoon has evaded rather than solved some of the pressing problems of writing autobiography. Nevertheless, the first two volumes contain many striking passages which should ensure them a significant place in the literature of the Great War, even if a rather lower one than that occupied by Sassoon's wartime poems. In many respects, too, his later autobiographical volume, *Siegfried's Journey, 1916-1920,* deserves mention, although it doesn't deal directly with the war: it is a work of some stylistic distinction, and usefully supplements the Sherston trilogy, though not always to the advantage of the latter.

Read and Blunden, Graves and Sassoon, were all infantry officers: most of the literary records of the war, whether in prose or verse, were written from that point of view. But one distinguished English writer has left a vigorous account of the artilleryman's experience. Wyndham Lewis, founder of the Vorticist movement and subsequently well known as a painter, novelist and amateur of politics and philosophy, joined up in 1916 and after some delay was commissioned in the Royal Garrison Artillery. He describes his wartime experiences in his magnificently entertaining autobiography, *Blasting and Bombardiering,* a work of a later date than the other books discussed in this chapter, since it did not appear until 1937. It was, perhaps, appropriate that Lewis, the belligerent propagator of the geometrical, anti-humanistic aesthetics of Vorticism should have found his place in the artillery; as, too, did Lewis's former associate, T. E. Hulme, who was serving at a battery about a quarter of a mile away from Lewis when he was killed. (The two men had become estranged, and Lewis regretted that he had not made an attempt at reconciliation before Hulme's death.) In *Blasting and Bombadiering* Lewis wryly commented about his choice of the artillery: 'I could not have been in the infantry: I am not nearly blood-thirsty enough.' In this book Lewis expressed anti-war sentiments almost as strong as those of avowedly pacifist writers like Aldington or Remarque, though his tone is dryly contemptuous rather than angry or hysterical: he frequently speaks of the stupidity of the operations he observed. His remarks are very much conditioned by the period at which he was writing: commenting from a strongly right-wing point of view, Lewis was aware that a new war was in preparation, and he wished to emphasize that he had had quite enough of the first one.

At his best, Lewis is one of the finest of modern prose

writers, and the war chapters in his autobiography contain some exemplary passages. The writing, though angular and even clumsy, is full of compelling visual detail, recalling Lewis's genius as a painter:

> I can only remember that in the air full of violent sound, very suddenly there was a flash near at hand, followed by further flashes, and I could see the gunners moving about as they loaded again. They appeared to be 11-inch guns— very big. Out of their throats had sprung a dramatic flame, they had roared, they had moved back. You could see them, lighted from their mouths, as they hurled into the air their great projectile, and sank back as they did it. In the middle of the monotonous percussion, which had never slackened for a moment, the tom-toming of interminable artillery, for miles round, going on in the darkness, it was as if someone had exclaimed in your ear, or something you had supposed inanimate had come to life, when the battery whose presence we had not suspected went into action.

Later, Lewis became an official war artist and gave expression to similar scenes in the medium of painting. His grimly sardonic sense of humour is very apparent in *Blasting and Bombardiering*, which contains some splendid anecdotes. There is a fine example in Chapter IX, called 'Hunted with Howitzers': Lewis and a small party of men are attempting to reach an observation-post in an unspeakably muddy section of the Passchendaele front. He notices that this post is in turn observed by another observer, situated in a German balloon not far above their heads; before they can reach the post they are subjected to the fire of a German howitzer battery, expertly directed by the aerial observer. It is particularly aimed at Lewis and a corporal, who are taking refuge in a very inadequate shell-hole, already bracketed by the enemy guns:

> I should think that you could count on the fingers of your hands the soldiers who have been fired at in this *personal* way by weapons of such dimensions—and a whole battery of them if it was the whole battery that was after us. For obviously for that to happen you have to have all the various factors that made it possible. First, a sausage-balloon

sitting with impunity up in the air above you, upon a nice clear day: secondly the Observer in the balloon with plenty of time on his hands, and in the mood for a little sport: and thirdly, two men practically underneath it, in an empty landscape. Again, were it a larger collection of people, then it would no longer be *personal*.

This jaunty detachment was characteristic of Lewis's temperament, which liked to give the impression of being a keen but contemptuous observer of the follies of humanity (not excluding himself), though it may have been helped by writing at twenty years' distance from the events he describes.

In 1933 there appeared a unique memoir of the war, written by one who had served with Graves and Sassoon in the Second Battalion of the Royal Welch Fusiliers. *Old Soldiers Never Die*, by Frank Richards, is a remarkable book for a number of reasons: its author was neither an officer not an idealistic volunteer; he served as a private from August 1914 to November 1918, most of that time at the Front, and survived without a scratch, although he was saved from death by what seems a whole succession of incredibly happy accidents. Richards had been a ranker in the old Regular Army, passing many years in India, and when the war broke he was in one of the first detachments of the British Expeditionary Force to see action in France. Although not a formally educated man, he was a natural writer, and *Old Soldiers Never Die* is a brilliant narrative. Richards's colloquial, salty, sardonic manner is far removed from the other retrospective accounts; he is not reflective, always keeps close to particular facets of the private soldier's experience, whether he is describing heroism under fire or some behind-the-lines episode of wenching or scrounging, and yet frequently he transcends his immediate context. Much of Richards's tough and comic narrative recalls the long-suffering humour of Shakespeare's humble soldiers; David Jones also caught this note in several passages of *In Parenthesis*, but Richards sustains it for a whole book. Some of its flavour can be seen in these remarks about a royal inspection, late in 1914:

No king in the history of England ever reviewed more loyal or lousier troops than what His Majesty did that day. To look at us we were as clean as new pins, but in our shirts, pants and trousers were whole platoons of crawlers.

Returning to the war books of 1928, 1929, and 1930, it is instructive to compare the English examples that I have mentioned with a German work of some distinction, Ernst Jünger's *The Storm of Steel*, of which the English translation appeared in 1929, with the sub-title, 'From the Diary of a German Storm-Troop Officer on the Western Front'. Jünger went through much the same experiences as his English counterparts, including the Somme fighting, but his attitude is remarkably different from theirs. He, too, records violent death, mutilation, and every kind of physical squalor and privation; yet at no point does his enthusiasm for the war falter; his patriotic fervour and idealism are unimpaired until the very end of the war—and subsequently. For Jünger, despite all he had seen and undergone—and he almost died of a lung wound—continued to exalt war as a great and ennobling experience. It is as though the subject-matter of Owen and Sassoon had been combined with the sentiments of Brooke and Grenfell. If one compares the following passage with the extract from Edmund Blunden's *Undertones of War* that I quoted on p. 153 the contrast is brought into sharp emphasis. They are both dealing with a similar topic, the fact that about the time of the Somme both armies adopted the steel helmet, and thereafter the character of the war changed:

> The spirit and the tempo of the fighting altered, and after the battle of the Somme the war had its own peculiar impress that distinguished it from all other wars. After this battle the German soldier wore the steel helmet, and in his features there were chiselled the lines of an energy stretched to the utmost pitch, lines that future generations will perhaps find as fascinating and imposing as those of many heads of classical or Renaissance times.

Whereas Blunden speaks ruefully of the helmet's 'ugly useful discomfort' and looks back nostalgically at the soldiers' soft caps and the primitive stage of the war associated with them, Jünger sees the helmeted German soldier as a figure of heroic energy, analogous to the heroes of the classical or Renaissance worlds. Jünger seems to think and feel instinctively in terms of heroic rhetoric in a way that would have been impossible for an English writer in the same situation; clearly, for him the heroic mode of perception had not yet been superseded. How far this is a question of Jünger's own temperament, and how far a matter of some such abstraction as the 'German national character', I would not care to discuss. Remarque's *All Quiet on the Western Front* (1929) represents another German picture of the war, and one rather closer to that of the English writers. Significantly, Jünger's final words form a nationalistic outburst that anticipates the Nazi spirit: 'Though force without and barbarity within conglomerate in sombre clouds, yet so long as the blade of a sword will strike a spark in the night may it be said: Germany lives and Germany shall never go under!' (The rhetoric of heroism received a forced efflorescence under fascism, and this further alienated it from the liberal consciousness.)

There were other kinds of war in 1914-18 from that of the trench-fighters, even though their experience was predominant. One of them, C. E. Montague, deploring the decline of chivalry during the struggle, had wistfully reflected that only amongst the airmen had the traditional habits of chivalry remained possible. This theme was enlarged on in *Sagittarius Rising* (1936), the autobiography of Cecil Lewis, who had served throughout the war as a pilot in the Royal Flying Corps. Lewis is an uneven writer, excellent in his descriptions of flying and aerial combat, but much less satisfactory in the purple passages that embody his reflections about life in general. His book gives a vivid picture of the aviator's life in the Great War, with its continual contrast between the luxury of life on the ground, many miles behind the lines, and the daily confrontation with death in the air, where the airmen were menaced not only by the Germans but by the instability of the rickety aircraft of the time. Lewis describes the joys of single-handed aerial combat, as against the impersonal slaughter of the trenches:

It was like the lists of the Middle Ages, the only sphere in modern warfare where a man saw his enemy and faced him in mortal combat, the only sphere where there was still chivalry and honour. If you won, it was your own bravery and skill; if you lost, it was because you had met a better man.

You did not sit in a muddy trench while someone who had no personal enmity against you loosed off a gun, five miles away, and blew you to smithereens—and did not know he had done it! That was not fighting; it was murder. Senseless, brutal, ignoble. We were spared that.

In his feelings about the romanticism of flying, Lewis has evident affinities with Antoine de Saint-Exupéry.

Other theatres of war also produced their literary memorials. Of these the most famous is, without doubt, T. E. Lawrence's *Seven Pillars of Wisdom*, first published in full in 1935 (a shorter version, *Revolt in the Desert* appeared in 1927).[1] This book, which describes Lawrence's part in organizing the revolt of the Arabs against the Turks and their German allies, is widely regarded as a classic of modern English prose writing. In the face of this reputation, I must register a certain personal dissent. As a writer of narrative, Lawrence undoubtedly had great gifts, and the scenes of action in his book are superb; but he was almost uncontrollably given to turgid reflections of an insufferably pretentious kind, which had a very corrupting effect on the quality of his prose. Lawrence is loath to let events speak for themselves; one is uncomfortably aware of his domineering personality, with its scarcely concealed pressures towards self-advertisement.

By contrast, another narrative from one of the minor sideshows of the war has had rather less than its share of recognition. Francis Brett Young's *Marching on Tanga*, a work of brilliant reportage rather than retrospective recollection, was published in 1917; it describes the campaign against the retreating German colonial army in German East Africa in 1916, carried out by Rhodesian and South African troops under the command of General Smuts. Young, one of the more interesting of the Georgian poets and a doctor by profession, was attached to the column as a medical officer. His simple, straightforward account describes an extraordinarily gruelling campaign: a rapid pace had to be kept up whilst contending with tropical heat, unexplored terrain, mosquitoes, fever, wild animals, as well as intermittent battles with the retreating enemy. Nothing could have been more remote from the characteristic experience of the troops bogged down in France, and no doubt many of them would have considered it a welcome change. Like them, Young brooded nostalgically about an ideal England that seemed all the more desirable in such exotic surroundings. In addition to the *Oxford Book of English Verse* he carried with him a Bartholomew map of England, 'and there I would travel magical roads, crossing the Pennines or lazing through the blossomy vale of Evesham, or facing the salt breeze on the flat top of Mendip at will'.

But the real war was being won or lost in the trenches of France and Flanders. It was here that the major crisis of English civilization was centred, and where most of the writers who responded to it underwent the experiences that were subsequently matured into autobiography or fiction.

9

RETROSPECT II
Fiction

THE difference between avowed autobiography and fiction with a strongly autobiographical flavour is often one of degree rather than of kind. Autobiography must, if it is to make any claims to literary attention, involve a good deal of selectivity and discrimination in ordering the writer's past experience; the novelist does much the same thing, but allows himself greater freedom in selecting and rearranging. The heavily autobiographical origin of some of the war novels of 1928-30 is unmistakable, and one or two books of the period could be placed in either category. This is particularly true of Sassoon's Sherston trilogy: it is usually regarded as a work of slightly disguised autobiography, but its fictional elements are sufficiently evident for a rather literal-minded librarian to consider classifying all three books as novels. Some writers treated their experience both directly and fictionally. Thus, C. E. Montague followed up *Disenchantment* with a collection of stories, *Fiery Particles* (1923), several of which gave a fictional embodiment to ideas and observations included in the earlier book. One of the most entertaining of them describes the wartime careers of two privileged young officers, both safely ensconced in staff jobs, who go through the war collecting a variety of medals for their administrative services and without ever going anywhere near the Front. The interest of the story lies in the contrast between their respective characters: one of them is clever, cynical and quite without self-respect; the other is stupid, complacent, and genuinely believes—unlike his rival—that he *deserves* the numerous decorations he is accumulating.

One of the principal differences between the autobiography and the novel is that the latter offers a wider angle of vision: the autobiographer is limited to the single thread of personal experience, while the novelist can supplement or enlarge on this by an imaginative penetration into the experience of others. Among war novels the ultimate ideal, of course, remains *War and Peace*, with its vast movements along the spectrum ranging from the utterly intimate to the cosmic impersonality of history. No English writer approached this scale, but one or two made attempts to render the war on a fairly broad canvas: notably R. H. Mottram in *The Spanish Farm Trilogy 1914-1918*, and Ford Madox Ford in *Parade's End*. Both works appeared between 1924 and 1928; Mottram's received an immediate though rather short-lived fame, whereas Ford's—a far more distinguished work of art—was subject to an almost total neglect from which it has still scarcely recovered, at least, among British readers (such contemporary esteem as Ford enjoys is very largely due to the efforts of American critics).

Mottram's first volume, *The Spanish Farm*, appeared in 1924, the second, *Sixty-Four, Ninety-Four!* in 1925, and the third, *The Crime at Vanderlynden's*, in 1926; in 1927 they were collected as a trilogy, together with some related short stories, in a single volume, which was reprinted several times in the next few years. Mottram has not attempted to provide a narrative of front-line life: his battle-scenes are infrequent and lack conviction. His principal characteristic is that he is imaginatively interested in the enormous effort and organization that goes to keep a great modern army in being. He saw the British Army in France as a self-contained civilization, with all its complex hierarchies and social codes. Mottram's three volumes are only loosely linked together, but each of them is centred round the Vanderlyndens' 'Spanish Farm', a relic of the seventeenth-century Spanish occupation of Flanders, and now not far behind a sector of the British line. The book's dominating character is Madeleine Vanderlynden, daughter of the house and its effective manager, who is an attractive but shrewd young Frenchwoman; Mottram makes her not only a representative of her class, nation and sex, but also something of an embodiment of the *Ewig-Weibliche*, who symbolizes the continuity of essential human concerns and remains indifferent to the ebb and flow of such trivialities as wars. The other principal figure of the two first volumes is Geoffrey Skene, a young English officer of the New Army, with whom Madeleine has a brief and tenderly described affair (though she remains in love with a local aristocrat, long since vanished in the French army). Skene is carefully characterized, but remains a somewhat shadowy figure.

As a literary artist, Mottram has affinities with his friend John Galsworthy, who contributed a preface to the trilogy. That is to say, he is—in a not necessarily pejorative sense—a superficial writer, who is most at home in rendering the characteristics of the social surface, rather than in plunging to moral or psychological depths. Like Galsworthy, his basic criteria are social. His presentation of Madeleine is convincing, but she remains a figure who has been very skilfully assembled from a number of constituent attributes; a certain imaginative fusion has undoubtedly taken place, but she lacks the totally autonomous quality of the great characters of fiction. Mottram remains at his best when he is writing about the army as a social organism, in respect of which the individuality of his characters is necessarily subordinated. His prose is unsubtle, even coarse-grained, but always clear, and moves forward with a steady narrative thrust—for all its length, the trilogy is remarkably readable. Many passages reveal the presence in Mottram of an essayist rather akin to C. E. Montague. The following extract, from near the end of *Sixty-Four, Ninety-Four!* describes Skene's response to the news of the Armistice; it shows Mottram's painstaking but somewhat unselective notation of physical detail, and it exactly echoes Montague's feeling that victory had come too late for anyone to feel much satisfaction in it:

Rounds! He went outside into the chill and darkness of that November night. At the small factory where his men were billeted, he found his sentry; in the little pay-office, his superior New Army Corporal, reading a paper-covered novel over a brazier;—beyond, in the low sheds where his men were sleeping, his mules tied up and his carts stacked, all was in darkness and silence. "Celebrations!" he thought. Emerging again into the little paved street, he met what to him was typical of war as he had waged it. In the lampless glimmer of the night, a string of square boxes on wheels, known as limbers, was being drawn with a springless rattle over the pavé, by weary mules, beside whom were men just sufficiently awake to guide them. At the head a muffled figure, for all the world like the leader of some North Pole Expedition, was plodding beside a somnambulistic horse.

Abreast of Skene he muttered:

"This'll get me to Werlies, I s'pose! Is it true they've chucked it?"

Skene nodded. "I believe the Bosche are going to sign the Armistice terms in the morning!"

"Good job. We should have chucked it, if they hadn't!" And he stumped on.

Skene pulled off his boots and got into his blankets. "Too long," he thought. "Who cares now?"

He had forgotten that this was Victory.

The third volume of the trilogy, *The Crime at Vanderlynden's*, is lighter in tone. It describes the efforts of a junior staff officer called Dormer to discover the perpetrators of a minor piece of damage at the Vanderlynden farm, for which a British soldier is allegedly responsible. The narrative forms, in effect, a humorous detective story, as Dormer travels the length and breadth of the British forces in France in vain pursuit of the criminal (or even of anyone who knows anything at all about the incident), himself chased by urgent directives from higher military authority, for by now the initially trifling incident has snowballed into a major issue affecting relations between the British army and the French civilian population. It affords Mottram the opportunity for some mild satire on the extra-military preoccupations of the Base that were such a vexation to the front-line troops; it also enables him to paint a large-scale picture, as we follow Dormer in his investigations, of the numerous ramifications of the army establishment behind the lines.

Henry Williamson, in an essay called 'Reality in War Literature' published in 1934,[1] has left a harsh judgment on *The Spanish Farm Trilogy*. Whilst admitting that it gives a fairly representative picture of the English soldier in France, he complains that 'the battle scenes are deficient and unsatisfying: they no more recreate actuality than a picture of paper and orange peel on Hampstead Heath or Coney Island beach after an August week-end recreates the life and turmoil of the happy masses'. Undoubtedly, Mottram is at his weakest in such scenes, and one can assume that his original experience was much less extensive than Williamson's. But his trilogy, though constantly faltering before the depths of experience, does convey an effective picture of the quality of life behind the lines, and indicates something of the relations between the British soldiers and the French population. He is skilful, too, in showing us his representative Englishman, Skene, through the eyes of the archetypal Frenchwoman, Madeleine. He is, at the very least, a remarkably competent story-teller.

Parade's End is a trilogy or a tetralogy, depending on whether one accepts the final volume, *Last Post*, as an integral part of the total design. The first section, *Some Do Not*, came out in 1924, *No More Parades* in 1925, and *A Man Could Stand Up* in 1926. *Last Post* appeared in 1928; it seems that Ford wrote it because of the importunate desire of a woman friend to know what happened to his characters, and a few years later he virtually disowned it, saying that if the work was ever to appear in a single volume he would like it to do so as a trilogy. In fact, the one-volume American edition of 1950 included all four volumes; the recent Bodley Head reprint was restricted to three. *Last Post* is, indisputably, very different in tone and technique from the first three volumes of the sequence: it represents a certain desire on Ford's part to tie up loose ends, and at the same time to adopt a radically different mode of narration. Ford's critics are very much at variance about the place of *Last Post* in the sequence: Robie Macauley and Richard Cassell believe that it is essential to round off the work; whereas John Meixner has argued vehemently against this opinion, claiming that *Parade's End* forms an artistic whole only as a trilogy, and he is supported in this by Graham Greene in his introduction to the Bodley Head edition.[2] My own view inclines towards the latter opinion; *Last Post* seems to be so loosely connected as to form a sequel rather than an integral part of the novel. As Meixner says, the trilogy, beginning with Ford's hero, Christopher Tietjens, travelling in a luxuriously appointed railway compartment, and ending, in the last paragraph of *A Man Could Stand Up*, with Tietjens celebrating Armistice Day in the empty flat from which his vindictive wife has stripped all the furniture, does have a distinct unity and symmetry.

Parade's End deals, in essentials, with the long martyrdom of Christopher Tietjens, officer and gentleman, who is subject to constant persecution, above all from his wife, the beautiful sexual terrorist, Sylvia, and, during the war, from his military superiors and from powerful civilians at home. *Parade's End* is, it seems to me, the finest novel by an Englishman to have been produced by the Great War; but at the same time, it can hardly be regarded simply as a 'war novel', as can some of the other books discussed in this chapter. Indeed, the whole of the magnificent opening section of *Some Do Not* takes place some years before the outbreak of war. Nevertheless, *Parade's End* does offer a profound imaginative grasp of the effect of the war on the traditional patterns of English life. In this novel we see a bringing together of the several dominant themes which, I have tried to suggest, characterized the literature of the Great War: the supersession of the Hero as a tangible ideal; a nostalgic love of rural England, combined with an anguished sense that centuries of English tradition were being overthrown; the alienation of the soldier from the civilians. Ford embodies all these themes in Christopher Tietjens, a deeply and intensely realized figure whose presence provides the necessary unity of the first three volumes (he is largely absent from the scene in *Last Post*), and who is at the same time made to bear an unusually wide range of significance: he is the last true Tory, the final anachronistic embodiment of the virtues of the eighteenth-century English gentleman, an Anglican saint, even something of a Christ-figure, turning the other cheek to his persecutors. And yet Tietjens is always recognizable as a living human being: fair, red-faced, large, slow-moving.

In the opening paragraph of *Some Do Not*, Ford brilliantly places Tietjens, and his friend Macmaster, in their appropriate context in the pre-war ruling class:

The two young men—they were of the English public official class—sat in the perfectly appointed railway carriage. The leather straps to the windows were of virgin newness; the mirrors beneath the new luggage racks immaculate as if they

had reflected very little; the bulging upholstery in its luxuriant, regulated curves was scarlet and yellow in an intricate,
minute dragon pattern, the design of a geometrician in
Cologne. The compartment smelt faintly, hygienically of admirable varnish; the train ran as smoothly—Tietjens remembered thinking—as British gilt-edged securities. It travelled
fast; yet had it swayed or jolted over the rail joints, except
at the curve before Tonbridge or over the points at Ashford
where these eccentricities are expected and allowed for, Macmaster, Tietjens felt certain, would have written to the company. Perhaps he would even have written to *The Times*.

They live in a world which is ordered, controlled, predictable
(even the railway upholstery's curves are both luxuriant and
regulated); a world, too, of security and conspicuous consump-
tion. And yet it is not entirely Tietjens's world, as the clear
note of distancing irony in this description suggests; the succeeding paragraphs show that it is the young Scottish *arriviste,*
Macmaster, who is the conscious upholder of Edwardian ruling-
class attitudes. Tietjens, on the other hand, moves through this
world with considerable indifference to the refinement of its
mœurs. He is in but not of it—a brilliant mathematician working
in the Imperial Department of Statistics—and his real all-
egiances are rooted in an older England, symbolized by the
family home, Groby, in the North Riding.
Unquestionably, Tietjens, and what he stands for, is heavily
romanticized by Ford. Half-German by birth, and the precocious
child of a cosmopolitan, artistic household, Ford had had little
opportunity to make extensive observations of the English gentry.
There is both a simplicity and a glamour in his picture of Tietjens's Tory ideals that suggests a foreigner's romantic image of
England; hence, perhaps, the high reputation of *Parade's End*
in America (William Carlos Williams claimed that the four
novels 'constitute the English prose masterpiece of their time').
Yet Ford's image is exaggerated rather than false: he shows us
a familiar subject in an unfamiliar light, which may distort but
also illuminates. Tietjens, the Yorkshire squire, stands for a
more remote England than the Liberal England, centred on the
week-end cottage in the Home Counties, of Forster and the
Georgian poets; he preserves something of the feudal manner.

M

In *A Man Could Stand Up*, Tietjens reflects in the trenches: 'The Feudal Spirit was broken. Perhaps it would therefore be harmful to Trench Warfare. It used to be comfortable and cosy. You fought beside men from your own hamlet under the leadership of the parson's son.'

One finds, too, an almost Gothic romanticism in Tietjens's conviction that there is a curse on Groby because the house was once dispossessed from its Catholic owners (the Tietjens family came over from Holland with William and Mary), and that the curse will not be lifted until Groby is once more in Catholic hands (as will happen when it is inherited by Tietjens's son, whom Sylvia is having brought up as a Catholic). Yet his visions of England have affinities with those entertained during the war years by writers of very different temperament. The following extract from one of Tietjens's reveries in the front line, evoked by hearing a cornet player practising an air by Purcell, recalls the passages from Lawrence's wartime letters quoted in a previous chapter:

> The only satisfactory age in England! . . . Yet what chance had it today? Or, still more, tomorrow? In the sense that the age of, say, Shakespeare had a chance. Or Pericles! or Augustus!
>
> Heaven knew, we did not want a preposterous drum-beating such as the Elizabethans produced—and received. Like lions at a fair. . . . But what chance had quiet fields, Anglican sainthood, accuracy of thought, heavy-leaved, timbered hedgerows, slowly creeping plough-lands moving up the slopes? . . . Still, the land remains. . . .
>
> The land remains. . . . It remains! . . . At that same moment the dawn was wetly revealing; over there in George Herbert's parish. . . . What was it called? . . . What the devil was its name? Oh, Hell! . . . Between Salisbury and Wilton. . . . The tiny church. . . . But he refused to consider the plough-lands, the heavy groves, the slow high-road above the church that the dawn was at that moment wetly revealing—until he could remember that name. . . . He refused to consider that, probably even to-day, that land ran to . . . produced the stock of . . . Anglican sainthood. The quiet thing!

In part, the random, fragmentary quality of the writing here may be regarded as expressive of Tietjens's disordered consciousness, still not properly recovered from shell-shock and amnesia. But at the same time, these stylistic devices occur with uncomfortable frequency in the later volumes of *Parade's End;* compared with the mastery writing of *Some Do Not,* their prose is often uncontrolled and fluid, and the use of dots as punctuation becomes obsessive.

Like Lawrence, Ford was very conscious of living in a doomed society, though some of the reflections by which Tietjens expresses this conviction read a little oddly. As when, in *Some Do Not,* Tietjens is in earnest conversation with his brother Mark, and glances at the fountain of the Inner Temple by which they are standing: 'He considered the base of the fountain that was half full of leaves. This civilization had contrived a state of things in which leaves rotted by August.' Unlike Lawrence, Ford dramatizes rather than describes his conviction of social decay; there is nothing equivalent to the retrospective diatribes of *Kangaroo.* Tietjens is constantly shown as the honourable man harried by the low, unworthy forces that manifest themselves when the opulent Edwardian upper-class world, so vividly evoked in the novel's opening paragraphs, becomes corrupt in the atmosphere of war. Macmaster, the energetic social climber whom Tietjens has befriended and helped, picks his friend's brains and rises to a pinnacle of bureaucratic eminence, whilst Tietjens remains an obscure infantry officer. Tietjens is disgraced when his bank unjustly refuses to meet his cheques. We learn that the banker responsible is one of Sylvia's admirers. She explains to Tietjens:

'But of course he hates you for being in the army. All the men who aren't hate all the men that are. And, of course, when there's a woman between them, the men who aren't do all they can to do the others in. When they're bankers they have a pretty good pull. . . .'

And from Sylvia, Tietjens suffers unspeakable humiliations; in his study of their relationship Ford shows unsurpassed psychological insight. For several years they have sustained a marriage without mutual love; indeed, Sylvia has actively despised

Tietjens. But when he falls in love with the young suffragette, Valentine Wannop, Sylvia's jealousy turns into a violent sexual passion for her husband, and when he fails to respond she turns to extremes of cruelty. Sylvia, though a monster, never entirely alienates the reader's sympathy. As V. S. Pritchett has shrewdly commented: 'One has a sneaking sympathy for his wife who at one moment complains that her husband is trying to be Jesus Christ as well as the misunderstood son of a great landowner. Her cruelties are an attempt to turn a martyr into a man.'[3]

The word 'martyr' is, indeed, significant. Ford is trying to write a novel about a particular kind of hero; not the towering martial heroes of the Renaissance whose insufficiencies for the life of the Western Front had been sardonically glanced at by Barbusse; nor the ardent young votaries of the early months of the war, whose spirit was summed up in Julian Grenfell's 'Into Battle'. In so far as Tietjens is intended by his creator to be more than a private man, to embody certain national traditions and habits of mind, he has remote affinities with the ancient heroes of epic, though he reflects a Virgilian *pietas* rather than an Homeric *virtù*. More specifically, Tietjens is a passive and suffering hero, whose triumphs arise, not from violent action, but from *patience* (derived, ultimately, from *patior*, to suffer). The most famous example in English of this kind of hero is the Christ of *Paradise Regained*. Yet Ford, working without Milton's theological frame of reference, is less able to convince us of Tietjens's ultimate triumph. The novel (as opposed to such sharply generic forms as the thriller and the western) is not an easy form in which to accommodate heroic figures; its natural bias is so much to the realistic, the typical, the ordinary, that the presence of any figure of conspicuous stature and virtue is liable to set up ironic tensions. The drama remains, still, a more convincing vehicle for such types. In our final glimpse of Tietjens in *Last Post*, he has retired into quiet country life with Valentine, as a small-holder and antique-dealer; Sylvia has at least abated her hostility, and this perhaps represents a triumph for Tietjens, but he is now purely a private man and not a representative figure. His ancestral home, Groby, is leased to a crazy and destructive American woman; the symbolism is unmistakable.

In those scenes of *Parade's End* that deal specifically with the war in France, Tietjens's role as a suffering figure is underlined. In the opening chapter of *No More Parades*, Tietjens refuses—for very good reason—to give compassionate leave to a Welsh private called O Nine Morgan. A few minutes later the man is killed by a shell splinter. Tietjens bends over the body:

> The heat from the brazier was overpowering on his bent face. He hoped he would not get his hands all over blood, because blood is very sticky. It makes your fingers stick together impotently. But there might not be any blood in the darkness under the fellow's back where he was putting his hand. There was, however: it was very wet.

Tietjens associates Morgan's death with his refusal of leave, and assumes a corresponding burden of guilt. Again, in the sustained section set in the trenches in *A Man Could Stand Up*, Tietjens rescues the young subaltern, Aranjuez, after he had been partly buried by a falling shell; he is carrying Aranjuez to safety when the boy suddenly runs off screaming, with his hands to his face. Tietjens thinks, disapprovingly, that Aranjuez has lost his nerve. Only later does he hear that he had been hit by a sniper and has lost an eye. Tietjens, already tormented beyond endurance by his private life, has to bear the infantry officer's common load of compassion and guilt for the sufferings of his men. He is also subjected to the animus of his new commanding officer, General Campion, a friend of Sylvia's, who transfers Tietjens to the ignominious task of guarding prisoners of war.

These trench scenes frequently manifest the fluidity of writing that is one of the major faults of the later sections of *Parade's End*. And Henry Williamson has attacked them, in 'Reality in War Literature', for inaccuracy of military detail and a general air of inauthenticity. Nevertheless, to an uninitiated reader, and despite their stylistic weaknesses, they convey a compelling impression of front-line life; more vividly, in fact, than many exact documentary descriptions. Ford was invariably an impressionistic artist rather than a reporter.

This discussion of *Parade's End* has only glanced at a few of its salient features, and has not done justice to its outstanding literary qualities. A full analysis, for instance, would trace

Ford's virtuoso use of the time-shift technique in the first part of *Some Do Not*, and would examine in detail the superbly sensitive effects he could achieve by his characteristically impressionist prose. One could also dwell on the breadth and richness of his characters; in which, although an avowed disciple of Flaubert and James, Ford showed himself a possibly unconscious follower of the great Victorians. Tietjens himself, Sylvia, Valentine, General Campion, Edith Ethel Duchemin, all have an instinctive vitality. At the same time, one must admit the work's unevenness: effects which were triumphant in the first volumes become weakly repetitive in later ones. In particular, some of Ford's uses of the time-shift seem like devices for evading a possibly tricky narrative climax. The great expanse of the three—or four—volumes makes it clear that Ford was weak at sustaining the architectonics of a large fictional structure; his numerous successes are all local rather than large-scale, and *Parade's End* is, *in toto*, rather less than the sum of its distinguished parts.

Yet the work's traditional novelistic virtues do, in my view, undoubtedly transcend its failures of technique. In contrast to other prose works produced by the Great War, *Parade's End* offers little concrete documentation but a great deal of brilliant insight into the effects of that war. Tietjens's romantic Tory England was, no doubt, an extravagant concept; but its affinities with the more modest visions of the poets in uniform are sufficient to produce a recognizable picture. As I have suggested, *Parade's End*, more than any other work, succeeds in combining the dominant literary preoccupations of the war.

In the course of discussing *Parade's End*, V. S. Pritchett has observed, 'As a character Tietjens escapes from the cliché of almost all the war novels of that time in which the hero conveys that the whole war has been declared against him personally'. This remark can take us on to consider a very different novel, written by one who had been a young acquaintance of Ford's in pre-war literary circles: Richard Aldington's *Death of a Hero*, published in 1929. If *Parade's End* is an attempt to delineate a hero of a rare and particular kind, then *Death of a Hero*, which is a very much cruder work, undertakes a savage debunking of the whole concept of heroism. As a very young man, before 1914, Aldington had been an Imagist poet

Fiction

of rather fragile delicacy; he was deeply embittered by the war, and his later literary personality became increasingly rancorous and disagreeable, though his autobiography, published in America in 1941—there was no British edition—contains some vigorous anecdotes and an absorbing account of Pound's early London circle.

On the face of it, *Death of a Hero* tells the life-story of George Winterbourne, a young painter, who grows up in and escapes from an atmosphere of stifling Victorian respectability, enjoys a brief taste of moral and cultural freedom in pre-war London bohemia, joins the army, and is killed a few days before the Armistice. It is a wilfully formless book, which Aldington unashamedly uses as a vehicle for his own lengthy first-person reflections on life and ideas. Indeed, a sizeable portion of the novel is taken up by these interpolated essays. Even in the dramatic and narrative portions, the pressure of the author's presence is always felt, and the total impression that the book makes can be described as a massive ejaculation of pent-up venom. Seldom can a work of fiction have been written in such a consistently sour and hectoring tone: Aldington hammers away with coarse sarcasm and derision at a large number of predictable targets: the Victorians, the Edwardians, the upper-classes and Establishment generally, civilians in the Great War, the higher command in the British Army. In one or two places, the author's intensity of feeling raises these interludes to a plane rather higher than nagging:

'You have a vendetta of the dead against the living.' Yes, it is true, I have a vendetta, an unappeased longing for vengeance. Yes, a vendetta. Not a personal vendetta. What am I? O God, nothing, less than nothing, a husk, a leaving, a half-chewed morsel on the plate, a reject. But an impersonal vendetta, an unappeased conscience crying in the wilderness, a river of tears in the desert. What right have I to live? Is it five million, is it ten million, is it twenty million? . . .

On Sundays the Union Jack flies over the cemetery at Etaples. It's not so big as it was in the old wooden-cross days, but it's still quite large. Acres and acres. Yes, acres and acres. And it's too late to get one's little lot in the acres. Too late, too late. . . .

183

In the face of such heavy auctorial intervention, George Winterbourne is not much more than a briskly manipulated puppet. Nevertheless, his adventures in the pre-1914 literary and artistic *avant-garde* are entertaining and illuminate the period: among various other lampoons, Aldington offers a vindictive portrait of Ford as Mr. Shobbe. Yet Aldington's own animus is always evident, giving an excessively personal flavour to the satirical observation. Winterbourne becomes heavily entangled with two beautiful girls—he marries one of them—and his attempts to maintain a *ménage à trois* fail miserably, despite their theoretical moral emancipation. He feels betrayed by them. This whole section is treated with a degree of emotional emphasis in excess of what the narrative seems to warrant, suggesting the nature of Aldington's own personal involvement.

After George has joined the army he looks admiringly at a group of seasoned front-line troops returning from leave; he is seized by an exalted sense of masculine exclusiveness and contempt for women, such as we have already observed in Sassoon and Owen:

> 'By God!' he said to himself, 'you're men, not boudoir rabbits and lounge lizards. I don't care a damn what your cause is—it's almost certainly a foully rotten one. But I do know you're the first real men I've looked upon. I swear you're better than the women and the half-men, and by God! I swear I'll die with you rather than live in a world without you.'

Here Aldington recognizes, in almost traditionally romantic terms, the heroic stature of the soldiers. But his main concern, in the battle sections of *Death of a Hero* (which take up less than half the total length of the novel) is to show how their heroism is consistently wasted and betrayed by the 'foully rotten' cause for which they are fighting. These chapters contain by far the best writing in *Death of a Hero*; less digressive and strident than the pre-war sections, conveying the nature of front-line experience, including such things as gas-attacks, with a harsh direct realism that is not much inferior to any of the prose accounts that I have so far mentioned. Yet to compare them with Blunden or Graves is to become aware of Aldington's limitations: he is concerned to impose, not merely to trace, a pattern of experience. He lacks the patient exactness and detachment of the finest autobiographical writers. Like many novels before it, *Death of a Hero* is written to advance a thesis; in this case, that the war was wholly pointless and fraudulent, and those who took part in it were wantonly robbed of life and its possibilities. The danger with didactic fiction is that one's attention is inevitably deflected from its quality as literary art to the nature of the argument. In Aldingon's novel, the approach is so crude, so oversimplifying, that the argument loses conviction by excess of emphasis. An attitude that seems altogether convincing when expressed in the brief compass of one of Sassoon's savage wartime lyrics seems merely rhetorical when blown up into a novel of over 400 pages. *Death of a Hero* does not, in short, make effective propaganda for the pacifist case.

One obvious reason lies in Aldington's use of a single vehicle of consciousness, and one very close to his own state of mind: inevitably one feels, in Pritchett's words, 'that the whole war has been declared against him personally'. Barbusse, another anti-war novelist, avoided this in *Under Fire*, sub-titled 'the story of a squad', by describing the effects of war on a group of comrades, rather than a single exacerbated sensibility. For George Winterbourne, the war seems merely the culminating element in a whole series of burdens that he has had to bear from childhood: his parents, his stultifying bourgeois background, the trying entanglement with the two girls he loves. Admittedly the war kills him, and Aldington turns him into a figure of significant pathos, by suggesting that, in effect, Winterbourne virtually committed suicide when under fire, and by placing his death only a few days before the Armistice; thereby giving him some of the terrible poignancy that, in real life, was acquired by Wilfred Owen.

In *Death of a Hero* we are aware of several successive stages in the development of Aldington's own attitudes: we have the young rebel who was one of the signatories of the *Blast* manifesto of 1914, eager to blow up the remains of Victorian respectability; the disillusioned soldier, turning to a Sassoon-like bitterness; the iconoclast of the 'twenties, taking part in the fashionable pursuit of debunking former idols, and with a strong flavour, too, of D. H. Lawrence's tirades against English hypocrisy and spiritual deadness. It was a strong mixture, too strong, in fact, for *Death of a Hero*, which lacks coherence and focus. Whatever its documentary interest, it fails as a work of art.

Like most writers who survived the war, Aldington wished to show the contrast between the glittering but fragile pre-war order and its violent destruction or corruption from within during the war years. He had this much in common with Ford, but, unlike Ford, was not able to focus his perceptions in a truly autonomous central character; Tietjens represents a class, a society, a tradition, without losing any of his humanity; whereas Winterbourne is no more than an isolated agonized consciousness. Yet both writers felt the need to show in some detail the pre-war order on the eve of its destruction: Aldington by his rambling excursion back into Victorian times, Ford by the brilliant packed microcosm of Tietjens's week-end at Rye in the first part of *Some Do Not*. A similar intention is evident in another novel, H. M. Tomlinson's *All Our Yesterdays*, published in 1930. Tomlinson was not, it seems to me, a novelist at all by conviction. He was a distinguished journalist who used the novel as a vehicle for reflections and observations, without any firmly established structure of plot, action and characterization. Yet his book, though imperfect as fiction, is extremely interesting and contains some admirable prose. It is narrated by a shadowy unnamed figure who combines his personal narrative with the prerogatives of the omniscient author. The story opens in the East End of London at the turn of the century, when we are introduced to a family called the Bolts, and this is followed by a spirited description of Mafeking night. Later, there is a lengthy Conradian interlude about the adventures of Jim Maynard, a journalist friend of the narrator's, in Darkest Africa. We learn, too, of the activities of Charley, the Bolts' eldest son, who has given up schoolteaching for journalism. But Tomlinson seems to have not much more than a perfunctory interest in these charaacters, and his notion of constructing a novel was artless in the extreme. Undeniably, these opening chapters, meant to give an impression of the multifariousness of the Edwardian world, are thin and slow-moving. They also show Tomlinson's less impressive attributes as a stylist: reared in the tradition of 'fine writing' he was liable to indulge in belle-lettristic embellishment of trivialities.

In the wartime section, however, the book comes triumphantly alive, and the writing, though always careful, even elegant, gains a new force and conviction. The plot still remains secondary—we are shown something of the everyday tragedy that befalls the Bolt family—but much of the narrative description is superb, and derived, no doubt, from Tomlinson's own experiences as a war correspondent. Particularly memorable is the account of a journey by train across the sunlit fields of Northern France in August 1914, just ahead of the advancing German army, culminating in a deserted, apprehensive Paris, which, before the Battle of the Marne, was hourly expecting the German entry. Tomlinson had a subtle, reflective mind, which was well able to grasp the complexities of experience. If, ultimately, *All Our Yesterdays* can be classed as an anti-war book it is in a very different vein from the hysterical outcry of *Death of a Hero*. Thus, in the passages to which I have just referred, Tomlinson vividly renders the excitement and confusion of war, as well as the fear of the advancing Germans. At the same time, he sets against this the calm unconcern of the peasants in the countryside through which the train is passing for such trifling irritations as war:

If they were not undismayed, they baffled the prompting to panic. Tough stuff, common men and women! An enemy, with terrors which could only be hinted, was at their doors. Yet it is hard to forsake one's door. There are the cows to be fed, and the legumes for the winter to be tended, the sick child, the gates to be watched at the road crossing, the lock at the canal, the barn to be roofed, the railway trucks to be shunted; therefore the unimportant ones continue to revolve this earth, without knowing why. Wheat must grow. The earth should not cease to turn from morning to night, and back to morning again, until a veritable comet smite it finally from the blue. They paused, these folk, and looked severely to the distance when we heard thunder begin on the skyline. The guns! They did not pretend that thunder was any better than it sounded; then they turned patiently to whatever belonged to the hour; they went about the next job.

This is a fine statement of the attitude of those who live closer to the rhythms of nature than to the changing movement of political organisms; it had been earlier expressed in the lines Yeats gave to his Irish airman:

> My country is Kiltartan Cross,
> My countrymen Kiltartan's poor,
> No likely end could bring them loss
> Or leave them happier than before.

Although he was lacking in a dramatic sense, Tomlinson had the gift of giving his perceptions a concrete imaginative embodiment, and his feeling for language was often genuinely poetic. One can, for instance, compare his account of the massive preparations for the Battle of the Somme with R. H. Mottram's description in *Sixty-Four, Ninety-Four!*: Mottram is lucid, detailed, but pedestrian; whereas Tomlinson's prose is metaphorically and linguistically vivid:

> The broad valley crawled with humans, cattle, and machinery, and distance merged horses, men and engines into a ceaseless stirring on the hairless hide of the planet. The interest of man had settled on the valley, and had worn it as dead as an ash-pit. From a distance, it was not an army of men you saw there, but merely an eddying of clusters and streams of loose stuff. It was not men, but man-power, which moved into that valley without ceasing, and the power was pumped into it from the reservoirs of distant cities to keep revolving the machinery of war. If life clotted, it was deflected into those hospital tents.

Here, Tomlinson's choice of words is instrumental in establishing the dehumanizing effect of the war, and prepares for the mass slaughter on the Somme and the subsequent concept of the 'war of attrition'. Or again, one may consider the bizarre but compelling juxtapositions in the following extract, which recalls Wilfred Owen's poem, 'Spring Offensive':

> With the hawthorn buds, we knew, must come the new crops of emplacements for guns and gas cylinders. Here again there appeared to be signs of it, though Easter was far away. Those signs were becoming familiar to us. The "Spring Offensive" was our name for the new interest of the vernal season; it was the adventual efflorescence, for us, of surgical

saws, bandages, and suppuration, as natural as the wind-flowers and little blue eggs in the shrubbery.

When he describes the fighting, or its effects, in terms of human destruction and mutilation, Tomlinson does so with a quiet exactness that, again, reminds one of Owen. He describes some singularly revolting episodes in a calm, unemphatic prose that makes their horror all the more striking, and is far more effective than Aldington's stridency. The total effect of Tomlinson's book is elegiac, for it culminates in an extended 'anthem for doomed youth':

> Maynard spied, lonely in a corner of a field, a gathering of wooden crosses. All young men, all young men! There must be something more important than life, thought Maynard, or else why are these boys there?
> There must be? Well, there ought to be; and if there ought to be something more important. . . !
> He was stopped, for a moment, by the appeal of that congregation of outstretched wooden army. All young men, all reluctant, and all lost! There must be something more important than life, or else the sun, moon and stars were nothing but an unintended joke, with nobody even to grin at it.

This was, indeed, the central dilemma that the war forced upon so many acute sensibilities: the conviction that life was the supreme value, in opposition to the traditional patriotic ethos that is eager to sacrifice it in a supposedly higher cause, was the driving motive behind much anti-war poetry and prose. In another passage, Tomlinson pin-points the change in attitude that the mechanization of war had brought about:

> "As things are," an officer explained, "a consumptive machine gunner, too scared in an attack to bolt, can sit in a lucky hole in the ground and scupper a company of the best as they advance. Courage isn't what it used to be. The machine runs over us and we can't stop it."

Despite its casual, episodic nature, and its deficiencies as a novel, *All Our Yesterdays* extracts a strange and memorable beauty from the common experiences of the Western Front.

The last of the war novels of the period 1928-30 that I shall discuss is Frederic Manning's *Her Privates We*, of which a new edition appeared in 1964. As I have previously remarked, there was nothing about the elegant aestheticism of Manning's earlier literary career that might have prepared one for the unrestrained realism of this, his single novel. Its verbal frankness had, indeed, to be slightly bowdlerized in accordance with the publishing conventions of the time (which had also accounted for the many rows of asterisks in *Death of a Hero*), but there was also an expensive limited edition called *The Middle Parts of Fortune*, typographically identical with *Her Privates We*, except for preserving unchanged the common obscenities of army speech which were, apparently, considered inadmissible in the ordinary edition. From the moment of its publication in 1930 the novel was a great success; it was acclaimed by Arnold Bennett, who wrote, 'it depends for its moral magic on a continuous veracity, consistent, comprehending, merciful and lovely.' By any standards, *Her Privates We* is a fine novel, with a timeless quality that contrasts with the period flavour that now characterizes so many books about the Great War. For all its concentration on detail and narrow range, *Her Privates We* rises in places to the universality that distinguishes major literature. Unlike most other literary records of the war, Manning's novel is written from the point of view of the ordinary private soldier; it is centred on a small group of infantrymen serving on the Somme during the late summer and autumn of 1916. The most usual kind of war writing was the work of young infantry officers, and reflected the anguished isolation and self-awareness of such a position; they shared and were yet separated from the experiences of their men, occupying an uneasy place between the mass of the other ranks and the higher military command. That such a viewpoint offered unique opportunities for observation and understanding I hope, by now, to have shown. Nevertheless, the infantryman's was the truly common experience of the war, even though it was rarely given articulate expression. When it was, as in *Her Privates We*, one has a momentary insight into a massive universal process, as opposed to the necessarily particularized and individual quality of the junior officer's response. Everything, in the end, rested on the private soldier; as Manning sardonically remarks at one point: 'That is what is called, in the British Army, the chain of responsibility, which means that all responsibility, for the errors of their superior officers, is borne eventually by private soldiers in the ranks.'

Her Privates We is marked by its austere concentration on the troops' existence at or near the Front, to the exclusion of any other kind of life; in this respect, it resembles *Undertones of War*. Unlike most writers who wrote retrospective accounts of the war, Manning does not establish any kind of contrast between the realities of battle and a nostalgically recalled England. Apart from one or two unflattering remarks about the home front, he does not even dwell on the alienation of soldiers from civilians. He shows the soldiers as immersed in a totally self-contained world with its own laws and values, in which civilian attitudes are best forgotten, and in which the only reminder that there is another kind of life comes with letters and food-parcels from home. Having established this world, Manning shows its workings with a wealth of convincing detail; in particular, he possessed a fine ear for dialogue, and a sensitive awareness of the various unexpected ways in which human qualities can appear in conditions of stress. At the same time, his use of Shakespearian chapter-headings indicates his desire to place the story on a universal plane, to underline the continuity of experience between the British troops on the Somme in 1916 and Henry V's battered army at Agincourt. *Her Privates We* is not an anti-war book; Manning does not flinch from rendering the brutality and bloody waste of battle, but he accepts the war as a total and inescapable experience and does not speculate about the possibility of things being otherwise. In his reflective passages, he has something of the tragic vision of some existentialist philosophers:

It was not much use telling them that war was only the ultimate problem of all human life stated barely, and pressing for an immediate solution. When each individual conscience cried out for its freedom, that implacable thing said: "Peace, peace; your freedom is only in me!" Men recognised the truth intuitively, even with their reason checking at a fault. There was no man of them unaware of the mystery which encompassed him, for he was a part of it; he could neither separate himself entirely from it, nor identify himself with it completely. A man might rave against war; but war, from among its myriad faces, could always turn towards him one, which was his own.

In his preface to the novel, Manning wrote: 'War is waged by men; not by beasts, or by gods. It is a peculiarly human activity. To call it a crime against mankind is to miss at least half its significance; it is also the punishment of a crime.'

Manning uses as his centre of consciousness a private called Bourne; we know nothing of his antecedents, nor even his Christian name, but he is obviously an educated man, a lover of good food and, particularly, of wine, and he seems to be fairly well off. At the same time, he is a good mixer and is thoroughly at home in the ranks; he is very popular with his comrades and the N.C.O.s, though rather less so with some of the officers, who resent the fact that a man of their own class and education should be serving as a private. He is urged to apply for a commission, but he is reluctant to leave the ranks, and only towards the end of the novel does he agree. Bourne is an interestingly complicated figure: an intellectual of a philosophical turn of mind, he is also, in the way of private soldiers, an expert scrounger, and possesses an Odysseus-like cunning; above all, he manages to be totally detached from his surroundings. Bourne has, in fact, elements of a type that has become familiar in more recent writing as the hipster, travelling light through the world. *Her Privates We* describes the adventures, in the trenches or in billets, of Bourne and his two comrades, Shem and Martlow; in essentials, Manning's novel is an exploration of comradeship, which, as so many writers testified, emerged as the supreme value amongst fighting men. As Manning insists, it was not the same as friendship; Bourne, Shem, and Martlow were very different types who would have had little in common in peace-time; but the shared experiences of war form a close union between them, which endures until it is bloodily broken.

Comradeship as an existentially lived value was meaningful to the men, whereas they were indifferent to all forms of patriotic and idealistic exhortation:

When at last Mr. Rhys left them, they relaxed into ease with a sigh. Major Shadwell and Captain Malet they could understand, because each was what every private soldier is, a man in arms against the world, a man fighting desperately for himself, and conscious that, in the last resort, he stood alone; for such self-reliance lies at the very heart of comradeship. In so far as Mr. Rhys had something of the same character, they respected him; but when he spoke to them of patriotism, sacrifice, and duty, he merely clouded and confused their vision.

Manning reveals another of war's 'myriad faces' in his portrayal of Weeper Smart, a superbly realized character: Smart is a lugubrious and shambling soldier who is an embodiment of envy, discontent, and defeatism. His attitude to fighting is an exact anticipation of Joseph Heller's Captain Yossarian: ' "All that a says is, if a man's dead it don't matter no more to 'im 'oo wins the bloody war," said Weeper.' On the face of it, Weeper is a thorough coward, and yet Bourne feels 'that in any emergency he would not let one down, that he had in him, curiously enough, an heroic strain'. And in the event, Weeper does prove himself capable of heroic behaviour. He is contrasted with the deserter, Miller (though even he has the energy and ingenuity to escape several times from captivity).

Her Privates We concentrates firmly on a small, clearly defined area of front-line life, and is saturated in that life: it avoids the significant contrasts posited by other novelists, and does not attempt to illustrate the decline in English civilization as a whole. And yet it treats of war with a Shakespearian inclusiveness, concretely presenting the humour as well as the horror and the pathos. Manning's close-textured prose maintains an effective balance between the salty vigour of the colloquial exchanges of the soldiers, and Bourne's probing, existential reflections; Manning's philosophical concern provides an additional dimension and unifies the novel's disparate realistic observations. This blend of the particular and the universal gives the book, at times, a certain epic flavour. Only in David Jones's *In Parenthesis* do we find anything approaching this particular quality.

There is one other work of the late 'twenties that needs to be mentioned, if only briefly, in the present discussion, and

N

that is R. C. Sherriff's famous play, *Journey's End*, first performed in December 1928—with Laurence Olivier in the role of Stanhope—and thereafter assured of a permanent place in the hearts of the public. On the face of it, Sherriff's play is a glib though competent theatrical contrivance, unpleasantly sentimental, and full of characters and situations which are none the less artificial for being found in a British dug-out on the eve of the German offensive in March 1918. At the same time, it glances at the issues that more genuinely imaginative writers were concerned with: in confronting the starry-eyed young subaltern, Raleigh, with the hard-drinking, nerve-shattered company commander, Stanhope, whom the boy had idealized when they were at school together, Sheriff is exhibiting the collapse of the public-school ethos under the pressure of war; and thus suggesting the breakdown of the traditional English values that had been sustained by this ethos. And in Stanhope's relation with Hibbert, Sherriff acknowledges, then evades, the whole difficult question of cowardice which writers such as Herbert Read had more deeply examined. On the whole, Sherriff was giving theatre audiences what they wanted: they were prepared, after ten years, to take a fresh interest in the war, and his play provided a degree of realism and affecting sentiment, without making any actively uncomfortable demands. The darkness that covers the stage after the final explosion is, no doubt, theatrically effective, and may faintly recall the civilization-occluding darkness of the closing lines of the *Dunciad*. Yet the inert clichés of Sherriff's final stage-direction emphasize the kind of predictable experience we have just passed through: 'very faintly there comes the dull rattle of machine-guns and the fevered spatter of rifle fire.'

The British writers of those years who returned to their wartime experiences were, as I have suggested, only one element in a large international wave of interest in the subject. This lies beyond the limited confines of the present study, but one can note that those writers who are most available to English readers, the Americans, exhibited a degree of protest and disillusion that was more extreme than the attitudes of most British writers. As Frederick J. Hoffman comments, in the excellent discussion of American war books in his *The Twenties* (1962):

Fiction

That sense of violation is present in each of the principal works of American war literature. (English writers were "disenchanted", disabused of their sacrifices *pro patria*, but in only a few cases had a comparable feeling of outrage.)

John Dos Passos's *Three Soldiers* had appeared in 1921 and E. E. Cummings's *The Enormous Room* in 1922. Hemingway published *A Farewell to Arms* in 1929, and this was to prove one of the most celebrated of all war—or anti-war—novels. After the retreat from Caporetto, Hemingway's hero abandons any vestige of attachment to a scheme of public values that had become meaningless to him, and is impelled only by the motive of self-preservation: he makes something rather like a psychotic withdrawal from the complexities of experience. He retreats to a small world of personal values, but even this fails when Catherine Barkley dies in childbirth. In *A Farewell to Arms* Hemingway registers the collapse of the heroic ideal; though in his later fiction we see him attempting to restore it, very much on his own terms.

Not all the international war books of 1928-30 were pacifist in their orientation, but many of them were, and those which were not dwelt on the grim rather than the conventionally glorious aspects of the Great War. Some notion of their general character can be gained from the attack on them contained in *The Lie About the War*, a pamphlet by the late Douglas Jerrold published in 1930. Jerrold was a right-wing journalist of romantic inclinations who had fought throughout the war and whose view of it was diametrically opposed to that of most of the writers he discusses. Jerrold's vigorous essay is a reminder that no matter how exigent the *Zeigeist* may seem to be, one can always find people who resist its pressures. He did not disapprove of all the writers he mentioned: he admired *Undertones of War*, and, with reservations, *Goodbye to All That*. Manning's novel had not appeared when Jerrold wrote, and it is possible that he would have looked favourably on that also. On the whole, however, he was concerned to denounce a wide range of distinguished writers, including Hemingway, Re_ marque, Aldington, Barbusse, and Arnold Zweig. Jerrold claimed that they gave a false picture of war; or even when they presented a fairly accurate picture, they distorted the underlying motives of the conflict:

> It is this obsession of futility, not any special depth of sympathy or humanitarianism which accounts for the piling up of the individual agony to so many poignant climaxes remote from the necessities or even from the normal incidental happenings of war.

It is undoubtedly true that the demands of dramatic intensity made many imaginative writers convey the certainly false impression that life in the line consisted of unbroken periods of bloody and destructive action, whereas for a great deal of the time it was fairly quiet. Jerrold complains that the 'frank' war books leave out the inactivity and boredom that made up nine-tenths of the life of the infantry soldier.

He also argues that, considered from the standpoint of the individual private or junior officer, the war must inevitably seem a meaningless muddle; only when regarded from the exalted position of the corps, or even army, commander, could its movements make any sense at all. He complains that nearly all the war books he discusses generalize from purely personal experience, without taking the broad view:

> These writers know as well as I do that the only possible tragedy of the war, *considered as war*, lay in its inevitability, that to deny the element of fatality must be to deny that it was a tragedy at all. Yet to accept the element of fatality would be to invest the war with a grandeur which these novelists are determined to deny it. Hence the frantic attempt to get the dramatic quality out of every kind of struggle except the struggle of one army against another and so to get a significant novel without having to admit that it was a significant war.

Jerrold seems to discuss the war with the detached tones of a critic describing the tragic grandeur of a play by Racine; but presumably his own wartime experiences were no less authentic than those of the writers he is attacking. The ultimate difference between them is that Jerrold remains secure in traditional habits of mind, which the others have abandoned. He regarded the conflict as both necessary and significant; they

Fiction

saw it as meaningless and so without significance. The concrete historical question of whether the war was unnecessarily prolonged, and might have been settled sooner by negotiation, is one which Jerrold avoids discussing in detail. He would certainly have claimed that the necessity and justice of the Allied cause meant that one *had* to accept all the slaughter and mutilation involved to achieve victory; his opponents would have claimed that no cause that involved such bloody destruction of life *could* be just or necessary. Between two such radically opposed points of view, rooted in such different ethical attitudes, there could be no common ground and so no argument.

Nevertheless, some of Jerrold's contributory points now seem unfortunate. In an attempt to show, for instance, that the war, terrible though it was, had good results, he points to the elimination of militarism and the establishment of parliamentary democracy in Germany. Three years later, the Nazis, deriving much of their strength from opposition to the Treaty of Versailles, were to come to power and begin preparing for another war. Some of Jerrold's other points are, however, valid as criticism. It is undoubtedly a limitation of the war novels he is discussing that they could only present the responses of a single, usually isolated consciousness, and made no attempt at a Tolstoyan largeness, though the reasons for this limitation were as much philosophical as literary.

As a final reflection on the anti-war books of 1928-30, one might add that many of those left-wingers who most enthusiastically espoused their sentiments were to abandon pacifism in 1936, on the outbreak of the Spanish Civil War. This, they said (as had been so often said in the past, on the outbreak of other wars), was an exception; this was a just and necessary war that *had* to be fought. (A sentiment certainly shared by Jerrold, though as a supporter of the other side.)

10

REMYTHOLOGIZING
David Jones's In Parenthesis

THE dominant movement in the literature of the Great War was, to adapt the terminology of some modern theologians, from a myth-dominated to a demythologized world. Violent action could be regarded as meaningful, even sacred, when it was sanctified by the traditional canons of heroic behaviour; when these canons came to seem no longer acceptable, then killing or being killed in war appeared meaningless and horrible. This, in essentials, is the difference between Brooke or Grenfell, and Sassoon or Owen; or, to take another contrast, between *The Storm of Steel* and *Death of a Hero*. Throughout the nineteenth century, poets had lamented the advance of scientific and positivistic modes of thought, which had stripped nature of her mysteries and her abiding myths. And yet the traditional pastoral mode obstinately endured, at least until the Georgians, when it gave a final flicker of life. Compared to the Georgians, the Imagists were the first poets of a demythologized world, concerned to make poetry from the naked, isolated object, stripped of all outworn mythical accretions. This, at least, was their theory; in practice, Imagist poets such as Pound, Aldington, and H.D., were heavily literary, drawing much of their inspiration from classical motifs. But we can see the logical working-out of the Imagist tenets in the poetry of William Carlos Williams, and his followers, the Objectivists, who concentrated on the naked object as it presented itself to the senses. Williams was, after all, living and working in an America that, he felt, owed nothing to the myths and literary conventions of Europe (though, curiously, Williams in his later years very beautifully translated an idyll of Theocritus, first of Western pastoral poets).

Similarly, the myths that had given value and significance to war were to be stripped away by the poets of 1914-18.

David Jones's In Parenthesis

As I have suggested, the process owed a great deal to the mass use of such unchivalrous and anti-heroic weapons as the machine-gun and heavy artillery. But this was certainly not the whole of the story: the bayonet was a fairly traditional weapon, and yet Herbert Read in his poem, 'The Happy Warrior', dwells on the gruesome business of stabbing a fallen enemy with a bayonet, whilst deliberately alluding to Wordsworth's poem, which complacently expounds the virtues of the soldierly life. Read describes the physical fact, whereas Wordsworth describes the attitudes that should, ideally, surround the fact. If one juxtaposes the two poems one can see clearly enough what the demythologization of war meant.

For a time this process seemed to have been brought to finality with the poetry of 1916-18 and those prose works of the 'twenties, which aimed, misleadingly, to 'tell the truth about war', as if there could be any such single, clearly defined entity. And this has proved a permanent shift of sensibility: the mood and the rhetoric of 1914-15 are now irrecoverably lost. But at the same time, war, as a subject, could not remain wholly stark and impoverished of all mythical accretions. Although the nineteenth-century rationalists and their literary opponents had both felt that the mythic mode of consciousness would be shrivelled up by the fierce light of science and positivistic thought, and might well disappear altogether, the twentieth century has seen events turn out rather differently. The philosophers of symbolic forms and the archetypal psychologists have shown that the mythopoeic faculty is deep-rooted in man, and is not likely to be weakened, even in a scientific and technological age; new myths arise, or old ones appear in new forms, as we see in such literary manifestations as science fiction. And in a more deliberate way, the most significant literature of our age is marked by its use of legendary and mythological material, often with an anthropological backing: one need only mention *The Waste Land* and *Ulysses*. Taken far enough, the demythologizing tendencies in movements like Imagism can transform themselves into new forms of mythic creation, as Northrop Frye has indicated. The literary use of myth by twentieth-century writers is, however, very conscious: instead of myth, as in other ages, being rooted in a system of public and shared beliefs, and so acting as a focus for the consciousness and aspirations of a community, it is used by the modern writer as a means of restoring contact with the past, of temporarily living and feeling in terms of vanished systems of value. Its use is therefore necessarily individualistic and fragmentary. Nevertheless, it serves as a means of escaping from the positivistic concentration on the naked thing-in-itself. It is in this context that one can, I think, profitably study the achievement of David Jones in *In Parenthesis*, which is an attempt to place the experience of war in a fresh mythic perspective.

David Jones, who was born in 1895, was known as a visual artist—principally an engraver and water-colourist—long before he became known as a writer. *In Parenthesis* was his first literary work, and took nine years to complete, for it was started in 1928 but did not achieve publication until 1937. Undoubtedly, it is one of the few works of literature by a native Englishman (or Anglo-Welshman) to contribute importantly to the twentieth-century Modern Movement (using the term, as does Mr. Stephen Spender in *The Struggle of the Modern* (1963), to denote a particular historical phenomenon). *In Parenthesis* owes a significant debt to *The Waste Land,* and at the same time has affinities with the later work of Pound and Joyce. It is an elaborate work which wholeheartedly obeys Pound's injunction to 'make it new'. Jones uses a combination of prose and free verse, and forms which can be regarded as either, though the difference is not deeply significant, for the prose resembles Joyce's in being so carefully wrought, with such care for the placing, resonance and interrelations of all his words, that in everything except external form it *is* poetry. Jones exploits all the possible resources of language in order to convey his meanings, in a way that utterly ignores conventional expectations about literary forms. At the same time, despite its complexity, *In Parenthesis* has a sharp simplicity of narrative line. Its substance has been well described in an excellent article by Mr. René Hague, who writes:

> The basic theme of *In Parenthesis* . . . is simple enough, treated with a classical plunge into action, and in each section, a classical respect for the unities: the story of how John Ball, a private in a new-army battalion of a Welsh Regiment (the choice of name, that of the priest executed for his share in the peasant rising of 1381, stresses the continuity of Welsh and

British tradition), parades with his battalion for overseas embarkation, of the journey to Flanders, the march up the line, the first day in the strange trench world, their assimilation to the alien rhythm, their march to the assembly point for the Somme offensive, and the final attack on Mametz wood, in which John Ball is wounded and many of his comrades are killed.[1]

Jones is at all times faithful to the material circumstances of an infantryman's life, for he has an Imagist's accuracy of response to the data of the physical world. But at the same time, John Ball's progress as a soldier is placed against a richly-textured background of multiple literary allusion; again, one may quote Mr. Hague:

> There is a close and natural association with Shakespeare (in particular with *Henry V*), with Welsh epic, with Malory, with biblical imagery, with the liturgy—a favourite metaphor is the hieratic order of soldierly manoeuvre.

In the preface of a later work, *The Anathemata* (1952), Jones described himself as 'a Londoner, of Welsh and English parentage, of Protestant upbringing, of Catholic subscription'. This rather unusual collocation of attributes underlies *In Parenthesis*, starting with the realistic observation that Ball's battalion is made up of a mixture of cockneys and Welshmen. Like Pound and Eliot and Joyce, Jones is an eclectic writer, who deals with disparate fragments of cultural deposits, working them into a closely woven tapestry. But he is a far more rooted writer than they are; certainly when compared with the deracinated Americans, Pound and Eliot, and even with Joyce, whose entire theme was Dublin but who could only cope with it in exile. Jones's interest in Celtic and early English literature, and in Catholic liturgy, is more than just 'a heap of broken images', because it springs directly from his origins and commitments as a man. Furthermore, Jones sees these interests as having their own interrelations and points of contact; in Mr. Hague's words:

> the Welsh element is presented not as something on the periphery of, or even extraneous to, England, but as the core of the British-Romano-British-Angle tradition, so that London, with the sister figures of Troy and Rome, is above all the city.

This, then, is a very limited degree of eclecticism, when compared with the shifts in Pound's *Cantos* from China to medieval Siena to Jefferson's America (and more recently to Ancient Egypt). Nevertheless, few readers are likely to possess precisely the same range of interests and knowledge as David Jones, so he has provided *In Parenthesis* with copious notes, which are more genuinely enlightening than those attached to *The Waste Land*. The question of how far a work is impaired by needing annotation of this kind is not easily settled; ideally, no doubt, a work should be self-contained but in an era of cultural fragmentation this is not always easily achieved. The best solution is to regard the notes to *In Parenthesis* as an integral part of the author's composition, rather as one regards Pope's notes to *The Dunciad*.

What, in particular, Jones does have in common with the other great practitioners of literary modernism is his use of the ideogrammatic method, the suppression of conventional narrative links in favour of the juxtaposition of two disparate images or phrases. Thus Jones points to a constant relation between Private Ball and his comrades and various soldiers of the past, such as Henry V's troops and, above all, the doomed warriors fighting a desperate foray described in *Y Gododdin*, a sixth-century Welsh heroic poem, which provides Jones with the epigraphs for each section of *In Parenthesis*. Jones was doubtless influenced here by the interpenetration of past and present in *The Waste Land*, and perhaps also by Eliot's stress, in 'Tradition and the Individual Talent', on the contemporaneity of significant literary experience. Yet unlike Eliot, Jones does not make his juxtapositions with ironical effect; there is no question of contrasting the sordid present with the beauties of a more or less legendary past: if anything, the humble infantrymen, enduring the misery of the trenches and then slaughtered in the attack on Mametz wood, are in some measure transfigured by the light of the earlier heroes.

In fact, Jones is concerned to restore the mythology of heroism, but with crucial differences. Whereas earlier literary representations of the hero, from Renaissance drama to the poetry of the early days of the Great War, had been rooted in an implicit but assured complex of assumptions and attitudes that were shared by the writer and his readers, Jones, writing in a post-heroic phase, has laboriously to construct an *ad hoc* frame of reference from his acquaintance with literature, showing the continuity of human attitudes in the conditions of battle. And

David Jones's In Parenthesis

this demonstration, this concrete embodiment of experience, is in no way rhetorical or assertive; thus, it is at the opposite pole from the expressions of the heroic mode that we find in the speeches of Tamburlaine or Hotspur, or, for that matter, in the sonnets of Rupert Brooke. It is unique and non-generalizable, valid only for Jones's particular purposes in writing *In Parenthesis*. This uniqueness means that the quality of epic that some critics have discovered in *In Parenthesis*, notably Mr. John H. Johnston in his *English Poetry of the First World War* (1964), needs to be discussed with some qualifications. As I have already suggested, in writing about Manning's *Her Privates We*, the private soldier's experience of total immersion in a vast inhuman process gave more scope for epic understanding than the officers' narratives; and this is true, also, of *In Parenthesis*; indeed, both Manning and Jones share a common element in their use of Shakespeare's picture of the soldier's life as a substratum in their narratives. Undoubtedly Jones does move towards the level of epic, in that he reproduces a sense of shared experience and transcends the limitations of the purely individual standpoint. But true epic, I take it, reaches out beyond the personal to appeal to a system of public and communal values which are ultimately collective, national, and even cosmic. And this Jones does not do; he may feel that Celtic myth is central and not peripheral to his understanding of British tradition, and he may have some success in persuading a discerning reader that this is so. Nevertheless, such knowledge will not already be there to provide a ready response in the consciousness of most of his readers. Quite apart from an author's subject-matter and treatment, the question of epic involves the author's relation with his audience. Jones, in this respect, was no differently placed from other twentieth-century *avant-garde* artists with a strictly minority appeal. Although he aspires towards the impersonality of epic, his perceptions remain individual, rooted in the accidents of his own experience and reading. One can reasonably doubt whether the conditions for epic—the existence of a shared scheme of communal values and assumptions—are ever likely to be fulfilled in modern society.

In Parenthesis remains, however, the nearest equivalent to an epic that the Great War produced in English. It is far more objective than the wartime poetry or the novels and memoirs of the 'twenties. Jones employs Private Ball simply as a focus for typical experience and not as a dominating vehicle of consciousness. In the first section the battalion is assembled and marches through the wet streets to embark for France—'The people of that town did not acclaim them, nor stop about their business— for it was late in the second year'; they reach France and journey on to a base behind the lines. This opening section employs Jones's stylistic narrative norm, a flowing descriptive prose largely derived from Malory, interspersed with the cockney that serves as the lingua franca of army life. In the later sections, the texture is less even, more broken up into verse and less regular forms, conveying disparate moments of violent experience.

In Part 2 the troops continue their training in France:

> They were given lectures on very wet days in the barn, with its great roof, sprung, upreaching, humane, and redolent of a vanished order. Lectures on military tactics that would be more or less commonly understood. Lectures on hygiene by the medical officer, who was popular, who glossed his technical discourses with every lewdness, whose heroism and humanity reached towards sanctity.

The image of the barn is significant: the great vaulted roof reminds us of the roof of a Gothic church, and both typify the pieties of an agrarian order. Jones's Catholicism is an important element in his work, though he is not a conventionally 'religious' writer. But he is deeply involved with the cultural forms that have grown up around Western Catholicism, and, in particular, the liturgy (considered, perhaps, in a somewhat external fashion). Like his friend and co-religionist, Eric Gill, Jones sees man as *homo faber*, who is closest to God when he is making order out of chaos, whether in building barns or cathedrals, or devising ecclesiastical ritual or military manoeuvres. The artefact is always a sign of something beyond itself—pointing to man's essential humanity as maker—and like Hopkins, whom he occasionally quotes in *In Parenthesis*, Jones sees the natural world as continually indicating its creator, God. As against the bleakness of the positivist *Weltanschauung* Jones posits not merely a mythic, but a sacramentalist view of the world.

Throughout *In Parenthesis*, the ritual element in military orders and words of command is stressed, as in this

extract from Part 3, where the troops are marching up to the
line, having to avoid shell-holes and the trailing field-telephone
wire. The repeated injunctions soon acquire a ritual quality:

> The repeated passing back of aidful messages assumes
> a cadency.
> Mind the hole
> mind the hole
> mind the hole to left
> hole right
> step over
> keep left, left.
> One grovelling, precipitated, with his gear tangled,
> struggles to feet again:
> Left be buggered.
> Sorry mate—you all right china?—lift us yer
> rifle—an' don't take on so Honey—but rather, mind
> the wire here
> mind the wire
> mind the wire
> mind the wire
> Extricate with some care that taut strand—it may
> well be you'll sweat on its unbrokenness.

Part 4 presents Ball and his comrades fully absorbed into the
life of the trenches. The section opens with a magnificent evo-
cation of a December daybreak in the front-line: its mingled
precision and richness shows that Jones is a master of language, and as conscious of the impact of the physical as any
Imagist (the opening words are from Malory):

> So thus he sorrowed till it was day and heard the foules
> sing, then somewhat he was comforted.
>
>   Stand-to.
>   Stand-to-arms.
> Stealthly, imperceptibly stript back, thinning
> night wraps
> unshrouding, unsheafing—
> and insubstantial barriers dissolve.
> This blind night-negative yields uncertain flux.
> At your wrist the phosphorescent dial describes the
> equal seconds.
>   The flux yields up a measurable body; bleached forms
> emerge and stand.

Where their faces turned, grey wealed earth bared
almost of last clung weeds of night-weft—
    behind them the stars still shined.
Her fractured contours dun where soon his ray would
show more clear her dereliction.
Already before him low atmospheres harbingered his
bright influence.
The filtering irradiance spread, you could begin to know
that thing from this; this nearer from that away over.
There at ten o'clock from that leaning picket-iron,
where the horizon most invented its character to their
eyes straining, a changing dark, variant-textured, shaped
to their very watching a wooded gradient.
Skin off those comforters—to catch with their
cocked ears
the early bird,
and meagre chattering of
December's prime
shrill over from
Biez wood.
Biez wood fog pillowed, by low mist isled, a play of
hide and seek arboreal for the white diaphane.
To their eyes seeming a wood moving,
        a moving wood advisioned.
        Stand-to.
        Stand-to.
      Stand-to-arms.
Out there,
get out there
get into that fire trench.
Pass it along to Stand-to.

Much of the distinctive quality of Jones's poetic writing lies in the often strange combination of a sharp registration of sense impressions and a mannered diction and syntax. Another aspect of it is seen in the lyrical compression of his account of Christmas morning ('his morning parapets', etc., are the Germans', always referred to by the collective 'he'):

It was yet quite early in the morning, at the time of Saturnalia,
when men properly are in winter quarters, lighting His
birthday candles—
all a green-o.

David Jones's In Parenthesis

> When children look with serious eyes on brand-new miracles, and
> red berry sheen makes a Moses-bush, to mirror in multiplicity
> the hearth-stones creature of fire.
>   But John Ball, posted as 1st Day Sentry, sat on the fire-step;
> and looking upward, sees in a cunning glass the image of: his
> morning parapets, his breakfast-fire smoke, the twisted
> wood beyond.

Such passages show much more clearly than any attempt at
paraphrase the nature of Jones's concern with myth and ritual.

At the same time he is capable of a novelistic realism in
rendering some of the stranger manifestations of the civilization
of the trenches:

> A man, seemingly native to the place, a little thick man,
> swathed with sacking, a limp, saturated bandolier thrown over
> one shoulder and with no other accoutrements, gorgeted
> in woollen Balaclava, groped out from between two tottering
> corrugated uprights, his great moustaches beaded with con-
> densation under his nose. Thickly greaved with mud so that
> his boots and puttees and sandbag tie-ons were become one
> whole of trickling ochre. His minute pipe had its smoking
> bowl turned inversely. He spoke slowly. He told the corporal
> that this was where shovels were usually drawn for any fat-
> igue in the supports. He slipped back quickly, with a certain
> animal caution, into his hole; to almost immediately poke
> out his wool-work head, to ask if anyone had the time of
> day or could spare him some dark shag or a picture-paper.
> Further, should they meet a white dog in the trench her
> name was Belle, and he would like to catch any bastard giving
> this Belle the boot.
>
>   John Ball told him the time of day.
>   No one had any dark shag.
>   No one had a picture-paper.
>   They certainly would be kind to the bitch, Belle.
>
> They'd give her half their iron rations—Jesus—they'd let her
> bite their backsides without a murmur. He draws-to the sack-
> ing curtain over his lair.

There is a Dickensian vigour here; whilst words like 'gorgeted'
and 'greaved' remind us that we are meant to see this appari-
tion in a perspective stretching back to Malory and beyond.

The earlier parts of *In Parenthesis* lead on to the Somme offensive and the unit's part in the assault on Mametz wood. Jones described the preparations without bitterness, but with the front-line soldier's customary sardonic intonation:

Private 21679, Map. 6 pla. 'B' Coy. temp. att. H.Q. Coy (office) pending present operations, key-fingered out the long roster of weapons to be borne and the last particular for the specialist details
for the chosen fire-eaters
for the co-opted runners
for the flank bombers with
their respective loads.
    And for the born leaders,
the top boys
the hero's grave squad
the Elect
the wooden-cross Dicks
    —for the White-men with Emergency Archie: all these types are catered for, but they must know exactly how to behave.

The book reaches a superb climax with the assault in Part 7. The state of mind of the men waiting to go over the top is rendered with acute sensitivity:

Racked out to another turn of the screw
the acceleration heightens;
the sensibility of these instruments to register,
fails;
needle dithers disorientate.
The responsive mercury plays laggard to such fevers—you
simply can't take any more in.
And the surfeit of fear steadies to dumb incognition, so that
when they give the order to move upward to align with 'A',
hugged already just under the lip of the acclivity inches below
where his traversing machine-guns perforate to powder
white—
white creature of chalk pounded
and the world crumbled away
and get ready to advance
you have not capacity for added fear only the limbs are leaden
to negotiate the slope and rifles all out of balance, clumsied
with long auxiliary steel
seem five times the regulation weight—
it bitches the aim as well. . . .

David Jones's In Parenthesis

As the attack proceeds Ball sees his comrades shot down
on either side of him, but he is so far unscathed. Jones can
describe death in battle with the brutal directness of a Sassoon
—'Wastebottom married a wife on his Draft-leave but the
whinnying splinter razored diagonal and mess-tin fragments
drove inwards and toxined underwear'—but his lengthier accounts of it have a stylized, ritual quality which makes them,
if anything, more moving—as with the death of the young
subaltern, Mr. Jenkins:

> He sinks on one knee
> and now on the other,
> his upper body tilts in rigid inclination
> this way and back;
> weighted lanyard runs out to full tether,
>   swings like a pendulum
>   and the clock run down.
> Lurched over, jerked iron saucer over tilted brow,
> clampt unkindly over lip and chin
> nor no ventaille to this darkening
>   and masked face lifts to grope the air
> and so disconsolate;
> enfeebled fingering at a paltry strap—
> buckle holds,
> holds him blind against the morning.

The last line of this extract possesses, I think, something of
the authentic *frisson* of the early heroic poetry that was such
an inspiration to Jones.

The detailed description of the savage fighting in the wood
contains scenes unsurpassed for energy and exactitude anywhere in the literature of the war. At the same time, Jones,
although unfaltering in his realism, also stresses the mythic
dimension. The wood, now the scene of carnage, is also, like
all woods, a traditional focus for the numinous, and we have
been reminded of this by earlier references in the book—'To
groves always men come both to their joys and their undoing'.
Eventually Ball is wounded in the legs and tries to crawl to
safety, but he finds his rifle an encumbrance:

> It's difficult with the weight of the rifle.
> Leave it—under the oak.
> Leave it for a salvage-bloke

O

let it lie bruised for a monument
dispense the authenticated fragments to the faithful.

He is reluctant to abandon the rifle, the well-loved artefact that
has shared his battle-experiences and which, as his instructors
have so often told him, is the soldier's best friend: 'You know
her by her bias, and by her exact error at 300, and by the deep
scar at the small, by the fair flaw in the grain, above the lower
sling-swivel——' but he must leave it. As Ball crawls away, among
the British and German dead he imagines the fallen in some way
commemorated by a local deity—'The Queen of the Woods
has cut bright boughs of various flowering.' He makes his
laborious way through the wood to the British lines:

Mrs. Willy Hartington has learned to draw sheets and so has
Miss Melpomené; and on the south lawns,
men walk in red white and blue
under the cedars
and by every green tree
and beside comfortable waters.
But why dont the bastards come—
Bearers!—stret-cher bear-errs!
or do they divide the spoils at the Aid-Post.
But how many men do you suppose could bear away a third
of us:
drag just a little further—he may yet counter-attack.

We are not told that Ball survives, but we must suppose he does
and is responsible for the narrative we have just read. At the
last, Ball and the author seem to become one. In the final words
of *In Parenthesis*, Jones quotes from the *Song of Roland*, indicating for the last time that the struggle we have just witnessed
must be regarded in the heroic perspectives of the past, and simul-
taneously emphasizing the front-line soldier's feeling of having
participated in a unique and non-communicable experience, which
sets him apart from other men: 'The geste says this and the man
who was on the field . . . and who wrote the book . . . the man
who does not know this has not understood anything.'

Jones is distinguished from the poets who wrote during the
course of the war both by his impersonality and by the far
wider emotional range of his work. As Mr. John H. Johnston
has observed, 'Unlike Owen, Jones found little poetry in pity;
pity was an emotion that might be aroused under certain cir-

cumstances, but the full reality of war was much too complex to be viewed through the eyes of pity alone.' Jones was, however, very aware of the sacrificial elements in the soldiers' experience, which he understood in Christian terms. Johnston acutely remarks:

> Positive, aggressive heroism of the epic character is seldom possible in modern war; a man may perform valiantly in action, but for every valiant moment there are weeks of inactivity, boredom, suffering, and fear. Thus the virtues of the modern infantryman are Christian virtues—patience, endurance, hope, love—rather than the naturalistic virtues of the epic hero.

As we have seen, this concept of the Christian hero had already been foreshadowed in Ford Madox Ford's Tietjens. Jones admits in his preface that the period of the war he was writing about—the early months of 1916—was still amenable to such treatment: it had not become entirely mechanized and depersonalized. Whether he could have written similarly about the post-Somme phase, so much more massive in its brutality, which produced the other war poets, is open to doubt.

Again, Jones resembles his contemporaries in seeing the actualities of the war against a background of traditional values, but differs from them in his manner of doing so. He looks much farther back than the nostalgically recalled Home Counties pastoral scenes of the Georgians, or even than Ford's Yorkshire squirearchy. Jones feels that his roots are British rather than narrowly English, and emphasizes the Romano-British elements in the national character (surviving in mythology if not in continuing social forms) rather more strongly than the Anglo-Saxon and subsequent strains. Thus, Jones establishes a comprehensive though eclectic frame for his action, whose closest parallel is perhaps to be found in the vision of the British past in Kipling's *Puck of Pook's Hill* (1906). As I have suggested, the degree of Jones's cultural eclecticism may, for many readers unfamiliar with his material, tend to obscure his comprehensiveness, though this difficulty diminishes on successive readings of *In Parenthesis*. In one other important respect, Jones's method differs from that of other war poets and prose writers: whereas they establish contrasts, whether nostalgic or ironical, between the past and the realities of the Front, Jones

O*

is concerned always to find parallels, to emphasize the underlying unity rather than the discontinuity of experience.

That Jones establishes this unity rather too easily is a point
that might be urged against him by his critics. His achievement in *In Parenthesis* is increasingly recognized, but some
readers may incline towards D. J. Enright's rather unfavourable comment that *In Parenthesis* is:

> a consciously 'literary' work: its style, tapestried and
> 'modernistic' at the same time, is at odds with its subject-
> matter (infantry life on the Western Front), and the allusions
> to ancient Welsh poetry and Celtic myths with their explana-
> tory but not always justificatory footnotes rob the account
> of most of its immediacy.[2]

This is a curiously superficial comment from a normally penetrating critic. If Jones has succeeded (as I would claim) then his style
is not at odds with but expresses in depth his subject-matter (it is
hard to see that any given subject inescapably *demands* one style
rather than another). Enright's crucial point is his assumption
that 'immediacy' is, or should be, the principal criterion of literary merit, at least in the literature of war. Jones, as I hope to have
shown, possesses as much concrete 'immediacy' as his more
avowedly realistic contemporaries, though he uses this as one
element in a complex of modes. The supremacy of the 'immediate'
was part of the implicit aesthetic of Imagism as well as of naturalistic fiction, and as a doctrine it has become a little threadbare;
it should at least be justified and not merely asserted. It is one
of the characteristics of the major work of art that it can modify
habitual responses and in some measure impose the criteria by
which it is to be assessed. This, I think, *In Parenthesis* succeeds
in doing; but like any major work it needs to be lived with before
all its meanings become fully alive.

In a recent letter defending *In Parenthesis* against a Welsh
critic, Mr. John Wain quoted Jorge Luis Borges's dictum that
'all literature begins in myth, and ends there'.[3] This forms
an apt conclusion to my discussion of a work which blends
myth and realism in a way that makes it one of the great
achievements of the Modern Movement, and which, at the
same time, has a rather greater depth of humanity than
some other masterpieces of post-symbolist literature.

11

Later Observations

THE First World War, and the Treaty of Versailles which officially concluded it, led in due course to the Second World War, which for several years drove much thought of the former conflict out of men's minds. The differences in attitude between the two wars are too marked, and too well known, to need much emphasis here. In place of the early heroics and subsequent savage disillusionment, there was from the beginning an unromantic acceptance, effectively crystallized in C. Day Lewis's 'Where are the War Poets?':

> It is the logic of our times,
> No subject for immortal verse—
> That we who lived by honest dreams
> Defend the bad against the worse.

The poets of 1939-45 knew more and expected less than their predecessors of 1914-18; indeed, the work of the earlier poets was an essential part of what they knew. The poetry produced during the Second World War by such writers as Alun Lewis, Keith Douglas and Roy Fuller was wryly ironical and understated rather than dramatic. And in the years since 1945 there have been few prose records of the Second World War that can approach the literary distinction of some of the autobiographies and novels that came out in the 'twenties and 'thirties. (Though there has been no shortage of vigorous but ephemeral narratives, escape stories, and so on.) The one exception is Evelyn Waugh's fine trilogy of army life, *The Sword of Honour*, which contains thematic echoes of *Parade's End*.

It is still the Great War, shorter, but, for Britain, far more traumatic and destructive of life, that seems to exercise the greater imaginative appeal. And in 1954 there appeared the first part of what must surely be the last substantial contribution to the literature of the Great War by a survivor:

Henry Williamson's *How Dear is Life*, part of his massive *roman fleuve*, *A Chronicle of Ancient Sunlight*, and the first of the five novels in the series that describe the experiences of his hero, Phillip Maddison, during the First World War. The subsequent volumes are *A Fox Under My Cloak* (1955), *The Golden Virgin* (1957), *Love and the Loveless* (1958), and *A Test to Destruction* (1960); all of them were revised for inclusion in the Panther paperback series in 1963-4.

There can be no doubt that the *Chronicle* is a heavily autobiographical work, and the author's identification with Phillip Maddison is complete. In fact, it must be regarded as a *Bildungsroman* of the same kind as *The Way of All Flesh*, as well as an extraordinarily detailed recapitulation of wartime experience. Three previous volumes, beginning with the marriage of Phillip's parents, have shown the boy growing up during the Edwardian years in a south-east suburb of London; in *How Dear is Life* he is in his late teens, working in a City insurance office, and is a Territorial: on the outbreak of war he is called up, and volunteers for overseas service. Phillip's character, as Williamson draws it, is complex: he is inconsequential and often light-hearted; at the same time, he is remarkably lacking in self-confidence and plagued by anxieties; and is liable, for the best of motives, to act in a foolishly rash or blundering manner. The principal key to his character is his unhappy relationship with his father, which has a lot in common with the similar relationship in several early twentieth-century novels and autobiographies. In Williamson's *Chronicle* the antipathy between Phillip and his father gives added and poignant emphasis to the customary alienation between front-line troops and the Home Front. As the war develops, we see Phillip maturing, though his character does not fundamentally change: he is transformed from the naïve young Territorial private of August 1914 to a seasoned soldier who, by the summer of 1918, has reached the exalted height of acting lieutenant-colonel, has been temporarily blinded in a gas attack, and awarded the D.S.O.

Phillip's career takes him through nearly all the principal campaigns of the British Army in France during the Great War. He gets to Flanders in November 1914, just in time to take part in the bloody First Battle of Ypres. The following year, as a young subaltern in charge of gas installations, he is present at the Battle of Loos, and takes a more active part in the fighting than he intends to. In 1916, he is wounded early in the Somme Offensive and sent back to England. In 1917, he is in the assault on the Hindenburg Line and then at Passchendaele. In 1918 he takes part in the British retreat before St. Quentin. In between these periods of activity at the Front he serves at a number of bases in England, and spends leaves with his family and friends in London.

Although Williamson waited so many years before embarking on a fictional treatment of his life in the Great War, his memories have lost none of their vividness. In fact, his narrative very much resembles an act of total recall by a patient undergoing analysis. The reader is all but swamped in a flood of indiscriminate detail, with the important and the trivial thoroughly mixed together. Nor is there much sense of fictional structure, for the constituent volumes seem merely to mark convenient intervals in the narrative flow, rather than to form separate artistic unities in themselves. The climaxes in Williamson's story are dictated by facts external to it—usually in the battles in which Phillip is involved—not by the inner necessities of the narrative. And in the unbroken outpouring of remembered material, considerations of style tend to become forgotten: throughout the *Chronicle*'s five wartime volumes, Williamson's prose is at best undistinguishedly adequate for his purposes, and at worst very slipshod. There are evident signs of hasty composition. This is true, also, in the matter of characterization. Williamson fills his fictional canvas with a very large number of people met by Phillip, either at home or in the Army. Some of them are very much alive, such as Phillip's parents, his admired company-commander, 'Spectre' West, or the ex-ranker, Colonel Moggerhanger. But many of the lesser figures are insufficiently realized, possibly because of the pressure under which Williamson is producing the series, and there are one or two irritating inconsistencies. Thus, the shell-shocked infantryman who is called 'Cutts' in *Love and the Loveless* becomes first 'Moggs' and then 'Mobbs' in successive references in *A Test to Destruction*.

Yet despite all these inadequacies and limitations, Williamson's novel, even if not in the front rank of fictional achievement, is an impressive work. It is compulsively readable, and, more important, its unremitting saturation in the atmosphere and material detail of life both in the Army and on the Home Front does leave an accumulative sense of 'felt life', prodigally unselective though it may be. And the amiable vagaries of Phillip, Williamson's principal vehicle of consciousness, relieve the deadening effect of prolonged stretches of rigorously naturalistic fiction. The five volumes are in fact given a certain moral unity by two linked themes. One of them lies in Phillip's attitude to his father, and the other stems from his experience of the Christmas-day truce in the front lines in 1914, when for a few hours British and German troops fraternized. Phillip is deeply impressed by his discovery that the ordinary German soldier is very like his British opposite number in his attitudes and aspirations; and the conclusion he draws from this is that the war is a wanton folly dividing two sets of brothers, though he never goes so far as an anti-war revolt in the manner of Sassoon. But whenever possible Phillip challenges the anti-Hun hysteria of the civilians, and particularly of his father; paying tribute to the qualities of the German Army and pointing out unpalatable facts such as that when, at Christmas 1915, some German soldiers attempted to repeat the truce of the previous year, gathering in their front line with carols and lanterns, they were shelled out of existence by British artillery. Williamson unites the two themes in Chapter 21 of *A Test to Destruction*, with the blazing row that Phillip has with his father in November 1919, on the first anniversary of the Armistice, a magnificently sustained piece of mutual haranguing; it ends with Phillip stalking out of the house with disastrous results.

Williamson is clearly anxious to produce an effect of verisimilitude, and he buttresses his own memories with fragments of undigested factual material: advertisements, songs, extracts from military despatches and newspaper reports. With, presumably, a similar end in view, he occasionally introduces actual personages into his narrative: Field-Marshal Haig is one, and Maurice Baring is another. These devices are sometimes obtrusive, and by no means always convincing or necessary. But at one point, in Chapter 19 of *The Golden Virgin*, Williamson makes a brilliant use of printed material. Phillip, wounded on the opening day of the Somme battle, is being transported in a hospital barge sailing down the Seine; still slightly delirious he starts turning the pages of a copy of *Nash's and Pall Magazine*, then amuses himself by annotating the advertisements:

On the first page there was a picture of an officer in the trenches stropping a safety razor. The loop of the strap was held by a tommy with rifle slung, while another looked on, grinning.

IN FRANCE, FLANDERS, GALLIPOLI—or wherever he is— send 'him' an Auto-Strop Safety Razor Set, the gift he most needs.

Comforts are few at the Front; therefore give 'him' the very real comfort of an Auto-Strop Shave. Send him the only razor that strops itself whether in Field, Camp, Dugout, or on Ship-board.

Opening his fountain pen, he gave the officer a beard; then the written comment, *If it strops itself, then what is the officer doing in the picture?*

The next advertisement was of a tommy holding an immense tin of Fry's Pure Breakfast Cocoa, while a shell burst behind him, and underneath the words, WHAT I HAVE I'LL HOLD. Then one of a small boy, finger in mouth, saying *I'se found out where Mummy keeps Ficolax.*

There is no need to cheat your children with nasty powders secreted in jam, or to give them horrid doses of castor oil . . .

Ugh, castor oil and licorice powder, given while Father stood by; for Mother alone could not get him to swallow such filthy stuff.

ONOTO the Pen. IT CANNOT LEAK. Do not make the mistake of sending the wrong pen to the front. The Military size exactly fits the Soldier's pocket, 10/6 in Black Vulcanite, £5/5/- in Gold.

Phillip took his pen and shook blots all over the advertisement, then smeared the blots, and wrote across the adverisement, PROOF!

FREE! *from Asthma.* Specially suitable for Children. Potters Asthma Cure, Artillery Lane, London E. Recommended by many doctors, it has proved its efficiency for Asthma, and also for Bronchitis, Whooping Cough, and other Lung Troubles.

Including Phosgene, Chlorine, and all Hot Air from Behind the Lines, he added.

Williamson's introduction of these advertisements—and the subsequent quotation from the editorial pages of some alleged notes from the Front, about which Phillip is very scathing—is an effective piece of *collage*, akin to the methods of some contemporary painters. Phillip's annotations, or mental comments, provide a sharp confrontation of the two opposed worlds of the civilian and the front-line soldier.

In general, Williamson writes better, or at least with greater intensity, when he is dealing with army life in France, and, in particular, in the battle sequences. In contrast, his accounts of Phillip's home-service and leaves in England are slacker and with a less compelling sense of authenticity; and the last chapters of *A Test to Destruction,* describing Phillip's life during the year following the Armistice, are written at manifestly low pressure (though, as I have suggested, Phillip's long row with his father, recorded in loving detail, is a memorable passage). The reason is, presumably, not difficult to find: memories of life at the Front were what principally fired Williamson's imagination and feeling when writing these books; and at the same time he conveyed the unreality that so many soldiers saw in civilian England by writing about it with less conviction—though Phillip's family and home are always rendered with a distinct—though sometimes grim—vitality. Similarly, Williamson may have been impelled to register the anti-climax that followed the Armistice by writing flatly and incoherently. If so, he is not the first author to have fallen into what modern critics have termed 'the fallacy of expressive form'.

In some ways it may be unfair to discuss only a part of what is by now an enormous and yet still unfinished fictional enterprise. But Williamson would probably agree that the wartime volumes are at the heart of *A Chronicle of Ancient Sunlight;* he has certainly implied in other writings that his whole life has been dominated by his memories of the Great War, and in particular by the momentary comradeship that the opposed sides enjoyed during the Christmas-day truce of 1914, the last occasion when the ancient chivalric spirit manifested itself in such a tangible fashion during a modern war.[1] (That his memory of this comradeship led Williamson to some rash judgments is undeniable; his admiration for the simple ex-soldier, Adolf Hitler, is the most notorious.) It is fitting that the last of the literary records of the Great War by a survivor of the British ranks should also be the most comprehensive: whatever their failings, the combined breadth of reference and minuteness of detail of the wartime volumes of Williamson's *Chronicle* give them an unforgettable quality.

Although Henry Williamson may have closed the account as far as survivors of the Great War are concerned, this is not to say that its literature is now complete. The immense wave of interest that it has aroused in the last few years has produced many works of military and political history, and a revival of old controversies; in the theatre there has been that popular extravaganza, *Oh What a Lovely War*. The reasons for this growing fascination, steadily mounting in intensity as the fiftieth anniversary of 1914 approached, are certainly complex. The Great War swept away the remnants of Victorian order, and brought into existence what is, more or less, the world we have had to inhabit ever since. In the 1960's Britain has been passing through a highly introspective phase of national self-examination, and a preoccupation with the catastrophic trauma that marked the beginning of the end of Britain's world dominance is part of that self-examination. The Great War is now remote enough to seem genuinely historical and not merely old-fashioned; yet it is well within living memory, and many families are still marked by its destruction of lives. At the same time, many of the attitudes it called forth seem unimaginably remote. This combination of relative closeness in time and remoteness in feeling is undoubtedly one of the things that gives the period its fascination.

J. B. Priestley has remarked that the Great War is now as far removed from us in time as the Napoleonic campaigns were from Tolstoy when he began *War and Peace*, adding that the subject would make a splendid challenge for an ambitious young novelist. So far, most recent treatment of the Great War has been in historiography rather than fiction, and there has been no sign of any attempt at a Tolstoyan grandeur of re-enactment. But one novelist who has evidently felt something of the challenge to which Priestley refers is John Harris, whose

Covenant with Death appeared in 1961. This novel, which can not unfairly be described as a highly competent piece of commercial fiction, tells in the first person the experiences of Mark Fenner, a young journalist in a Yorkshire city, from the moment he joins the city's volunteer battalion of the New Army in August 1914 to the point when he is one of the handful of survivors of the battalion's desperate attack in the face of German machine-gun fire on the morning of 1st July 1916. Almost all of his comrades are wiped out in the effort to reach the German lines: 'Two years in the making. Ten minutes in the destroying. That was our history.' *Covenant with Death* is a remarkably painstaking piece of reconstruction by an author who has had to rely on printed sources—which he has studied exhaustively—and the testimony of survivors. It reads grippingly, and might almost be the record of someone who actually went through the New Army and the Somme, though when one places it against actual autobiographical or fictional records, there is an excess of neatness about its development, a rather too well rounded quality, that suggests its synthetic nature. Under the fidelity of documentary observation, and the massed horrors of the final section, there remains a somewhat conventional story and characterization. But the novel is an extremely interesting sign of the way in which the Great War can capture the imagination of a writer of a later generation.

Among poets, less concerned with surface realism and more attuned to the mythic implications of the subject, there have been some significant recent treatments of the Great War. Whereas David Jones ordered his memories of the war by mythologizing it, poets now in their thirties or forties see the Great War, with all its familiar literary and historical associations, as in itself a potent myth, symbolizing the crisis of a civilization. Thus, Peter Porter writes in 'Somme and Flanders':

> Who am I to speak up for the long dead?
> Three uncles I never knew say I'm right.
> Their tongues are speaking in my head
> I'm related to their flesh by fright.
>
> Their world was made of nerves and mud.
> Reading about it now shocks me—Haig
> Gets transfusions of their blood,
> Plum-and-apple feeds them for the plague.

Later Observations

Those Harmsworth books have sepia'd
Their peasants' fields sown with barbed-wire.
In Nineteen-Nineteen, crops of crosses appeared
Seeded by bodies ripened in shell-fire.

One image haunts us who have read of death
In Auschwitz in our time—it is just light,
Shivering men breathing rum crouch beneath
The sandbag parapet—left to right

The line goes up and over the top,
Serious in gas masks, bayonets fixed,
Slowly forward—the swearing shells have stopped—
Somewhere ahead of them death's stopwatch ticks.

A similar attitude is exhibited at greater length in Vernon
Scannell's fine poem, 'The Great War':

Whenever war is spoken of
I find
The war that was called Great invades the mind:
The grey militia marches over land
A darker mood of grey
Where fractured tree-trunks stand
And shells, exploding, open sudden fans
Of smoke and earth. . . .

Scannell concludes the poem with a beautiful confluence of
images:

And through the misty keening of a band
Of Scottish pipes the proper names are heard
Like fateful commentary of distant guns:
Passchendaele, Bapaume, and Loos, and Mons.
And now,
Whenever the November sky
Quivers with a bugle's hoarse, sweet cry,
The reason darkens; in its evening gleam
Crosses and flares, tormented wire, grey earth
Splattered with crimson flowers,
And I remember,
Not the war I fought in
But the one called Great
Which ended in a sepia November
Four years before my birth.

A possible, but, I think, incorrect way of responding to such poems might be to consider them as pastiche of genuine war poetry, merely rearranging familiar, even well-worn references. It would be truer to say that the poets, familiar with these images from childhood, are exploiting the fact that they are now, after fifty years, so ineradicably rooted in the common consciousness that they have acquired a mythic quality. It is surely in this direction that the literature of the Great War, if it is to continue, will most fruitfully develop.

The Great War is not likely to be forgotten: the memory of its waste and dumb heroism is part of twentieth-century sensibility. It started as a war to end wars, but instead it pointed forward to the totalitarian state, to an even greater war and a concept of unlimited conflict in which not merely uniformed armies but whole populations, down to the smallest child, are regarded as appropriate victims for destruction on a scale that makes the slaughter on the Somme appear ordinary. The poets sensed some of this, though, in Owen's phrase, all they could do was warn. If we now regard war as, on occasion, still necessary, in the way that abattoirs and operating-theatres are necessary, we do not feel the need to adorn it with the tinsel of a factitious glory. This much we have learnt from the writers of the Great War, who absorbed its shock and employed their art to change a generation's modes of feeling. In the course of doing so, they undermined a whole range of traditional responses: heroism, as a kind of behaviour, might still be possible, but not the rhetoric and gestures of heroism. The response of the English writers was perhaps more acute than that of other nations. As Mr. John Terraine has suggested, for centuries the English were in the habit of letting other people do their fighting for them, and the initial exposure of the civilian volunteer soldiers of 1914 and 1915 to the realities of large-scale technological war was all the more painful. But the best of them did more than register a hopeless trauma: in confronting unimagined degrees of horror they discovered new modes of order and even beauty. In their writing they have preserved the images by which men endeavour to crystallize and shape experiences, and so have enabled us to understand more deeply both the men and their experiences.

Appendix
War as Literary Experience

AMERICANS who write about English culture often get it wrong, in ways that jar on the British reader. They may not know enough, and even if their information cannot be faulted they may still miss the point or convey a false impression. On the other hand, some Americans have achieved a broader and more perceptive view of English affairs than most English writers, precisely because they can look at the situation with an unprejudiced eye.

The necessary blend of detachment and knowledge and sympathy was, I think, shown by William Abrahams and Peter Stansky in their studies of the 1930s and the early career of George Orwell, and it is equally apparent in Paul Fussell's remarkable book *The Great War and Modern Memory*. He is interested in the inter-penetration of literature and history in the British experience of the Western Front in 1914-1918, in the way in which the soldiers' immediate experience was often apprehended in literary terms, and the literary means in which it was later recalled, codified and, ultimately, mythologized. In Mr Fussell's words, 'I have tried to understand something of the simultaneous and reciprocal process by which life feeds materials to literature while literature returns the favour by conferring forms upon life.'

Methodologically, this is a very up-to-date book, since it rests on assumptions that are much more common now than fifteen or twenty years ago. I refer, first, to the idea that 'reality' is not some kind of raw, unformed flux but is necessarily shaped and limited in the very act of understanding by the pre-existing categories of the mind; and secondly to the belief that a poem, or other literary text, can never be a totally unique entity, however original in theme and feeling, since it inevitably uses and modifies existing literary codes and conventions. Mr Fussell brilliantly illustrates these considerations in a series of chapters on the various categories through which front-line experience was mediated. He is marvellously illuminating about simple instances. Thus, as a matter of history, the most crucial parts of the day at the front were dawn—when attacks might be launched—and dusk—when raiding parties would set out. The sky was always visible from the trenches, and sunrise and sunset were much more apparent to the soldier than to the civilian town-dweller. The peculiar significance of dawn is conveyed in one of the finest front-line poems, Isaac Rosenberg's 'Break of Day in the Trenches.' Mr Fussell reminds us that a whole tradition of describing skies and sunrises and sunsets had grown out of Ruskin's *Modern Painters*—it is conspicuous, for instance, in Hopkins's letters and journals—and during the war it directed both the observation of such things, and the literary response to them, whether in poems or memoirs or private letters. It was, as Mr Fussell says, a very literary war. The Englishmen of 1914 were at a high pitch of literacy. The young officers, who wrote most of the literature of the war, had received a classical education, and were extremely well read in English poetry, so that Shakespeare and Milton, Wordsworth and Keats, would be constantly quoted or alluded to when they wrote about the war, either publicly, in established literary forms, or privately, in their correspondence. English poetry provided a sense of identity and continuity, a means of accommodating to life in a bizarre world as well as a mode of consolation. To quote Mr Fussell again, 'the *Oxford Book of English Verse* presides over the Great War in a way that has never been sufficiently appreciated.'

The private soldiers, though less well educated and less given to literary allusions, were still part of a traditional verbal culture, not yet affected by the electronic media, and many of them naturally expressed themselves in the idiom of the English Bible and *Pilgrim's Progress*. Englishmen of all classes, enduring a seemingly endless war, could readily see the water-logged battlefields of Passchendaele as a literal Slough of Despond. Again, many of the poems by Wilfred Owen and others, lamenting the premature deaths of fine young men were in an ancient tradition reaching back to classical pastoral. But they had a more immediate source in the curious *fin de siècle* cult of the Uranian love which produced poems of sublimated devotion to young men, usually called 'boys' or 'lads.' This mode

224

of feeling, the author suggests, might be called 'homoerotic' rather than overtly or consciously homosexual, and it has evident roots in the culture of the English public school. Housman was a distinguished poetic exponent of such sentiments, and there is a striking sense in which Owen gives a terrible new content to the literary wistfulness of *A Shropshire Lad*. As Mr Fussell notes, Owen's 'sad shires' sounds like a deliberate distorted echo of Housman's 'coloured counties.' Such a realization does not detract at all from the originality of Owen's poems; but it indicates the complex fusion of tradition and unprecedented reality that formed them.

Owen and Rosenberg did not survive the war. Others, such as Siegfried Sassoon, Robert Graves, Edmund Blunden and David Jones, did, and in later years returned to their wartime life in autobiographical works.These records are in no way unmediated transcripts of personal experience; they are carefully formed, directed and controlled by literary categories, and have in turn helped to shape our own understanding of the Great War. Graves's *Goodbye to All That*, so vivid and relaxed a narrative, might well strike an unwary reader as simply 'telling it like it was.' But, as Mr Fussell shows, it is a most conscious and crafty book, where practically everything that Graves sees and undergoes is presented as a form of Jonsonian farce, and where the narrative is a tissue of tall stories. It is also profoundly true; but it has the truth of literature rather than of unadorned documentary. The Great War lives on, in all sorts of unsuspected ways, even in the casual clichés of our bureaucratized daily life, where one is 'bombarded with forms' or faces a 'barrage of complaints'; where negotiators adopt 'entrenched positions' but still hope for a 'breakthrough'; and where such once precise terms as 'to go over the top' or be in 'no man's land' survive as metaphors whose original force is half-forgotten. Pursuing his argument, Mr Fussell finds many elements of the First World War surviving as myth or convention in American novels about the Second, by Mailer and Heller and Pynchon.

I found this book totally fascinating and almost totally convincing. My occasional reservations arose from a suspicion that Mr Fussell sometimes claims too much. I readily believe that irony as a dominant mode of modern literary consciousness arose from the bitter disappointments and betrayed idealism of 1914-18; but

I doubt if implacable oppositions in cultural models were also, as he argues, a result of the war. After all the 'class war,' perhaps the most implacable and enduring instance of such oppositions was, as a concept, a product of Victorian England. The chapter where Mr Fussell tries to establish this case, called 'Adversary Proceedings,' seemed to me weaker than the rest, and it is the one place where Mr Fussell seems slightly to fudge the evidence. At least, he implies that the violent rhetoric and antagonisms expressed by Ezra Pound and Wyndham Lewis in *Blast* were a wartime phenomenon, whereas the first issue of *Blast* came out before the war, if only by a few weeks. Otherwise, Mr Fussell displays only the defects of his qualities; that is to say, he has read so widely and throws out so many ideas that he sometimes tries to follow too many at once and so loses the thread of his argument. This apart, his book is a *tour de force*, a superb combination of acute critical analysis and informed cultural history.

(Reprinted from *Commonweal*, 9 April 1976)

NOTES

CHAPTER 1
1. *Further Speculations* (ed. Sam Hynes), 1955, pp. 200-202.
2. For a shrewd analysis of the inconsistencies of *Catch - 22*, see Norman Podhoretz, *Doings and Undoings*, 1964, pp. 228-36.

CHAPTER 2
1. *The New Poetic*, 1964, p. 85.
2. Mr..Pound has now disowned 'Altaforte' and does not wish it to be reprinted.
3. Ezra Pound, *Gaudier-Brzeska: A Memoir*, 1960, p. 69.
4. Ibid., p. 72.
5. Ibid., pp. 27-8.

CHAPTER 3
1. *Margin Released*, 1962, p. 82.
2. *Further Speculations*, p. 175.
3. *Reputations*, 1920, p. 90.
4. *The Strange Death of Liberal England 1910-1914*, 1961, p. 430.
5. *The New Poetic*, 1964, p. 87.
6. *Tradition and Change*, 1919, p. 150.
7. Reprinted in *The Prose of Rupert Brooke* (ed. Christopher Hassall), 1956, p. 195.
8. *Poetry of the First World War* (Taylorian Lecture), 1961.
9. *The Modern Age* (Volume 7 of *The Pelican Guide to English Literature* [ed. Boris Ford]), 1961, p. 155.
10. *The Letters of Charles Sorley*, 1919, p. 263.
11. *Pages from a Family Journal 1888-1915* (privately printed), 1916, p. 37.
12. This and subsequent extracts from Grenfell's letters are from *Pages from a Family Journal*, pp. 452-526.

CHAPTER 4
1. *Crisis in English Poetry*, 1951, p. 142.
2. *Vision and Rhetoric*, 1959, p. 141.
3. *War Poets 1914-1918* (Writers and their Work), 1958, pp. 26-7.
4. *Stand* (iv, 3), p. 50.
5. *The New Poetic*, 1964, p. 101.

CHAPTER 5
1. 'The Fight to a Finish in 1914-1918' (*Sunday Times*, 24th February 1963).
2. *Stand* (iv, 3), p. 39.
3. *The Modern Age*, p. 161.

CHAPTER 6
1. *Collected Works of Isaac Rosenberg* (ed. G. Bottomley and D. Harding), 1937, p. 305.
2. Foreword to *Collected Poems of Isaac Rosenberg*, 1949, p. vii.
3. *Experience Into Words*, 1963, p. 100.
4. *Stand* (iv, 3), p. 38.
5. *A Tribute to Wilfred Owen* (compiled by T. J. Walsh), 1964, p. 60.

6. *The Later Life and Letters of Sir Henry Newbolt* (ed. Margaret Newbolt), 1942, p. 314. (I am indebted to C. K. Stead's *The New Poetic* for this reference.)
7. *A Tribute to Wilfred Owen*, pp. 34-42.
8. Ibid., p. 28.
9. 'Owen, Rosenberg and the War' (*Stand* [vi, 4], pp. 26-42).
10. *Stand* (vi, 4), p. 7.
11. Possibly Owen was anticipating C. E. Montague's later sentiments about post-war vindictiveness:

> The old spirit of Prussia was blowing anew, from strange mouths. From several species of men who passed for English—as mongrels, curs, shoughs, water-rugs, and demi-wolves are all clept by the name of dogs —there was a rising chorus of shrill yelps for the outdoing of all the base folly committed by Prussia when drunk with her conquest of France. Prussia, beaten out of the field, had won in the souls of her conquerors' rulers; they had become her pupils; they took her word for it that she, and not the older England, knew how to use victory.
>
> (*Disenchantment*, 1922, p. 181)

CHAPTER 7
1. *Reputations*, p. 92.
2. *Kipling's Mind and Art* (ed. Andrew Rutherford), 1964, pp. 271-4.
3. Quoted by Noel Stock in *Poet in Exile: Ezra Pound*, 1964, p. 96.
4. *The Modern Age*, p. 326.
5. *Collected Letters of D. H. Lawrence* (ed. Harry T. Moore), 1962, Vol. I, p. 460.

CHAPTER 8
1. A privately printed edition of *Seven Pillars of Wisdom* had been given a limited circulation in 1926.

CHAPTER 9
1. *Linhay on the Downs*, 1934, pp. 224-62.
2. See Robie Macauley, 'Parade's End', in *Modern British Fiction* (ed. Mark Schorer), 1962; Richard A. Cassell, *Ford Madox Ford: A Study of His Novels*, 1961; and John A. Meixner, *Ford Madox Ford's Novels*, 1962.
3. 'Talented Agrarians' (*New Statesman*, 2nd August 1963).

CHAPTER 10
1. 'David Jones: A Reconnaissance' (*Twentieth Century*, July 1960, pp. 27-45).
2. *The Modern Age*, p. 169.
3. *Encounter*, July 1964, p. 94.

CHAPTER 11
1. *Aylesford Review* (ii, 2), 1957-8, pp. 34-5.

CHRONOLOGY OF PUBLICATIONS

1914   H. G. Wells: *The War That Will End War*

1915   Rupert Brooke: *1914 and other poems*
       Arthur Machen: *The Bowmen*
       Robert Nichols: *Invocation*

1916   Robert Graves: *Over the Brazier*
       F. W. Harvey: *A Gloucestershire Lad*
       Charles Hamilton Sorley: *Marlborough and other poems*
       H. G. Wells: *Mr. Britling Sees It Through*

1917   Henri Barbusse: *Under Fire*
       G. H. Clarke: *An Anthology of War Poetry*
       Robert Graves: *Fairies and Fusiliers*
       Ivor Gurney: *Severn and Somme*
       F. W. Harvey: *Gloucestershire Friends*
       Frederic Manning: *Eidola*
       Robert Nichols: *Ardours and Endurances*
       Ezra Pound: *Homage to Sextus Propertius*
       Siegfried Sassoon: *The Old Huntsman*
       Edward Thomas: *Poems*
       Francis Brett Young: *Marching on Tanga*

1918   Rupert Brooke: *Collected Poems*
       Ford Madox Ford (Hueffer): *On Heaven*
       Siegfried Sassoon: *Counter-Attack*

1919   Richard Aldington: *Images of War*
       Ivor Gurney: *War's Embers*
       Herbert Read: *Eclogues*
                   Naked Warriors
       Bernard Shaw: *Heartbreak House*
       The Letters of Charles Sorley
       Arthur Graeme West: *The Diary of a Dead Officer*

1920   D. H. Lawrence: *The Lost Girl*
       Wilfred Owen: *Poems* (ed. Siegfried Sassoon)
       Ezra Pound: *Hugh Selwyn Mauberley*
       Edward Thomas: *Collected Poems*

1921   John Dos Passos: *Three Soldiers*

1922   E. E. Cummings: *The Enormous Room*
       T. S. Eliot: *The Waste Land*
       C. E. Montague: *Disenchantment*
       Isaac Rosenberg: *Poems* (ed. Gordon Bottomley)

1923   D. H. Lawrence: *Kangaroo*
       C. E. Montague: *Fiery Particles*

1924   Ford Madox Ford: *Some Do Not*
       R. H. Mottram: *The Spanish Farm*

1925   Ford Madox Ford: *No More Parades*
       R. H. Mottram: *Sixty-Four, Ninety-Four!*
       Herbert Read: *In Retreat*
1926   Ford Madox Ford: *A Man Could Stand Up*
       R. H. Mottram: *The Crime at Vanderlynden's*
1927   T. E. Lawrence: *Revolt in the Desert*
       R. H. Mottram: *The Spanish Farm Trilogy 1914–18*
1928   Edmund Blunden: *Undertones of War*
       Ford Madox Ford: *Last Post*
       Siegfried Sassoon: *Memoirs of a Fox-Hunting Man*
       R. C. Sherriff: *Journey's End* (first performed)
1929   Richard Aldington: *Death of a Hero*
       Robert Graves: *Goodbye to All That*
       Ernest Hemingway: *A Farewell to Arms*
       Ernst Jünger: *The Storm of Steel*
       E. M. Remarque: *All Quiet on the Western Front*
1930   Frederick Brereton: *An Anthology of War Poems*
       Douglas Jerrold: *The Lie About the War*
       Frederic Manning: *Her Privates We*
       Siegfried Sassoon: *Memoirs of an Infantry Officer*
       H. M. Tomlinson: *All Our Yesterdays*
       Henry Williamson: *The Patriot's Progress*
1931   Wilfred Owen: *Poems* (ed. Edmund Blunden)
1933   Guy Chapman: *A Passionate Prodigality*
       Frank Richards: *Old Soldiers Never Die*
1935   T. E. Lawrence: *Seven Pillars of Wisdom*
1936   Cecil Lewis: *Sagittarius Rising*
       Siegfried Sassoon: *Sherston's Progress*
1937   David Jones: *In Parenthesis*
       Wyndham Lewis: *Blasting and Bombardiering*
       Collected Works of Isaac Rosenberg (ed. G. Bottomley and D. Harding)
       Siegfried Sassoon: *The Complete Memoirs of George Sherston*
1938   Siegfried Sassoon: *The Old Century*
1942   Siegfried Sassoon: *Weald of Youth*
1943   Robert Nichols: *Anthology of War Poetry 1914–1918*
1945   Siegfried Sassoon: *Siegfried's Journey*
1947   Siegfried Sassoon: *Collected Poems*
1949   Isaac Rosenberg: *Collected Poems* (ed. G. Bottomley and D. Harding)
1954   Ivor Gurney: *Poems* (ed. Edmund Blunden)
       Henry Williamson: *How Dear is Life*
1955   Henry Williamson: *A Fox Under My Cloak*

1956   *The Prose of Rupert Brooke* (ed. Christopher Hassall)
       T. E. Hulme: *Further Speculations* (ed. Sam Hynes)

1957   Henry Williamson: *The Golden Virgin*

1958   Edmund Blunden: *War Poets 1914–1918*
       Henry Williamson: *Love and the Loveless*

1960   D. S. R. Welland: *Wilfred Owen: a Critical Study*
       Henry Williamson: *A Test to Destruction*

1961   C. M. Bowra: *Poetry of the First World War*
       John Harris: *Covenant with Death*

1962   J. B. Priestley: *Margin Released*

1963   *Oh What a Lovely War* (first performed)
       Wilfred Owen: *Collected Poems* (ed. C. Day Lewis)
       Harold Owen: *Journey From Obscurity: I: Childhood*
       Herbert Read: *The Contrary Experience*

1964   Christopher Hassall: *Rupert Brooke*
       John H. Johnston: *English Poetry of the First World War*
       Harold Owen: *Journey From Obscurity: II: Youth*
       Up the Line to Death: the War Poets 1914–18
       (ed. Brian Gardner)

1965   Harold Owen: *Journey from Obscurity: III: War*
       Men Who March Away: Poems of the First World War
       (ed. I. M. Parsons)
       Robert H. Ross: *The Georgian Revolt*

1966   Michael Thorpe: *Siegfried Sassoon*

1967   Wilfred Owen: *Collected Letters* (ed. Harold Owen and John Bell)

1968   Rupert Brooke: *Letters* (ed. Geoffrey Keynes)

1970   William Cooke: *Edward Thomas: A Critical Biography*

1971   David Blamires: *David Jones: Artist and Writer*

1972   Jon Silkin: *Out of Battle: the Poetry of the Great War*

1973   M. C. Grecius: *Prose Writers of World War I*
       The Poems of Ivor Gurney 1890–1937

1974   David Jones: *The Sleeping Lord and Other Fragments*
       Jon Stallworthy: *Wilfred Owen*

1975   Paul Fussell: *The Great War and Modern Memory*
       Joseph Cohen: *Journey to the Trenches: the Life of Isaac Rosenberg*
       Jean Liddiard: *Isaac Rosenberg: a Half-Used Life*
       Jean Moorcraft Wilson: *Isaac Rosenberg: Poet and Painter*

1976   Holgar Klein (ed.): *The First World War in Fiction*
       Nicholas Mosley: *Julian Grenfell*

1978   Michael Hurd: *The Ordeal of Ivor Gurney*
       Jan Marsh: *Edward Thomas*
       Collected Poems of Edward Thomas (ed. R. G. Thomas)

1979   *Collected Works of Isaac Rosenberg* (ed. Ian Parsons)
       Andrew Rutherford: *The Literature of War*
       The Penguin Book of First World War Poetry (ed. Jon Silkin)

ACKNOWLEDGEMENTS

RICHARD ALDINGTON: For extracts from *Death of a Hero*, to Rosica Collin Ltd., Mme. Catherine Guillaume, and Mr. Alister Kershaw; for quotations from *Images of War* to George Allen & Unwin Ltd.

HENRI BARBUSSE: For extract from *Under Fire* to J. M. Dent & Sons Ltd.

LAURENCE BINYON: For extract from 'For the Fallen' to the author's estate and Hodder & Stoughton Ltd.

EDMUND BLUNDEN: For extract from *War Poets 1914–1918* to Longmans for the British Council; for extracts from *Undertones of War* and *After the Bombing* to A. D. Peters & Co.

RUPERT BROOKE: For extracts from the *Collected Poems* and *The Prose of Rupert Brooke* to the estate of Rupert Brooke and Sidgwick & Jackson Ltd.

G. K. CHESTERTON: For extract from *The Napoleon of Notting Hill* to A. P. Watt & Son and Miss D. E. Collins.

CYRIL CONNOLLY: For extract from *Enemies of Promise* to Routledge & Kegan Paul Ltd.

D. J. ENRIGHT: To Penguin Books Ltd., for extracts from 'The Literature of the First World War' included in *The Modern Age*, edited by Boris Ford.

FORD MADOX FORD: For extracts from *Of Heaven* and *Parade's End* to the author's estate and the Bodley Head Ltd.

E. M. FORSTER: For extract from *Howards End* to the author and Edward Arnold Ltd.

ROBERT GRAVES: For extracts from *Goodbye to All That* to A. P. Watt & Son, International Authors N. V., and Cassell & Co.; for extract from 'The Fight to a Finish in 1914–1918' to A. P. Watt & Son, International Authors N. V., and the *Sunday Times*. Acknowledgements are also due to Mr. Graves in respect of quotations from 'It's a Queer Time', 'Big Words', 'Dead Boche', and 'Goliath and David'.

JULIAN GRENFELL: For extracts from poetry and letters, to Lady Salmond.

IVOR GURNEY: For extract from *War's Embers* to the author's estate and Sidgwick & Jackson Ltd., and from *Poems* to the author's estate and Hutchinson & Co.

RENÉ HAGUE: For extract from 'David Jones: A Reconnaissance' to the author and *Twentieth Century*.

D. W. HARDING: For extracts from *Experience Into Words* to the author and Chatto & Windus Ltd.

THOMAS HARDY: For extract from *The Collected Poems of Thomas Hardy* to Macmillan & Co., Ltd.

F. W. HARVEY: For quotations from *A Gloucestershire Lad* to the author's estate and Sidgwick & Jackson Ltd.

JOSEPH HELLER: For extract from *Catch–22* to the author and Jonathan Cape Ltd.

T. E. HULME: For extracts from *Further Speculations* to the University of Minnesota Press.

DOUGLAS JERROLD: For extracts from *The Lie About the War* to the author's estate and Faber & Faber Ltd.

J. H. JOHNSTON: For extract from *English Poetry of the First World War* to the author and Princeton University Press.

DAVID JONES: For extracts from *In Parenthesis* to the author and Faber & Faber Ltd.

ERNST JÜNGER: For extract from *The Storm of Steel* to Chatto & Windus Ltd.

RUDYARD KIPLING: For extracts from 'Tommy', 'The Islanders' and 'All We Have and Are' to A. P. Watt & Son, Mrs. George Bambridge, and Methuen & Co., Ltd.

D. H. LAWRENCE: For extracts from *The Collected Letters*, *Kangaroo* and *The Lost Girl* to Laurence Pollinger Ltd., and the Estate of the late Mrs. Frieda Lawrence.

CECIL LEWIS: For extract from *Sagittarius Rising* to the author and Peter Davies Ltd.

C. DAY LEWIS: For extract from 'Where Are the War Poets?' to the author and Jonathan Cape Ltd.

WYNDHAM LEWIS: For extract from *Blasting and Bombardiering* to the author's estate and Methuen & Co., Ltd.

FREDERIC MANNING: For extracts from *Eidola* to John Murray Ltd., for extracts from *Her Privates We* to the author's estate and Peter Davies Ltd.

C. E. MONTAGUE: For extracts from *Disenchantment* to the author's estate and Chatto & Windus Ltd.

R. H. MOTTRAM: For extracts from *The Spanish Farm Trilogy* to the author and Chatto & Windus Ltd.

SIR HENRY NEWBOLT: For extracts from *Later Life and Letters* to A. P. Watt & Son, the author's executor and Faber & Faber Ltd.

ROBERT NICHOLS: For extract from *Ardours and Endurances* to the author's estate and Chatto & Windus Ltd.

WILFRED OWEN: For extracts from *Collected Poems* to the author's estate and Chatto & Windus Ltd.

PETER PORTER: For extract from *Once Bitten, Twice Bitten* to the author and Scorpion Press.

EZRA POUND: For extracts from *The Cantos* and *Hugh Selwyn Mauberley* to the author and Mr. A. V. Moore; acknowledgements are also due to the author in respect of three lines quoted from 'Sestina: Altaforte'; for extracts from *Gaudier-Brzeska: A Memoir* to the Marvell Press, Hessle, Yorkshire, England.

J. B. PRIESTLEY: For an extract from *Margin Released* to the author and A. D. Peters & Co.

SIR HERBERT READ: For extracts from *The Contrary Experience* and *Collected Poems* to the author and Faber & Faber Ltd.

EDGELL RICKWORD: For extracts from *Collected Poems* to the author and the Bodley Head Ltd.

ISAAC ROSENBERG: For extracts from *Collected Works* and *Collected Poems* to the author's estate and Chatto & Windus Ltd.

SAKI (H. H. MUNRO): For extract from *When William Came* to the author's estate and the Bodley Head Ltd.

SIEGFRIED SASSOON: For extracts from *Collected Poems* and *The Complete Memoirs of George Sherston* to the author and Faber & Faber Ltd.

VERNON SCANNELL: For quotation from 'The Great War' to the author.

BERNARD SHAW: For extract from *Heartbreak House* to the Public Trustee and the Society of Authors.

R. C. SHERRIFF: For extract from *Journey's End* to Curtis Brown Ltd.

SIR OSBERT SITWELL: For extract from *Selected Poems—Old and New* to the author and Gerald Duckworth & Co., Ltd.

GEORGES SOREL: For an extract from *Reflections on Violence* to George Allen & Unwin Ltd.

CHARLES SORLEY: For extracts from *Marlborough and Other Poems* and *The Letters of Charles Sorley* to the author's estate and Cambridge University Press.

EDWARD THOMAS: For extracts from *Collected Poems* to Mrs. Helen Thomas and Faber & Faber Ltd.

H. M. TOMLINSON: For extracts from *All Our Yesterdays* to the Society of Authors as the literary representative of the estate of the late H. M. Tomlinson.

H. G. WELLS: For extracts from *Mr. Britling Sees It Through* to Cassell & Co., A. P. Watt & Son, and the executors of H. G. Wells, and from *The World Set Free* to A. P. Watt & Son and the Executors.

ARTHUR GRAEME WEST: For extracts from *The Diary of a Dead Officer* to George Allen & Unwin Ltd.

HENRY WILLIAMSON: For extracts from *The Golden Virgin* to the author and Macdonald & Co.

W. B. YEATS: For extract from 'An Irish Airman Foresees His Death' to Mrs. Yeats and Macmillan & Co., Ltd.; for extract from *The Letters of W. B. Yeats* to Mrs. Yeats and Rupert Hart-Davis Ltd.

Acknowledgements are also due to those copyright-owners whom it has not been possible to trace.

Index

Index

Eliot, T. S.: 38, 122, 201; 'The Love Song of J. Alfred Prufrock', 39; *The Waste Land*, 144, 199, 200, 202; 'Tradition and the Individual Talent', 202; contributes to *Blast*, 29; on Owen, 132

Encounter, 224 n.

Enright, D. J.: On Brooke, 43-4; on Sassoon, 96, 108; on Jones, 212

Flaubert, G.: 182

Ford (Hueffer), Ford Madox: 84, 91, 211; *The Good Soldier*, 29, 79; *Parade's End*, 79, 81, 144, 172, 186, 175-82; trilogy or tetralogy, 175-6; Ford's vision of England, 177-9; personality of Tietjens, 180, 213; *Collected Poems*, 79; 'Antwerp', 79-80; *On Heaven*, 80; 'That Exploit of Yours', 81; wartime service, 80; caricatured by Aldington, 184

Forster, E. M.: 35, 177; *Howards End*, 21-2, 30, 40

Fraser, G. S.: 67; *Vision and Rhetoric*, 223 n.

Frye, Northrop: 199

Fuller, Roy: 213

Galsworthy, John: 173; *The Man of Property*, 39; *A Modern Comedy*, 145

Gaudier-Brzeska, Henri: 27-8, 29, 30

Gibson, W. W.: 60

Gill, Eric: 204

Goldring, Douglas: *Reputations*, 223 n., 224 n.; on Wells, 34, 137; on war poets, 61-2; on Nichols, 64; on Graves, 66; on Ford, 80

Graves, Robert: 44, 65, 85, 86, 91, 106, 120, 150, 164, 166; *Over the Brazier*, 65, 93; *Fairies and Fusiliers*, 65, 89, 91; 'Goliath and David', 65; 'It's a Queer Time', 66; 'Big Words', 67; 'Dead Boche', 67; *Goodbye to All That*, 68, 93, 97, 99, 146, 154-8, 184, 195; 'The Fight to a Finish in 1914-1918', 223 n.; as Georgian, 65; and myth, 65-7; officially reported killed, 67, 157-8; on Robert Nichols, 63; on Sassoon, 93-4, 97-8, 155; on a negotiated peace, 100-1; interest in ritual, 155-6; and the White Goddess, 156

Gray, Thomas: 68

Greene, Graham: 175

Grenfell, Julian: 17, 18, 56, 58, 67, 91, 167, 198; 'Into Battle', 42, 45,
49-51, 180; 'Prayer for Those on the Staff', 48-9; letters, 47-8; personality, 45-6; wartime heroism, 47

Gurney, Ivor: 88-90, 91; *Severn and Somme*, 89, 91; *War's Embers*, 89; 'The Target', 89; *Poems*, 90; 'War Books', 90

Hague, René: On David Jones, 200-1; 'David Jones: A Reconnaissance', 224 n.

Harding, D. W.: On Rosenberg, 110-11, 112-13, 115, 117, 118; *Experience into Words*, 223 n.

Hardy, Thomas: 'Men Who March Away', 32

Harris, John: *Covenant with Death*, 220-1

Harvey, F. W.: 90, 91; 'The Soldier Speaks', 90; 'To the Devil on His Appalling Decadence', 90

Hassall, Christopher: On Brooke, 37, 39

Heller, Joseph: *Catch-22*, 18-19, 193

Hemingway, Ernest: *A Farewell to Arms*, 146, 195

Henley, W. E.: 'The Song of the Sword', 22-3, 33

Hill, Geoffrey: On Owen, 133-4

Hitler: 219

Hoffmann, Frederick J.: *The Twenties*, 194-5

Hopkins, G. M.: 125, 204

Housman, A. E.: 57, 58, 105, 131

Hulme, T. E.: 29, 94; *Further Speculations*, 223 n.; defends heroic values, 16-17, 28; dispute with Bertrand Russell, 17; and Georges Sorel, 28; on Wells, 34

Hunt, Violet: 80

Huxley, Aldous: *Antic Hay*, 144

Inge, Dean: 41

James, Henry: 182

Jefferies, Richard: 68

Jerrold, Douglas: *The Lie About the War*, 195-7

John Bull: 144

Johnson, Geoffrey: 62

Johnston, John H.: 210-11; *English Poetry of the First World War*, 203

Jones, David: 220; *In Parenthesis*, 193, 198-212 *passim*; cultural eclecticism, 201-2; ideogrammatic method, 202; epic elements, 203;

238

Index

Index

Index

Shaw, Bernard: *Arms and the Man*, 16; *Heartbreak House*, 139
Shelley, P. B.: 121; *Revolt of Islam*, 132
Sherriff, R. C.: *Journey's End*, 194
Silkin, Jon: On Sassoon, 103; on Owen, 133, 134
Sitwell, Sir Osbert: 132; 'The Trap', 99; 'Hymn to Moloch', 99–100, 123; on Owen, 121
Sitwell, Sacheverell: 99
Song of Roland: 210
Sorel, Georges: *Reflections on Violence*, 28
Sorley, Charles Hamilton: 44, 51–9 *passim*, 81, 91; Letters, 44, 51–5; 'Rooks', 55; *Marlborough and other poems*, 55; 'To Germany', 56; 'All the Hills and Vales Along', 57, 113; *The Letters of Charles Sorley*, 223 n.
Spender, Stephen: *The Struggle of the Modern*, 200
Stand: 223 n., 224 n.
Stead, C. K.: 21, 39, 85; *The New Poetic*, 38, 223 n.
Stendhal: 23, 126; *La Chartreuse de Parme*, 14–15
Stewart, J. I. M.: On Kipling, 33
Stock Noel: *Ezra Pound: Poet in Exile*, 224 n.

Tate, Allen: 75, 79
Tennyson, Alfred Lord: 'Charge of the Light Brigade', 16, 17
Terraine, John: 222
Thackeray, W. M.: 15
Thomas, Edward: 85–6, 91; 'No Case of Petty Right or Wrong', 86; 'A Private', 86
Tolstoy, Leo: 36; *War and Peace*, 15, 172, 219
Tomlinson, H. M.: *All Our Yesterdays*, 186–9

Wain, John: 212

Wadsworth, Edward: 29
Watson, Sir William: 39, 60
Waugh, Arthur: 40; *Tradition and Change*, 223 n.
Waugh, Evelyn: *The Sword of Honour*, 213
Welland, Dennis: 58; on Owen, 121, 132
Wellesley, Dorothy: 124
Wells, H. G.: *The War of the Worlds*, 24; *The War in the Air*, 25; *The World Set Free*, 25, 33–4; *The War That Will End War*, 33–4; *Mr. Britling Sees It Through*, 136–7, 138; *God the Invisible King*, 137; *The Soul of a Bishop*, 137
West, Arthur Graeme: 17, 86–8, 91; *The Diary of a Dead Officer*, 86; 'God! How I hate you, you young cheerful men', 87; 'The Night Patrol', 87–8
Williams, William Carlos: 177, 198
Williamson, Henry: *A Test to Destruction*, 107, 214, 216, 218; *A Chronicle of Ancient Sunlight*, 123, 213–19; 'Reality in War Literature', 174–5, 181; *A Fox Under My Cloak*, 214; *The Golden Virgin*, 214, 216–18; *Love and the Loveless*, 214, 215; *Linhay on the Downs*, 224 n.
Woolf, Virginia: *Mrs. Dalloway*, 144–5
Wordsworth, William: 68, 73, 78, 199; 'Thanksgiving Ode', 13

Yeats, W. B.: 57–8, 122, 141; 'An Irish Airman Foresees His Death', 188; On Owen, 124–5
Young, Francis Brett: *Marching on Tanga*, 169–70

Zweig, Arnold: 195